ROCKS,
CRYSTALS,
MINERALS

ROCKS, CRYSTALS, & MINERALS

complete identifier

Edited by Rosie Hankin

CHARTWELL
BOOKS, INC.

A QUINTET BOOK

Published by **Chartwell Books**
A Division of **Book Sales, Inc.**
114, Northfield Avenue
Edison, New Jersey 08837

This edition produced for sales in the U.S.A.,
its territories and dependencies only.

ISBN 0-7858-1031-5

This book was designed and produced by
Quintet Publishing Limited
6 Blundell Street
London N7 9BH

Creative Director: Richard Dewing
Art Director: Silke Braun
Designer: Rod Teasdale
Project Editor: Amanda Dixon
Editor: Rosie Hankin

PICTURE CREDITS
Geoscience Picture Library, Natural History Museum, London
Christopher Pellant, Paul Forrester, Vaughan Flemming, Peter Nixon, C M Dixon,
Dougal Dixon, Earth Satellite Corporation, NASA, Diamond Information Centre.
While every effort has been made to ensure this listing is
correct, the Publisher apologizes for any omissions.

The material used in this publication previously appeared in *Crystal Identifier* by Peter Darling,
Collecting Gems & Minerals by Chris Pellant, *Gems & Precious Stones* by Cally Hall, *The Practical
Geologist* by Dougal Dixon, *Rocks & Minerals* by Basil Booth, and *Rocks, Shells, Fossils, Minerals,
& Gems* edited by Harriet Stewart-Jones.

Typeset in Great Britain by
Central Southern Typesetters, Eastbourne
Manufactured in Singapore by Eray Scan Pte Ltd
Printed in China by Leefung-Asco Printers Limited

CONTENTS

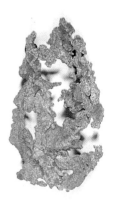

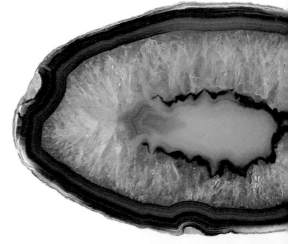

ABOUT THIS BOOK

The durability, beauty, variety, and widespread availability of minerals and rocks make them ideal subjects for the amateur collector or for the aspiring geologist who wants to find out more about the planet on which we live.

In this book we have put together two sections on minerals and rocks with carefully selected entries to give as wide as possible a range of the types of mineral and rock from the hardest diamond to the softest clay. Detailed information on the form, color, and occurrence of each sample is given along with a clear color photograph.

We have also provided detailed introductions to each section in order to explain how minerals and rocks are formed, and how to identify them in the field and at home, with suggestions for the best ways to collect and prepare specimens.

GEOLOGICAL BACKGROUND

History of the Earth

The Earth is made of stardust, as is all it contains, including ourselves. We cannot actually trace the Earth's history, but the following is agreed to be a rough approximation.

The Development of the Solar System

About 15,000 million years ago there was a vast mass of dust and gas in one of the spiral arms of our galaxy, and this mass began to contract. The spaces between the stars are not empty; they contain gases and tiny dust particles in varying concentrations. The arms of the galaxy are not static, but spin and pulsate, with waves passing through them, although very slowly by our standards. A random concentration of gas and dust, caught up by one of these waves, would have been compressed to such an extent that the miniscule gravitational forces between the particles would come into operation, and the particles would have begun to move together. The original movement of the cloud in its orbit around the galaxy would have caused the contracting mass to begin to spin.

Two main forces then came into play. The first was the gravitational force between the particles, and this caused all the matter to compress toward the center where the greatest mass was accumulating. The second was a centrifugal force that spun the matter outward again along a plane perpendicular to the axis of rotation. As a result of both these forces the matter began to form in a broad spinning disk which was our solar system in embryo.

The greatest mass of material gathered at the center, and the energy released by the collision of particles and the compression of the material caused the mass to heat up. This action would have taken only a few million years—a very short time in geological terms—and the Sun was "switched on."

The disk of matter was not stable. Eddies appeared across its face, disrupting the local speed of the spin. As a result, the material on the inner arms of the eddies was orbiting at a smaller angular velocity and tended to fall toward the "protosun" while that on the outer arms was orbiting faster and was thrown outward. The mass of the disk was thus separated into a number of discrete stable rings around the protosun, similar to the rings around some of our planets. Only a few hundred thousand years would have been needed to create this ring system—a system that would eventually become the nine planets of the solar system.

The Earth Solidifies

The rings of gas and dust particles around the protosun were subjected to the same random wave effects as the galaxy arms, and in any area where the concentration became particularly great the matter began to gravitate together to form lumps, probably around 100 yards in diameter. Eventually these lumps began to collide and stick together. The larger accumulations scooped up the smaller pieces as the rings revolved, and in each ring all the ring matter began to accumulate into a single large mass—a "planetesimal."

Let us now concentrate on the planetesimal that eventually became the Earth. There are two main theories about the process of accretion. According to the first—the "homogeneous accretion model"— all the particles accumulated in a random mass, with every component spread throughout the planetesimal without a pattern of any sort. The same action that generated the heat of the protosun then generated heat in the embryonic Earth. The heat melted the iron and nickel in the mass and the droplets of these, being heavy, sank toward the center. The stony material—the silicates—being lighter, would have remained on the outside.

The alternative theory—the "heterogeneous accretion theory"—suggests that the iron and nickel gathered together to form the first planetesimal while the silicate material was still drifting about as the remains of the ring. The silicate then settled on the outside.

Whatever the process, the result is that we now have an Earth that is divided into a number of layers. There is an inner core of solid iron and nickel, an outer core of molten iron and nickel, a mantle of dense stony silicate material, and a crust of lighter silicate material.

From away out in space we can see little of the Earth but cloud and haze.
It looks blue because of reflection from the atmosphere and the oceans.
The shapes of the continents can be glimpsed through the cloud cover.
Astronauts in a low orbit can see the mountain ranges, the river courses,
the island chains. The geologist on the ground can actually touch the
Earth's substance, and make deductions about our planet's history.

Inside the Earth

Oceanic crust

- Outermost 3–6 miles below oceans
- Solid
- Average composition similar to that of basalt. High in silica and magnesium—sometimes referred to as SIMA. Distinguished from mantle composition by having more silica.
- Density 233 lb/cubic ft
- Temperature 1,148–32°F

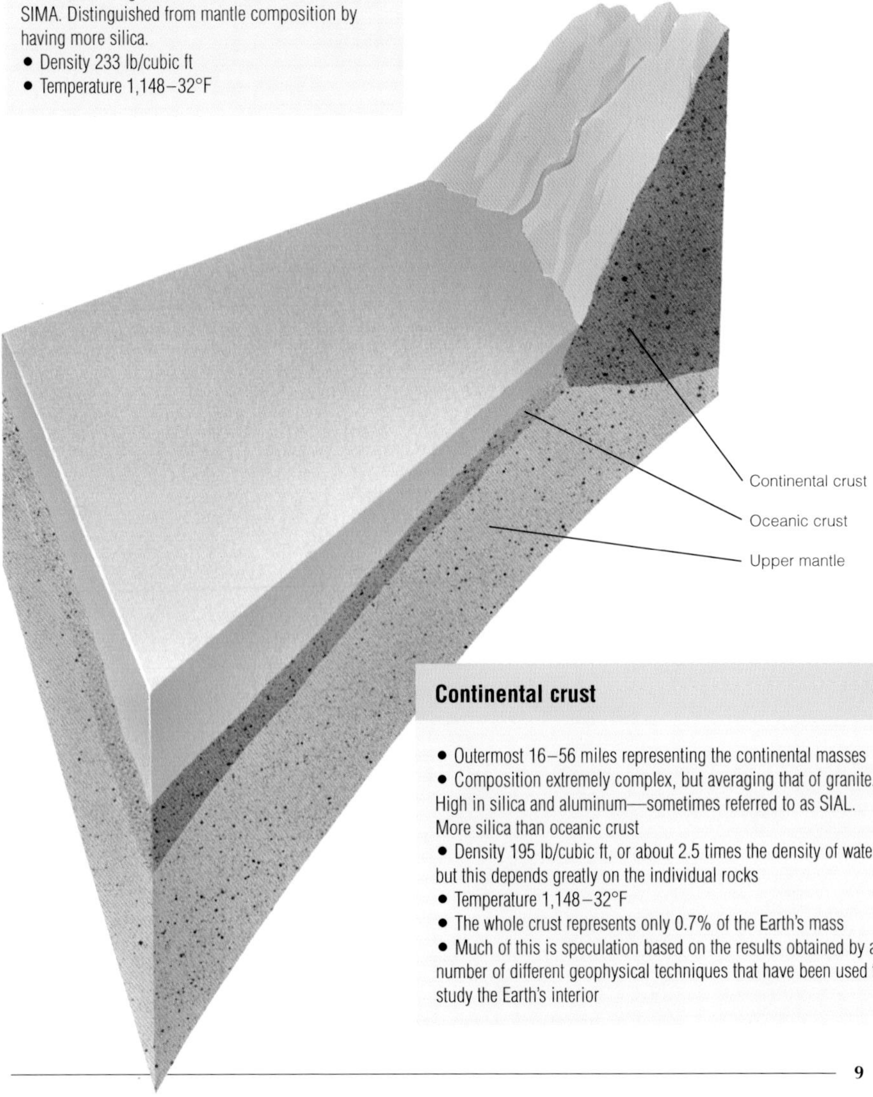

The Earth is composed of layers with distinct physical and chemical properties. The chemical compositions are more easily compared to those of common materials, which appear later in the book.

Continental crust

Oceanic crust

Upper mantle

Continental crust

- Outermost 16–56 miles representing the continental masses
- Composition extremely complex, but averaging that of granite. High in silica and aluminum—sometimes referred to as SIAL. More silica than oceanic crust
- Density 195 lb/cubic ft, or about 2.5 times the density of water, but this depends greatly on the individual rocks
- Temperature 1,148–32°F
- The whole crust represents only 0.7% of the Earth's mass
- Much of this is speculation based on the results obtained by a number of different geophysical techniques that have been used to study the Earth's interior

Upper mantle

- 249 miles to anything between 56 miles beneath continents and 3 miles beneath oceans
- Solid except for a squashy layer near the outside, especially below the oceans, where some of the minerals are molten
- Similar composition to rest of the mantle but richer in the mineral olivine
- Recognizable minerals, such as spinel and garnet, sometimes extruded by volcanoes
- Density 233 lb/cubic ft
- Temperature 2,340 – 1,148°F

Transition zone

- 652–249 miles
- Solid
- Similar composition to the rest of the mantle but showing changes between very compact mineral phases to looser, less dense phases
- Density 358 – 268 lb/cubic ft
- Temperature 3,240 – 2,340°F

Lower mantle

- 1,793–652 miles
- Solid
- Composition similar to the minerals olivine (60%), pyroxene (30%), and feldspar (10%). Fairly even composition throughout
- Density 420 – 358 lb/cubic ft
- Temperature 5,040 – 3,240°F
- The whole mantle represents 68.3% of the Earth's mass

Outer core

- 3,762–1,793 miles
- Liquid. Moving about by convection and producing the Earth's magnetic field
- Iron-sulfur mixture
- Density 950–770 lb/cubic ft
- Temperature 5,760°F
- 29.3% of the Earth's mass

Inner core

Center of the Earth
- 3,958–3,762 miles
- Solid
- Iron-nickel alloy
- Density 1,017 lb/cubic ft, or about 13 times the density of water as we know it
- Temperature 8,100°F
- 1.7% of the Earth's mass

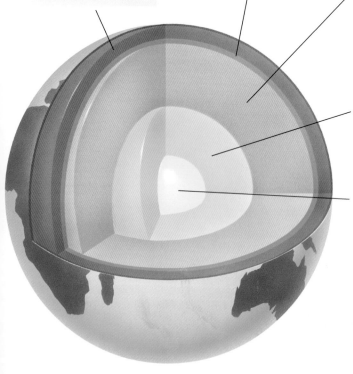

Evidence for the Theories

The interior of the Earth is as inaccessible to us as the interior of the Moon. Yet there are indirect ways of obtaining information about the subsurface features of our planet.

Meteoritic evidence Particles of the nebula that spawned the Earth and the rest of the solar system are still falling onto the surface of our planet. Occasionally these come in blocks large enough to survive the destructive heat of friction as they pass through the Earth's atmosphere, and so land as meteorites. Two types of meteorite are known: iron meteorites and stony meteorites. We can regard iron meteorites as remains of the substances that formed the core of our planet, and stony meteorites as representing the material of the mantle.

Eruptions of mantle material to the surface These rare occurrences give us the opportunity to analyze mantle material directly. Sometimes nodules of mantle appear in the basaltic lavas of oceanic volcanoes. The material for the basaltic lavas is

Above The Big Hole at Kimberley, South Africa, excavated in the diamond rush of the late 1800s, looks huge but is only 975 feet deep—a pinprick in the Earth's crust.

extruded from the mantle but usually it changes completely through cooling and lowering of pressure before coming anywhere near the surface. The unaltered mantle nodules carried in it contain silica, but in a much smaller proportion than in crystal rocks. Other nodules, called peridotites, are found in a particular kind of ancient volcano, called a kimberlite pipe. These nodules are interesting from an economic viewpoint because they contain diamonds, which are formed at depths of around 60 miles.

Seismic surveys The principle of studying the refraction of shock waves can be used on a local scale by generating artificial earthquakes. Controlled explosions are set off and the vibrations that are refracted through the various layers in the crust are then recorded by geophones and analyzed by computer.

Drilling An international team, led by the United States, has, since 1969, been drilling into the ocean crust. No one has yet succeeded in reaching the Mohorovičić (Moho) discontinuity, the boundary between the crust and the mantle.

Scientists can use bore holes to discover several things. They can analyze the core samples that are brought up. Instruments can be lowered to test the electrical properties of the various layers penetrated. A sonic generator can be lowered into the hole to produce a sound source for acoustic logging—similar in principle to seismic refraction. Sensors can be lowered to record the differences in natural radioactivity between the layers. In practice all of these techniques are used in combination to produce as complete a picture as possible.

Gravity studies The denser a material is, the greater will be its gravitational force. It takes a sensitive instrument to detect any difference in

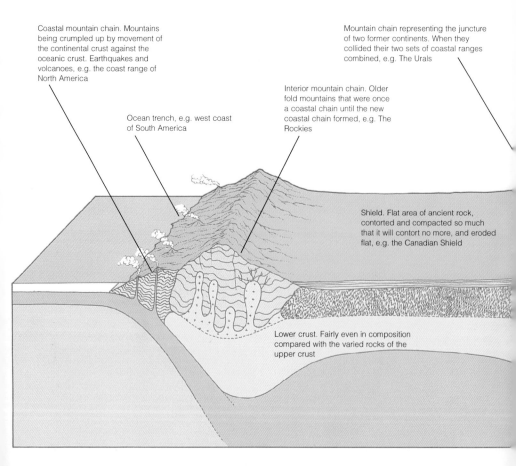

Coastal mountain chain. Mountains being crumpled up by movement of the continental crust against the oceanic crust. Earthquakes and volcanoes, e.g. the coast range of North America

Ocean trench, e.g. west coast of South America

Mountain chain representing the juncture of two former continents. When they collided their two sets of coastal ranges combined, e.g. The Urals

Interior mountain chain. Older fold mountains that were once a coastal chain until the new coastal chain formed, e.g. The Rockies

Shield. Flat area of ancient rock, contorted and compacted so much that it will contort no more, and eroded flat, e.g. the Canadian Shield

Lower crust. Fairly even in composition compared with the varied rocks of the upper crust

gravity between one place and another (a gravity anomaly), but it can be done.

The device used is called a gravimeter. It consists of a weight suspended on a spring. A region of high gravity—a positive anomaly—will pull the weight and the spring farther downward than a negative anomaly, and the difference can be measured. The various geophysical results show that the crust beneath the ocean is thin and dense. In the region of the continents, the crust is thick

and light. A typical continent will consist of a solid contorted mass of extremely ancient rock at its heart, surrounded by ranges of progressively younger mountains, and there may be very young mountains by the sea. Old mountains may lie across the continent, separating one shield area from another. This is the broad picture of a continent—a structure built of rocks. And it is these rocks that will constitute the subject of the rest of this book.

Below A typical continent is made up of a number of parts—usually a core of ancient metamorphic rock surrounded by the remains of mountain ranges. Not all continents exhibit all the features shown here.

Block mountains. Formed by cracking and shifting of the crust associated with a rift valley

Rift valley. Where earth movements are beginning to tear the continent apart. Earthquakes and volcanoes here too, e.g. The Great Rift of East Africa

Continental shelf. Edge of a continent that represents one flank of a rift valley—the other having been torn away. Continental mass broken into a steplike structure covered by younger rocks and shallow sea, e.g. the coast of the British Isles

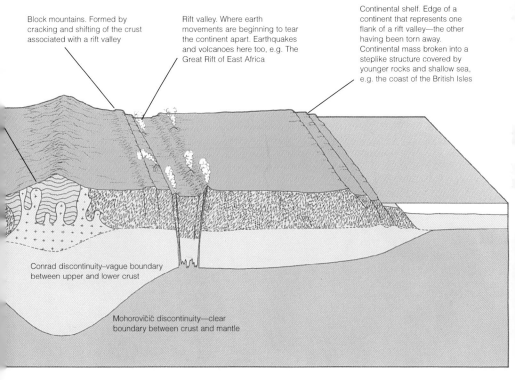

Conrad discontinuity–vague boundary between upper and lower crust

Mohorovičić discontinuity—clear boundary between crust and mantle

Substance of The Earth

Pick up a stone. In your hand you have a piece of the Earth's crust, made up of minerals produced by the chemical reactions that formed the planet.

Minerals—Rock Components
If you take a rock and look at it through a hand lens or a microscope, you will see that it is made up of a mosaic of interlocking particles. Sometimes, in rocks such as granite, these are so big that you can see them with the naked eye. These particles are the minerals, naturally occurring homogeneous solids which have been inorganically formed. They have definite chemical compositions and definite atomic structures.

When a rock forms, the chemicals organize themselves into a number of different minerals. There are hundreds of different types, each with its own particular chemical composition, but some are more common than others. Every rock is made up of a mixture of different minerals—but usually no more than a half dozen or so.

For convenience we can divide the minerals into two broad classifications—the rock-forming minerals and the ore minerals. The latter are those that usually come to mind when the word mineral is mentioned, those that can be mixed and processed for a product, but they are a very minor constituent of the Earth's crust.

As we have seen, silica (SiO_2) is the most common chemical component of the earth, so the most common rock-forming minerals are

Left and right Some minerals are economically important. These are called the ore minerals. Iron ore, for example, comes in several mineral forms, including the yellowish powdery limonite **left** and the unevenly shaped kidney ore **right**.

Left When we look closely at a rock we can see that it is made up of much smaller components. Sometimes they form good crystal shapes, and sometimes irregular chunks. These components are called the minerals.

Right Most minerals, however, are referred to as the rock-forming minerals, since they make up the bulk of the rocks. Calcite is a common rock-forming mineral, but rarely does it produce the well-shaped crystals seen here.

silicates—minerals containing silica. Silica can take part in complex chemical reactions and so there are many different types of silicate material.

The simplest silicate material is quartz, which is pure silica. More commonly there are metallic elements combined with the silica. Magnesium forms a high proportion of the oceanic crust, and so the magnesium-iron silicate material called olivine ($(Mg,Fe)_2SiO_4$) is common here.

Continental crust is rich in aluminum, and so continental rocks tend to be rich in the aluminum silicate minerals called the feldspars, such as orthoclase ($KAlSi_3O_8$) and albite ($NaAlSi_3O_8$).

Carbonates—compounds containing carbon—are also important rock-forming minerals. Perhaps the most important is calcite ($CaCO_3$). This tends to be unstable when exposed to the weather and so rocks containing large proportions of carbonate tend to be eroded more quickly than those containing the more robust silicate minerals.

The silicates contain metals. However, their chemical nature is such that the metals are almost impossible to remove. Olivine therefore cannot be regarded as a source of magnesium, any more than feldspar would be a useful storehouse of aluminum. Ore minerals must contain a metal that is easily extracted. Sometimes a mineral contains the metal and nothing else. Such "native ores" include gold nuggets.

Oxides—formed when the metal combines with oxygen—are important ore minerals. Most of the iron ores are oxides, such as magnetite (Fe_3O_4) and hematite (Fe_2O_3).

A metal combined with sulfur forms a sulfide mineral, many of which are ore minerals. These include iron pyrites (FeS_2) and the lead mineral galena (PbS).

BUILDING, LOOKING AFTER, AND DISPLAYING YOUR COLLECTION

Collecting Minerals

Rocks and minerals are the very substance of the Earth, and finding, identifying, and collecting them can be a rewarding hobby. You should never lose sight of the scientific aspects of what you are doing. Collecting is more than an end in itself; it will help you to understand what has happened on the particular piece of ground you are exploring.

The Field Trip
Before going on a field trip, do some research. Local museums, study centers, gem stores, and geologists will tell you where to go and what to look out for. A vital aid will be local geological maps. These come in two types: those that show the solid geology of the area and those, called drift maps, that show the distribution of loose surface sediment spread by glaciers, rivers, and erosion. Geological maps will show you not only the type of rock to be found, but its structure and angle of strata. They will not show features such as roads, buildings, and woods.

Above Scree slopes have plenty of loose rocks, but they are dangerous places to hunt for minerals because debris may fall at any time.

Tools and Equipment
For the field you will need a compass as well as maps. Essential tools are a geologist's hammer (the sharp end is for cleaning not smashing), chisel, hand lens, and penknife. Bubble wrap and plastic containers, as well as a cloth bag, for specimens are useful. Protective goggles, a hard hat, and strong gloves will stop you being harmed by stone chips or falling rocks. The scientific value of a find will be lost if its surroundings go unrecorded, so take a pen and notebook and a camera. Rock falls, scree slopes, and alluvial deposits are the best places to find minerals rather than solid rock faces which in any case should not be damaged.

At home you will need to identify your specimens before cleaning them. Halite, for example, will dissolve in water and must not be washed. You will need a streak plate (see page 34) and a hardness points kit (see page 25). For cleaning you will need a toothbrush and, for very fragile specimens, a blower brush as used by photographers to clean lenses.

Polishing and Cutting

You can polish pebbles in a machine called a tumbler, available from specialty stores. It costs as much as a small camera, but if you want to make a display, or turn samples into presents, it can be a worthwhile investment. A tumbler is a drum rotated by an electric motor. You place your pebbles in the drum with abrasive grit and water. When you switch on, the drum rotates slowly, and the grit grinds the pebble. After a few days' grinding, you change to a finer grit. After a few changes of grit and a final polish, you end up with shiny specimens. Even small beach pebbles look exceptional after this treatment.

An advanced piece of equipment for the serious collector is a diamond-impregnated saw for cutting agate into slices. This is driven by a motor which can also drive a tumbler. Once cut, slices can be polished on a horizontal circulating disk treated with different grades of abrasive grit. You can make these slices thin enough for light to shine through them.

Left Never search for minerals in such dangerous places as high unstable cliffs.

Below The basic equipment for cleaning samples is a nailbrush or toothbrush and a bowl of water with a drop of detergent. However, a range of scrapers and tweezers is invaluable.

Displaying Your Collection

Minerals and gems vary in hardness and may scratch or chip if knocked against each other. The simplest solution is to store samples individually in cardboard boxes or sturdier plastic boxes that can be bought from a gem store. Keep the boxes in a shallow box or drawer.

Minerals and gems look their best when they are clean and sparkling, so a cover is important if you want to keep them dust-free. Prized items can be displayed in a glass-fronted cabinet, or even on an open surface, supported on mounts, which can be bought from a specialist supplier. It is best to reserve polished specimens of simple shapes for open display because they are easier to keep clean.

Cataloging your Collection

1 Put a reference number on each specimen: dab a spot of white paint or correcting fluid on an inconspicuous part of the specimen, wait for this to dry, and write the number on it.

2 Log the identification number for each mineral in a card file. Write the name and characteristics of each specimen, date and place found or bought, on the card. Arrange the cards in numerical order.

3 If you keep your collection in a drawer to protect them from dust, you could arrange them thematically; by family, by color, or in numerical order to tie in with your card index system.

GEMS, CRYSTALS, AND MINERALS— INTRODUCTION

The Earth's crust consists of rock which itself is an aggregate of minerals. These minerals have developed—and are still developing—from the basic material in the star dust that formed our solar system. If a mineral is allowed to develop unhindered it will form a characteristic three-dimensional shape called a crystal. This development is an inorganic chemical process caused by elements and compounds coming into contact with one another in conditions of varying intensity. Only if a crystal satisfies the three requirements of beauty, durability, and rarity it is classified as a gemstone.

The growth of crystals is similar to that of a pearl which develops layer by layer from a grain of sand within an oyster. It is hard to believe that crystals form one atom at a time, but this process takes place in three dimensions and is repeated thousands of times a second. Depending on the size of the crystal, they can take anything from a day to a year to be completed.

Crystals are formed from cases, molten rock, or aqueous solutions which are usually created far below the Earth's surface. Sometimes they are re-formed from previously solid material which has been heated and pressurized until it liquefies, only resuming a solid state when the pressure and/or the heat source is removed. Such re-formed crystals may not resemble their original form due to the addition or subtraction of elements, or because of a change in the heat and/or pressure of the growth environment.

Crystals are often formed as a result of hydrothermal action. A super-hot solution heavily charged with chemical elements is forced by high temperature through microcracks and veins. As this solution is displaced, its temperature and pressure are dissipated. When the conditions are right and

Below A fine example of a Brazilian agate geode that has been infilled with quartz, followed by further infilling to give a central core of opal. (Magnification × ½)

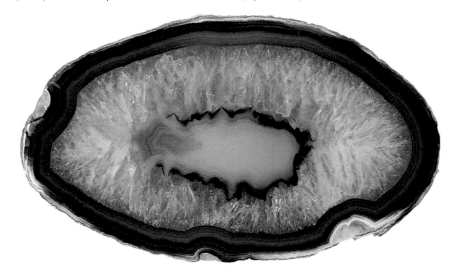

less "turbulent," crystals will start to grow out of the solution.

Crystals are also formed from solutions of elemental salts which become steadily more concentrated as they exceed their saturation level. This usually happens when the inlet or outlet of an inland lake or sea is altered by geological uplift and the resulting solution becomes progressively more concentrated as natural evaporation occurs. This continues until saturation is achieved and crystallization then follows.

The size of crystals depends on the rate of growth: the slower they grow, the larger they will be. This may be due to evaporation, a cooling off of the solution, or the bleeding off of pressure. Sometimes the results of slow crystal growth are spectacular; in Brazil a beryl crystal weighing 200 tons was found and in Siberia a milky quartz crystal of 13 tons was uncovered. Slow growth rate also causes the crystal to be shaped more regularly because the atoms have more time in which to

assume some orderly arrangement.

The faces of a crystal do not necessarily grow at the same speed. This difference in the rate of face growth, if very pronounced, will result in elongated crystals. A faster accumulation of atoms in one direction, due possibly to a strong electrical attraction, will be exaggerated as the atoms are being attracted to a small face-end rather than to a long side. Similarly if a crystal grows from a solid base, as is so often the case with amethysts and halite, only half of the crystal is in a position to receive new unit-cells. It is astonishing that these crystals are not more frequently malformed and irregular in shape.

Even under ideal conditions, few minerals form regular shapes. Instead they simply assume a more rigid form of the liquid phase. When such minerals are formed from a gel, they are usually composed of tiny crystals which, given time and stable conditions, will join together to form solid masses or aggregates.

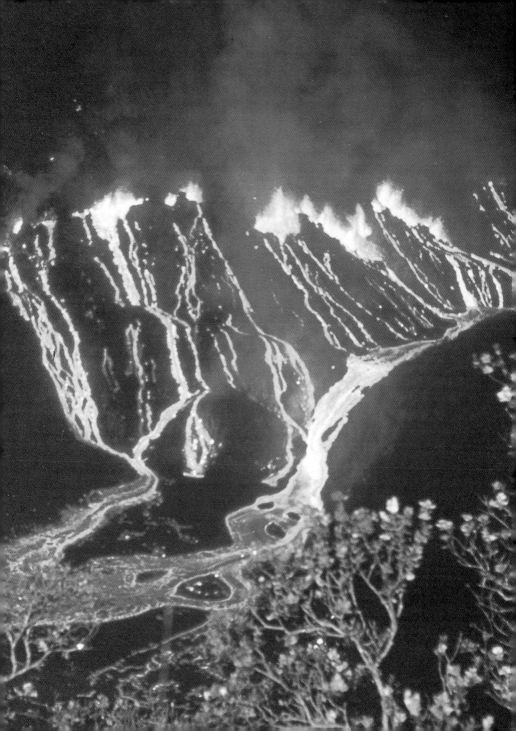

Properties of Crystals

Crystal Systems

When a cube is held by its two opposite square faces it can be rotated so a different square face presents itself four times (four-fold symmetry). There are three such axes of four-fold symmetry (written as 3iv). The cube has 13 symmetry axes— 3iv, 4iii, 6ii—but only the 3iv axis is characteristic of the cubic (or isometric) crystal system.

There are seven crystal systems, based on the number of axes of symmetry developed. These are:

Cubic System Three axes at 90 degrees, all equal in length

Tetragonal System Three axes at 90 degrees, two of equal length, plus one longer axis

Orthorhombic System Three axes at 90 degrees, all of different length

Monoclinic System Two axes at 90 degrees, plus one axis at a different angle, all of different length

Triclinic System Three axes of different length, none at 90 degrees

Hexagonal and Trigonal Systems Three axes of equal length in one plane at 120 degrees, plus a longer axis at 90 degrees to the plane containing the other three (these two systems are distinguished by their differing symmetry—the hexagonal system has one six-fold symmetry and the trigonal has one three-fold symmetry).

Crystallographic axes are lines that intersect crystal faces. The isometric or cubic system has four such axes at 90 degrees to each other and the crystal faces that intersect these axes are identified by Millar indices—100 for the cube face intersected by the A$_1$ axis, 010 for the face intersected by the A$_2$ axis and 001 for the face intersected by the A$_3$ axis. Where the A$_1$ axis intersects a face, the Millar index is 100; when all three axes intersect a crystal face, the Millar index is 111. A Millar index of 210 indicates that the A$_1$ axis cuts the face at a different distance to that of the A$_2$ axis.

All axes are divided into positive and negative portions which start at the point of intersection—or origin—of the axes. The negative axis is represented by a bar above the index (e.g. 10$\bar{1}$); the positive portion of the axis has no bar (e.g. 101).

Related to the crystal structure is a property called the cleavage. Planes of weakness in the crystal lattice reveal themselves in the tendency for the crystal to split in a certain direction.

A crystal may grow in two different directions from one face. The result is called a twin. Twinned crystals can be recognized by the presence of re-entrant angles. Commonly, twinning occurs in the cubic system, where one cube penetrates another.

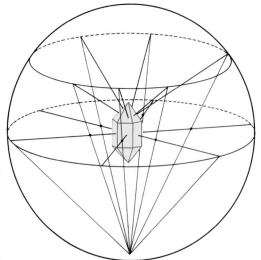

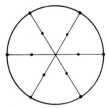

The faces of a crystal can be plotted on a plane. The mathematics are complex but the theory is simple. Imagine a crystal placed at the center of a sphere **left**. Project lines from the center at right angles to each face to meet the surface of the sphere. Connect each of these surface points to the south pole of the sphere. The pattern formed where these lines cut the equatorial plane of the sphere is the stereographic projection. It does not matter how distorted the crystal is, the resulting stereographic projection is the same, because of the constancy of interfacial angles.

In practice stereographic projections are plotted on a kind of circular graph called a Wulff net.

Classification	Face Shape and Axis Orientation	Form	Examples
ISOMETRIC OR CUBIC		All three axes are the same length and are at right angles to each other.	garnet (icositetrahedron) spinel (octahedron)
TETRAGONAL		Three axes which are at right angles to each other. The two on the same plane are equal in length while the third is perpendicular to this plane and of different length.	zircon scapolite
HEXAGONAL		Three of the four axes are in one plane and intersect at 60°. The fourth axis is perpendicular and unequal in length to the others. There are six planes of symmetry.	apatite beryl
TRIGONAL		Similar to the hexagonal system. There are three axes at 60° to each other in the same plane. The fourth axis is perpendicular. There are three planes of symmetry.	quartz sapphire
ORTHORHOMBIC		Three axes of unequal length. Two are at right angles to one another and the third is perpendicular.	peridot topaz
MONOCLINIC		There are three axes of unequal length. Two intersect at an oblique angle in one plane and the third is perpendicular.	orthoclase feldspar epidote
TRICLINIC		Three axes of unequal length all inclined to one another at different angles.	alkali feldspar (amazonite) rhodonite

Millar Indices

ISOMETRIC/CUBIC

012
102
201
210 210 021
201

TETRAGONAL

001
111 111
110 110
111 111

HEXAGONAL

1011 0110
1101
1100
1010 0110
1011 0111
1101

Regularity

The regularity with which crystals form was first noted by Nicolaus Steno, the Danish scientist, in 1669. He found that at a specific temperature and pressure, all crystals of the same substance possess the same angle between corresponding faces. This is known as the law of constancy of interfacial angles. It was further clarified by Reinhard Bernhardi, in the early nineteenth century, who showed that the angle referred to was taken at right angles to the faces toward the central point of the crystal.

Above Different sections through the main axes of quartz crystals. The crystal on the left has developed regularly while the other two have developed unequally but still comply with the law of constancy of interfacial angles.

Left Bright, vitreous pyrope crystals look like spots of blood in this greenish quartz. In some the crystal shape is clear; in others it is rounded by erosion. Pyrope gets its blood-red color from traces of iron and chromium. The word pyrope comes from the Greek word for fire.

Hardness

Hardness, an inherent and easily determined characteristic of a mineral, is measured using a resistance to scratching method known as Mohs' Scale, named for Freidrich Mohs (1773–1839), a Viennese mineralogist. Frustrated by the existing method of describing minerals in such scientifically imprecise terms as "soft" or "hard" (with the prefixes of "medium," "very," or "extreme"), Mohs decided that a more scientific approach to hardness measuring was required. If mineralogy was to be considered a true science it would have to meet science's exacting standards in nomenclature to begin with.

Accordingly, Mohs chose 10 minerals of varying degrees of hardness, and allocated each a "hardness number," ranging from 1 as the softest to 10 as the hardest. Each mineral in the series is capable of scratching the mineral below it in the scale, as well as itself being scratched by the one above. Those with a hardness of 1 to 2 are called soft, 3 to 6 are termed medium-hard, 6 to 8 are hard, and 8 to 10 have "precious-stone" hardness status.

Mohs' Scale

	Comparison Mineral	Mineral Test	Rosiwal's Grinding Hardness
1	Talc	Powdered by fingernail	0.03
2	Gypsum	Scratched by fingernail	1.25
3	Calcite	Scratched by copper coin	4.5
4	Fluorite	Easily scratched by pocket knife	5.0
5	Apatite	Just scratched by pocket knife	6.5
6	Orthoclase	Scratched by steel file	37
7	Quartz	Scratches glass window	120
8	Topaz	Easily scratches quartz	175
9	Corundum	Easily scratches topaz	1,000
10	Diamond	Cannot be scratched	140,000

Mohs' Scale ranges from 1, whose comparison mineral is talc (**top**), to 10, whose comparison mineral is diamond (**above**).

Traditionally, a geologist would carry samples of most of the minerals in the scale in order to be able to field-test rocks. Today, it is possible to buy a set of what are known as hardness pencils; these consist of splinters of the appropriate mineral set into a mineral holder with the hardness value clearly indicated on the holder. Care should be taken when conducting a hardness test that only a sound surface is tested.

The advantage of Mohs' scratch hardness test is its simplicity and ease of application. However, it is an empirical scale and does not bear any relationship to hardness in the strict scientific sense of that term. This can be seen by consulting the right-hand side of the table above which lists the Rosiwal cutting resistance or grinding hardness of the materials used in Mohs' Scale. The Rosiwal Scale was devised by August Karl Rosiwal (1860–1923), and is a scientific scale of hardness.

The hardness of a material depends on the atomic bonding of the crystal structure. These bonds can vary depending on their crystallographic direction. Hardness variations are displayed by striated, laminated, or weathered crystals, among others. The most celebrated example of hardness variation occurs in the kyanite crystal which displays a hardness of 4 to 5 along the length parallel to the C axis but a value of 6 to 7 across the width parallel to the B axis.

Specific Gravity

The specific gravity of a crystal (sometimes referred to as its relative density) is defined as the weight per unit volume, i.e. the ratio of the weight of an object to that of an equal volume of distilled water. Consequently, a crystal with a specific gravity of 4 is four times as heavy as the same volume of water.

The specific gravity of a crystal can be measured in a number of ways. Firstly, using a hydrostatic balance, the crystal is weighed in air (W1) and then in distilled water (W2). Its specific gravity can then be calculated as:

$$\text{specific gravity} = \frac{W1}{W1 - W2}$$

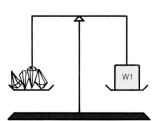 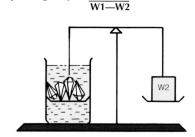

Above Using a hydrostatic balance.

An alternative method uses a pycnometer (density measurer). This device is a bottle with a tightly fitting stopper which has a capillary hole in it. The procedure adopted consists of first weighing the crystal on scales (see diagram, W1). The pycnometer is then filled with distilled water, and, with the stopper in place, is also weighed (W2).

Next, the crystal is placed in the pycnometer and the stopper replaced. The excess water is now removed, and the pycnometer and its contents weighed once more (W3). The specific gravity of the crystal can now be calculated using the formula:

$$\text{specific gravity} = \frac{W1}{W1 + W2 - W3}$$

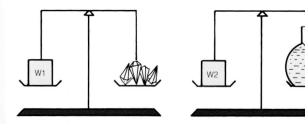 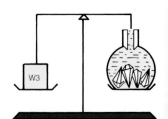

Above The three stages of using a pycnometer.

The density of a material is a function of how closely together the atoms are packed. It is often used by the mineral processing engineer as an easy and reliable way of separating a useful mineral from a worthless one, especially if there is a large differential in their respective specific gravities.

Comparable pieces of calcite and galena. These two samples are pretty much the same size, but the lead-rich galena **far right**, with its high specific gravity is much heavier than the calcite **left**.

Color

Some colors are striking and serve a diagnostic purpose, while others are less useful for identification purposes. The colors of the following minerals help identify them:
Galena lead gray
Malachite green
Pyrites brassy yellow
    The colors of the following are variable and therefore of less diagnostic value:
Barytes
Fluorspar
Quartz

Luster

Luster is the way light is reflected from a mineral's surface. A surface may be very shiny, almost like glass, or it may hardly reflect the light at all. There are a number of special words used to describe luster, and, for the most part, they are self-explanatory.
Adamantine brilliant, like diamonds, e.g. cassiterite
Vitreous like broken glass, e.g. quartz
Resinous like resin or wax, e.g. sphalerite
Greasy like the surface of margarine or butter, shiny but not as bright as glass, e.g. halite
Pearly like pearls, e.g. stilbite
Silky like silk, e.g. satin spa
Splendent brilliant reflectivity, e.g. specularite
Shining reflects an image, but not clearly, e.g. selenite
Metallic like polished metal, e.g. pyrites
Glistening reflects light, but not an image, e.g. chalcopyrite
Glimmering has imperfect reflections from points on the specimen, e.g. flint
Dull with little reflection

Left Pyrite displays a metallic to glistening luster.

Fracture

When a specimen breaks smoothly and evenly along certain planes, these are called cleavage planes. Other specimens break randomly, while some may give a distinctive type of break or fracture:
Conchoidal breaks with concentric cavities, e.g. quartz
Subconchoidal indistinct conchoidal, e.g. tourmaline
Even surface flat, but slightly rough, e.g. barytes
Uneven surface rough and irregular, e.g. pyroxene
Hackly surface has sharp points, e.g. specularite
Earthy surface dull and crumbly, e.g. limonite

Right A mineral's fracture can be diagnostic. Conchoidal fracture, such as in this obsidian, produces patterns of concentric ridges.

Tenacity

Another related test is for tenacity. Minerals are termed:
Sectile if they are easily cut by a knife, e.g. gypsum
Brittle if they crumble when hit by a hammer, e.g. calcite
Malleable if cut slices can be flattened by hitting them with a hammer, e.g. copper
Flexible if they will bend without breaking, e.g. chrysotile

Right Galena, a member of the sulfide group, is very brittle.

Refraction and Reflection of Light

The behavior of light entering a crystal is dependent upon the internal atomic structure of the mineral. Values for different gem minerals can be measured and used as a means of identification.

Isometric minerals and non-crystalline minerals are isotropic (have the same optical properties in all directions). When light enters them it is slowed down and its course is changed (the light ray is bent or refracted). Each ray of light is slowed down and refracted by the same amount and the mineral is said to be singly refractive. Light entering minerals crystalizing in any of the other six crystal systems (see pages 22–23) is split into two rays and each ray is refracted by a different amount. These crystals are said to be doubly refractive.

Doubly refractive gemstones may appear to be different colors and different shades of the body color when viewed from different directions. They are said to be pleochroic. Gemstones that show two colors are dichroic and belong to the tetragonal, trigonal, or hexagonal crystal symmetry classes. Gemstones that show three colors are trichroic and belong to the orthorhombic, monoclinic, or triclinic crystal symmetry classes. An instrument called a dichroscope can be used to see two colors side by side through the eyepiece.

Above A cut sinhalite stone showing double refraction because it has a range of refractive indices.

Above Pleochroism in an iolite cut stone. The stone shows blue and colorless as it is turned.

Stones with strong pleochroism, which can be seen easily with the naked eye, include iolite (yellow, pale blue, dark blue) and tourmaline (two shades of the body color).

The refractive index (RI) indicates the amount that the light rays are bent by a mineral and it is measured by a refractometer. A singly refractive mineral has one refractive index but a doubly refractive mineral has a range of refractive indices. The difference between the minimum and maximum refractive indices in such a crystal is called its birefringence. When the birefringence is high, the light rays can be seen to reflect off different parts of the back of the stone, causing an apparent doubling of the back facets when viewed through the front facet.

Light that is reflected from fibers or fibrous cavities within the mineral may appear as a cat's-eye (chatoyancy) or a star (asterism) when cut with a domed top (*en cabochon*). Cat's-eyes can be seen when the light is reflected from parallel arrangements of inclusions as in chrysoberyl cat's-eyes. Star stones are seen when several sets of parallel fibers reflect light. A four-rayed star has two sets of parallel fibers and a six-rayed star has three sets of parallel fibers. Occasionally, a twelve-rayed sapphire star stone can be cut.

Above Chrysoberyl cat's-eyes or chatoyants reflect light from parallel arrangements of inclusions.

Left Calcite is a mineral which may be transparent and objects can be seen through a crystal — some clear calcite crystals, called Iceland Spar, give a double image when you look through them.

Right Blue aquamarines showing different styles of faceting.

Analyzing Minerals with Light

If you slice a rock or a mineral thinly enough, it is transparent and, when mounted on a glass slide, can be examined through a special kind of microscope. This technique is the main one used by professional geologists to identify the different minerals and rocks.

A petrological microscope is basically a conventional desk-mounted optical microscope, with attachments. Below the microscope stage is a polarizing filter—called the polarizer—so only polarized light passes through the specimen. In the barrel of the microscope is a removable polarizing filter—called the analyzer—mounted at right angles to the first, that blocks the polarized light coming up the barrel. As a result, no light is visible to the user. A slice of mineral on the stage, however, may affect the polarization of the light passing through, and it becomes visible to the viewer in a false color—called an interference color. This repolarization of the light by the mineral depends on its crystal symmetry, and the angle at which it lies. The specimen stage of a petrological microscope is a turntable, so that a specimen can be rotated and the effect examined.

Refractive index This is studied without using the analyzer. Light passing from one medium into another is refracted, or bent, toward the denser medium. The principle is the same as the study of shock waves passing through the Earth after an

Right With polarized light passing through, a thin section of the rock schist reveals the individual minerals. Certain kinds of mica show up brown, while large irregular crystals of garnet are a pinkish-gray. Black opaque crystals are tiny fragments of iron ore.

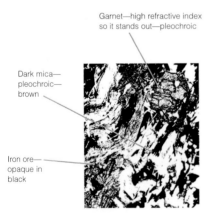

Garnet—high refractive index so it stands out—pleochroic

Dark mica— pleochroic— brown

Iron ore— opaque in black

earthquake. In a rock slice, where minerals of different refractive indices abut one another, light passing up through the sample is refracted into the mineral with the higher RI. As a result, those minerals with high RIs appear to have a band of brightness around the insides of their margins—the so-called Becke line.

Isotropic minerals Thin sections of some minerals do not affect the polarity of the light passing through. Polarized light passing through is blocked by the analyzer, so these minerals show up as dark shapes.

Anisotropic minerals Most minerals affect the polarity of the polarized light passing through them, and show up in their interference colors. When that mineral is turned a particular way, the effect on the polarity is minimal and the mineral becomes dark. When the microscope stage is turned to this extinction angle the effect is like a light going out. Some minerals turn dark when they are lined up parallel to the polarization of the light—they show straight extinction. Others go dark when the crystal lies at an angle to the polarization—showing oblique extinction. Studies of these angles are important in identifying individual minerals.

All micas (dark and light)—twisted grain—gaudy interference colors

Iron ore—still black

Left When a polarizing filter is put in place, affecting the polarized light already passing through the specimen, most of the minerals show up in false colors that can help to identify them. The garnet becomes completely black and the twisted crystals of mica show the strain under which the rock formed. A mass of quartz crystals shows up as a mosaic of gray crystals.

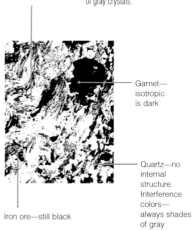

Garnet—isotropic is dark

Quartz—no internal structure. Interference colors—always shades of gray

Streak

A mineral's streak is the color of its powder. While many minerals vary in color to look at, their streak typically remains the same color. Fluorite, for instance, comes in many colors, but its streak is always white. Some minerals that are the same color, such as

magnetite and chromite, can be told apart by their streak. Magnetite has a black streak and chromite a buff or brown streak.

To find the streak you need a streak plate. You can buy a streak plate from a specialty store—or simply use the unglazed back of a porcelain kitchen or bathroom tile. To create a streak, rub the mineral along the tile. This won't work with very hard minerals, which just scratch the plate.

Above To test for streak you need a porcelain kitchen or bathroom tile. Turn it over and use the unglazed back. Break the rock down into individual minerals if you can. If you use a lump of rock, as here, scratch with the mineral you want to identify.

Transparency

Just as you can see through glass, you can see through some solid minerals. Such minerals are said to be transparent. Calcite is transparent but gives a double image of things when you look through it. Other minerals, like aquamarine, you may not be able to see through, but light shines through them. Such minerals are said to be translucent. If no light shines through at all, the mineral is said to be opaque.

Left Some crystals demonstrate an optical characteristic called birefringence, in which an object viewed through the crystal is seen double. In this instance, the transparent crystal is calcite from Iceland.

Birthstones

Month	Color	Official stone	Month	Color	Official stone
January	Dark red	Garnet	July	Red	Ruby
February	Purple	Amethyst	August	Pale green	Peridot
March	Pale blue	Aquamarine	September	Deep blue	Sapphire
April	White (transparent)	Diamond	October	Variegated	Opal
May	Bright green	Emerald	November	Yellow	Topaz
June	Cream	Pearl	December	Sky-blue	Turquoise

This decorative box is set with a large citrine and other gemstones. The lizard is carved from cat's-eye quartz.

Gem, Crystal, and Mineral Color Key

Over these pages, you will find the information you need to identify a wide range of gems and minerals. If you have a good idea what a specimen is, you can go straight to the appropriate page and check if it fits the facts. Make sure all the facts fit, not just most of them—even a small difference can indicate a different mineral's identity. If you have no idea what the sample is, look for each key factor in turn, starting with color. Below, stones are grouped vertically according to their common color to help you get started. It is worth making your own charts of other properties, such as luster. Remember though, that many minerals occur in a wide variety of colors.

Colorless
Diamond

White
Milky quartz

Kunzite

Ruby

Zircon

Calcite

Morganite beryl

Spinel

Rock crystal-quartz

Pink
Rose quartz

Red
Agate

Almandine

Yellowish
Citrine

Amber

Jade

Lapis Lazuli

Amber-brown
Heliodor beryl

Green
Emerald

Peridot

Turquoise

Carnelian

Garnet

Amazonite

Topaz

Caingorm
(smoky quartz)

Malachite

Blue
Aquamarine

Purple
Amethyst

Fashioning Gemstones

Gemstones may be found as rough crystals or rolled pebbles. They are cut and polished by lapidaries whose aim is to make the stone as attractive as possible while retaining as much of its weight as they can.

When deciding how best to cut a gemstone, the lapidary must have a knowledge of the properties of the stone being dealt with. Lapidaries must be aware of the stone's strengths (including hardness, dispersion "fire," and birefringence) and weaknesses (cleavage), and must carefully observe the stone for any flaws or inclusions. It is important to orient the stone so that the best color of a pleochroic stone is seen and flaws or inclusions are hidden.

The oldest and simplest cuts are cabochons. A stone cut *en cabochon* has a smooth polished surface with a rounded or curved outline. The cabochon cut is used mainly for opaque or translucent stones, for stones with a strong body color, iridescence or sheen, or to show cat's-eyes or star stones to best advantage.

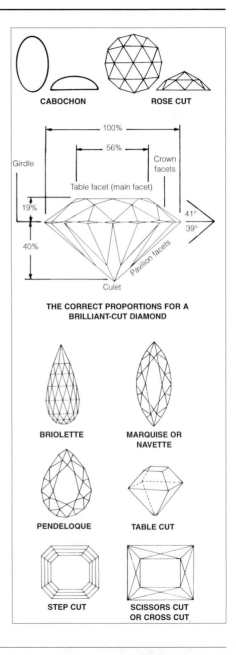

CABOCHON   ROSE CUT

THE CORRECT PROPORTIONS FOR A
BRILLIANT-CUT DIAMOND

BRIOLETTE   MARQUISE OR
NAVETTE

PENDELOQUE   TABLE CUT

STEP CUT   SCISSORS CUT
OR CROSS CUT

A collection of star-stone and cat's-eye cabochons.

Transparent stones are cut to show a number of flat polished faces (faceted). The brilliant cut is one of the most popular and is ideal for diamonds because it makes the most of the high dispersion and adamantine luster. In an ideal cut, all the light that reaches or enters a stone is reflected. The facets at the front of the stone (crown facets) reflect light off the surface, seen as the luster. The large central facet on the crown is the table facet. Light that enters the stone is reflected off the back facets (pavilion facets) to show the color and fire. If the angles are not correct, some light may be lost through the back facets.

The step cut (or trap cut) style of faceting has been developed for stones where the color is the most important feature. It is used for emeralds and rubies. There are a number of other cuts, some of which are illustrated. A rare or interesting stone may be fashioned in an unusual cut to add to its interest or to keep as much weight as possible.

Imitations

A number of different materials can be used to copy or imitate gemstones. These imitations may be manmade or natural.

Imitations may simply be pieces of glass colored to look like gems, or they may be more complex and made up of several different materials (composite stones). The bubbles and swirls characteristic of paste may be seen even without the help of a hand lens, and scratches on the surface of the glass are often apparent. Glass is singly refractive and many of the stones it imitates are doubly refractive.

Diamond Imitations

Imitation	In comparison with diamond
Spinel	less fire than diamond
Sapphire	less brilliant
YAG	heavy, lacks fire
Sphene	soft, birefringence too strong
Synthetic scheelite	soft
High zircon	birefringence too strong
Cubic zirconia	heavy
Strontium titanate	soft, more fire than diamond
Synthetic rutile	strongly birefringent, excess fire
Paste	soft
Rock crystal	lacks fire

Above Dispersion and light in **from left to right**: strontium titanate, cubic zirconia, diamond, yttrium aluminum garnet (YAG), and synthetic white sapphire.

Above Rock crystal is used to imitate diamonds.

The garnet-topped doublet was regularly used in Victorian times to imitate gemstones of various colors. These were made by cementing a piece of almandine garnet on top of a piece of glass; the garnet and glass together was then faceted to imitate ruby, sapphire, or emerald. The joint between the two pieces can often be seen in the top part of the stone and the difference in luster between the parts is usually distinctive.

Soudé emeralds are composite stones made to imitate emerald by cementing two pieces of pale beryl or rock crystal together with a green cement. The junction is often concealed in a closed setting. Other composite stones include opal doublets and triplets.

Synthetics

Synthetic stones are manmade materials that have the same chemical composition and therefore almost the same physical and optical properties as the naturally formed gemstone. Synthetics are made in laboratories using a number of techniques which include melting or dissolving powdered chemicals before allowing them to cool and crystalize.

Synthetic corundum has characteristic internal

Three Types of Composite Stones

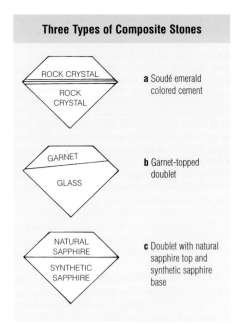

a Soudé emerald
colored cement

b Garnet-topped doublet

c Doublet with natural sapphire top and synthetic sapphire base

features that may be seen using a hand lens or a microscope. Curved growth lines (instead of the straight growth lines of natural corundum) and inclusions of small bubbles can be used to help distinguish between natural and synthetic stones. Synthetic emeralds also have distinctive inclusions, including liquid-filled cavities and two-phase inclusions (a liquid and a gaseous bubble).

Pierre Gilson produced black-and-white opals with a structure similar to that of natural opal and giving the same play of color. Under a microscope the Gilson opals have a distinctive mosaic pattern with a "lizard skin" appearance. Gilson synthetic turquoise can be recognized by its characteristic structure of dark blue angular particles on a whitish background. Gilson synthetic lapis lazuli can be distinguished from natural lapis lazuli by its low density and high porosity.

Left Brownish yellow synthetic diamonds manufactured at the De Beers Diamond Research Laboratory.

Crystal Uses, Past and Present

Crystals were originally used by primitive man as a cutting edge; they were attached to a wooden shaft or handle, which could be used as a formidable weapon or tool. They were also used by cave dwellers in the paintings they made on the sides of rocks and cave walls, some of which still exist in southern France, northern Spain, and eastern Australia. These paints were made from ground and powdered hematite (red), limonite (yellow), and pyrolusite (blue-black) which were mixed with water or animal fats to produce a paste. They have also been used in this form as a body paint to be worn in battle, at ceremonies, or as a religious decoration.

Over 5,000 years ago in Ancient Egypt, the Pharaohs employed thousands of slaves to work the turquoise mines located within the Sinai Peninsula. These were perhaps the first commercially operated crystal mines. In addition to their quest for turquoise, the Egyptians had an almost fanatical desire for lapis lazuli. As the demand for this beautiful crystal could not be met by local production, supplies were carried from Afghanistan, some 2,500 miles away. Imitations

Below Long sought after for its beauty and endurance, gold is a rare metal which may be found in crystal form. This gold dredge is working a river bed in South Island, New Zealand.

were also produced to help meet the demand.

Today, some of the most commonplace materials, such as plaster of Paris and rock salt, come from crystal sources. Crystals are used in the metals industry not only as a source of most metal ores, but as the main ingredient of refractory bricks and the fluxes used in metallurgical refining. High quality crystals continue to be used as gemstones.

A revolutionary step in crystal engineering has recently come about as a direct consequence of the interest shown in ceramics as an alternative material to steel alloys. Ceramic materials and powdered metal are pressed into a mold at such high temperatures and pressures that they fuse into a solid mass. The resulting mass is machined to precise tolerances and may be used as, say, an engine block. The reduction in weight and the degree to which the original powdered mass can be sculptured have been welcomed as a breakthrough in materials engineering. The next stage in this exciting development was the growing of a single crystal into the shape of an engine block or turbine blade using a heavily charged solution as the source medium. Work is continuing in this field and encouraging progress has already been made.

Above Crystals were often carried into battle, as with the garnets on this belt buckle found in a 6th century Viking grave in Norway.

Left This wooden box contains a selection of typical Egyptian jewelry and amulets, featuring such crystals as gold and lapis lazuli.

GEMS, CRYSTALS, AND MINERALS— IDENTIFIER

How to Use this Section

The minerals in the identifier section are listed in the following order:
Native metals and nonmetals
Sulfides
Borates
Oxides
Hydroxides
Halides
Carbonates
Silicates
Phosphates
Sulfates
Tungstates
Hydrates
Organics

To find the reference to a specific gem or precious stone, refer to the index at the back of the book.

Key to Symbols

Each identifier entry has information on:

Crystal Structure

Crystal Structure

 isometric/cubic   orthorhombic

 tetragonal   monoclinic

 hexagonal   triclinic

 trigonal   amorphous

Specific Gravity

Specific Gravity 3.16–3.20

Hardness on Mohs' scale

Mohs' Hardness 6–7

NATIVE METALS AND NONMETALS

Natives are single elements, not compounds which are made up of several elements. Gold, silver, copper, platinum, and mercury are metallic; diamond, graphite, and sulfur nonmetallic. Metals are dense and opaque, and are good conductors of electricity, unlike nonmetallic natives which are translucent and tend to form more distinct crystals. Some natives, such as arsenic and antimony, have metallic and nonmetallic properties and are classified as semimetals.

Gold Au Native Metals and Nonmetals Group

Mohs' Hardness 2.5–3	Specific Gravity 15.6–19.33, pure form	Crystal System Isometric

Distinctive features Malleability, color, association with pyrites, galena, and chalcopyrite.
Color Deep gold-yellow to pale yellow.
Luster Metallic.
Streak Golden-yellow to reddish.
Transparency Opaque.
Cleavage None.
Fracture Hackly.
Tenacity Ductile, malleable.
Forms Flat plates, arborescent, crystals rare.
Varieties Usually alloyed with silver: ordinary gold is 10 percent silver, electrum is 38 percent silver and is, therefore, a pale yellow to silvery color, while

other varieties contain up to 20 percent copper and palladium.
Uses Monetary standard, jewelry, electronics, aircraft window screening.
Occurrence Worldwide, mostly in quartz veins and placer deposits, although it does occur in igneous, metamorphic, and sedimentary rocks. Particularly prevalent in the Ural Mountains, Siberia, the Alps, India, China, New Zealand, Queensland, South Africa (Transvaal), Colombia, Mexico, Yukon, USA (along mountain ranges in western states).

Gold is sometimes confused with pyrite (fool's gold). But gold is usually a much richer golden yellow color, and is much softer than pyrite. Its streak is also golden yellow, whereas pyrite leaves greenish black streaks. Gold rarely tarnishes or is altered by the weather.

Gold is one of the few pure elements to occur naturally. It does form cube-shaped crystals but these are rare, and you can see them only in museums. More often it forms small grains and flakes on other minerals. Often small glittering patches of gold can be found on quartz grains in mineral veins, and you may be

Above When a prospector panned river shingle from the Quillabamba river in Peru, these tiny grains of gold were left behind in the pan. Occasionally, panning may turn up a nugget. The largest pure nugget, weighing 156 pounds, was the "Welcome Stranger" found at Moliagul, Victoria in Australia in 1869.

lucky enough to find some by searching carefully in a known gold locality. But the specks are often tiny and you will probably need to look at many pieces of quartz with a hand lens to spot even the smallest patch. Gold like this can sometimes be extracted industrially by crushing the rocks, and then using mercury or cyanide to dissolve away the rock fragments.

Besides mineral veins, gold can be found in sandstones and pebbly conglomerates, where it is washed after the rock in which it

first developed is broken down by the weather. Because gold is one of the densest minerals it settles among sand and shingle in stream beds in lumps called nuggets. Nuggets like these can be retrieved by panning.

Gold has been a measure of wealth for over 5,000 years. The ancient Egyptians learned how to work gold and used it in religious ornaments. In the last century there were a number of "gold rushes" in the USA and Australia, when people went in search of a fortune to places where chance

Above Wires of gold sometimes grow on quartz like this in mineral veins where hot watery liquids cool in cracks. More often, gold forms almost microscopically small specks scattered throughout the native rock. Gold can be extracted from such rocks industrially with chemicals—or the rocks may be weathered naturally, leaving the grains to be washed into rivers as "placer" deposits.

discoveries of gold had been made. In 1848, for example, tens of thousands of people flocked to California to prospect for gold.

Silver Ag Native Metals and Nonmetals Group

Mohs' Hardness 2.5–3	Specific Gravity 10.1–10.5, pure form	Crystal System Isometric

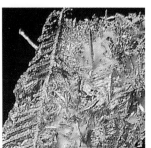

air creates a black coating of silver oxide. Silver is so easily bent and worked that it has been used for making jewelry, ornaments, and various other objects since ancient times. The largest producer of silver today is the Guanajaro mine in Mexico, where silver has been mined continuously for more than 500 years. Silver also forms the light-sensitive compounds that are the basis of photographic film and prints. Today, the photographic industry is the world's biggest consumer of silver. But silver is also the best natural conductor of both heat and electricity, and is playing an increasingly important role in the electronics industry.

Below Silver, like gold and a few other metals, is one of the few elements that occur naturally in pure form—that is, as "native elements."

Distinctive features Malleability, color, and specific gravity.
Color Silvery white.
Luster Metallic.
Streak Silvery white.
Transparency Opaque.
Cleavage None.
Fracture Hackly.
Tenacity Ductile, malleable.
Forms Distorted crystals, reticulated, and arborescent.
Varieties Usually alloyed with gold or copper.
Uses Coinage, jewelry, ornaments, electronics.
Occurrence Native silver is rare and is often associated with silver minerals. Norway, central Europe, Australia (New South Wales), Chile, Mexico, Canada (Ontario), USA (Michigan, Montana, Idaho, Colorado).

This precious metal sometimes occurs as small, cube-shaped crystals, but more often as nuggets or wires. Silver forms in veins with other minerals, and is often extracted by crushing and refining galena, the ore of lead. Silver is also found with copper minerals such as chalcopyrite. When exposed to air, silver quickly tarnishes as oxygen in the

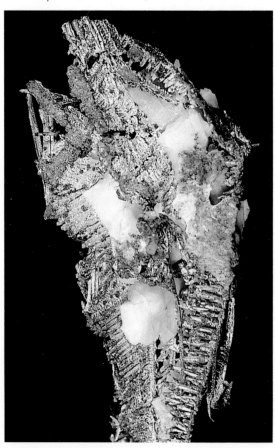

Copper Cu Native Metals and Nonmetals Group

Mohs' Hardness 2.5–3	Specific Gravity 8.8–8.9	Crystal System Isometric

Distinctive features Color, malleability, ductility, association with malachite and other copper ores. Soluble in nitric acid, producing red nitrous fumes (care is needed for this test).
Color Copper-red.
Luster Metallic.
Streak Metallic, coppery, shining.
Transparency Opaque.
Cleavage None.
Fracture Hackly.
Tenacity Ductile, malleable.
Forms Twisted, wirelike, platy, crystals uncommon.
Varieties Veins, strings, sheets, crystal masses.
Uses Electrical conductor in wires, electronics, alloyed with tin—to produce bronze—and zinc—to produce brass.
Occurrence Native copper is usually of secondary origin in copper ore veins, sandstone, limestone, slate, and near igneous rocks. Southwest UK, Russia, Australia (New South Wales), Chile, Bolivia, Mexico, USA (Lake Superior area, Arizona, New Mexico).

Copper is a vital component of modern industry. For example, one automobile requires between 50 and 80 pounds of copper in its construction. Chile is the world's largest copper producer with the USA second. Copper mining is vital to economies around the globe, including Russia, Indonesia, Australia, Peru, China, Zambia, Poland, Kazakstan, the Philippines, and Zaire.

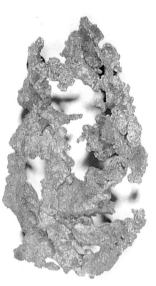

Below The massive Kennecott open-pit copper mine in Utah.

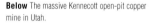

Diamond c Native Metals and Nonmetals Group

Mohs' Hardness 10	Specific Gravity 3.516–3.525	Crystal System Isometric

Distinctive features Brilliant luster and extreme hardness.
Color Colorless, white or, rarely, pink, yellow, orange, blue, or green.
Luster Adamantine to greasy.
Streak None.
Transparency Transparent, but may be translucent to opaque.
Cleavage Octahedral, perfect on lll.
Fracture Conchoidal.
Tenacity Not applicable.
Forms Octahedral and more complex crystals; also spherical and massive.
Varieties None.
Uses Gemstone, abrasive, cutting tools and drill bits, polishing gemstones.

Occurrence The ancient diamond mines in the Golconda area of southern India have been the source of some of the most famous diamonds such as the Koh-i-nor and Jehangir. Diamond is widespread in Brazil and most gems, although small, are of good quality. Carbonado is an unusual black microcrystalline diamond found in river gravels in Bahia, Brazil. Ballas (boart) is another important type of industrial diamond found in Brazil and South Africa.

Alluvial diamonds have been found in almost every state of the USA and the largest north American diamond (weighing 40.23 carats) was found in a now abandoned mine at Murfreesboro, Arkansas. Until recently Australian diamonds were small and yellowish, but white and fancy-colored stones, such as pink and pinkish brown, are now mined at Argyle in the Kimberley district of northern

Western Australia. Probably the most famous diamond bearing country is South Africa. The first diamond was reported in 1866. In 1869 the Star of South Africa was found weighing 83.5 carats and later cut into a pear-shaped brilliant weighing 47.74 carats. Other localities include Borneo, Botswana, China, Ghana, Guinea, Guyana, Russia, Tanzania, Venezuela, Zaire, and Zimbabwe.

Diamond crystals form as cubes, octahedra, and dodecahedra, the octahedra being the form most commonly used for gems. Diamond has an adamantine luster and very good "fire" (dispersion), which makes it

Above Raw diamonds surround a spectacular rose cut specimen.

the most popular gemstone.

The bluish-white fluorescence of most diamonds under ultraviolet light is used in identification. Colorless to yellow diamonds which show a blue fluorescence and have the strongest absorption line in the violet part of the spectrum are members of the Cape series. Other diamonds may show a green or yellow glow under ultraviolet light and have absorption lines in other parts of the spectrum.

The World's Largest Diamonds

The World's Largest Rough Diamonds

Rank	Carats	Name	Discovery date	Place	Cut Into
1	3,106.00	Cullinan	1905	South Africa	Cullinans I-IX; 96 others
2	995.20	Excelsior	1893	South Africa	21 gems (largest 69.80)
3	968.90	Star of S. Leone	1972	Sierra Leone	–
4	890.00	The Incomparable	1984	Zale Corp.	Incomparable; 14 others
5	770.00	Woyie River	1945	Sierra Leone	30 gems (largest 31.35)
6	755.50	Unnamed Brown	1984	South Africa	Unnamed Brown
7	726.60	Vargas	1938	Brazil	Vargas (48.26); 22 others
8	726.00	Jonker	1934	South Africa	Jonker (125.65); 11 others
9	650.25	Reitz	1895	South Africa	Jubilee (245.35); one other
10	609.25	Baumgold Rough	1923	South Africa	14 gems (sizes unknown)

The World's Largest Cut Diamonds

Rank	Carats	Name	Color	Shape	Last reported owner or location
1	545.67	Unnamed Brown	dark brown	fire-rose	De Beers Consolidated Mines Ltd
2	530.20	Cullinan I	white	pear	British Crown Jewels—Tower of London
3	407.48	Incomparable	brownish yellow	triolette	Auctioned in New York, October 1988
4	317.40	Cullinan II	white	cushion	British Crown Jewels—Tower of London
5	277.00	Nizam	white	dome	Nizam of Hyderabad—1934
6	273.85	Centenary	white	modified heart	De Beers Consolidated Mines Ltd
7	245.35	Jubilee	white	cushion	Paul-Louis Weiller
8	234.50	De Beers	light yellow	cushion	Auctioned in Geneva, May 1982
9	205.07	Red Cross	yellow	square brilliant	Auctioned in Geneva, November 1973
10	202.00	Black Star of Africa	black	–	Exhibited in Tokyo, 1971

Platinum Pt Native Metals and Nonmetals Group

Mohs' Hardness 4–4.5	Specific Gravity 14–19	Crystal System Isometric

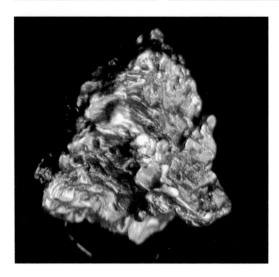

Distinctive features Malleable, weakly magnetic, soluble in aqua regia, and very high specific gravity.
Color Metallic gray.
Luster Metallic.
Streak White/gray.
Transparency Opaque.
Cleavage None.
Fracture Hackly.
Tenacity Malleable.
Forms Grains, nuggets, scales, crystal rare.
Varieties Platinum group metals.
Uses Chemical catalyst.
Occurrence In ultrabasic and basic igneous rocks and, rarely, in contact aureoles. Also occurs in placer sediments because of its very high specific gravity. Principally South Africa, also Belarus, Australia, Canada, and Alaska.

Mercury Hg Native Metals and Nonmetals Group

Mohs' Hardness 0	Specific Gravity 13.6	Crystal System Hexagonal at -38.2°F

Distinctive features Liquid at room temperature, high specific gravity, soluble in nitric acid.
Color Metallic, red when found in cinnabar.
Luster Metallic.
Streak None.
Transparency Opaque.
Cleavage Not applicable.
Fracture Not applicable.
Tenacity Not applicable.
Forms Crystallic at -38.2°F.
Varieties None.
Uses Explosives, batteries, gold and silver recovery.
Occurrence Volcanic vents, regularly with cinnabar, in Italy, Spain, and Croatia.

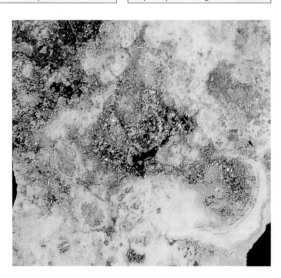

Graphite C Native Metals and Nonmetals Group

Mohs' Hardness 1–2	Specific Gravity 2.09–2.23	Crystal System Trigonal

Distinctive features Silvery-black color with pencil black streak. Very soft with greasy feel. Extremely dirty to handle.
Color Steel black to gray.
Luster Metallic, dull, earthy.
Streak Black.
Transparency Opaque.
Cleavage Perfect basal.
Fracture Rough when not on cleavage.
Tenacity Not applicable.
Forms Tabular crystals—six-sided, foliated masses, granular to compact masses.
Varieties None.
Uses Lead in pencils, graphite lubricants, paints, high temperature crucibles, electrodes.
Occurrence In gneiss, schists, limestones and quartziles.

Siberian gneisses, Ceylon granulites, Finnish limestones, Mexico, USA (Adirondack

quartzites and gneisses, Rhode Island limestones, Pennsylvania, Montana, and New Mexico).

Sulfur S Native Metals and Nonmetals Group

Mohs' Hardness 1.5–2.5	Specific Gravity 2.05–2.09	Crystal System Orthorhombic

Distinctive features Yellow color, melts and burns readily with blue flame, giving off choking sulfur dioxide fumes. Often contaminated with clay or bitumen.
Color Bright yellow to red or yellow-gray.
Luster Resinous.
Streak White.
Transparency Transparent to translucent.
Cleavage On 001, 110, 111.
Fracture Conchoidal to sectile.
Tenacity Ductile when heated.
Forms Pyramidal to tabular.
Varieties None.
Uses Making sulfuric acid, gunpowder, fireworks, insecticides, and fungicides, vulcanizing rubber, medicines.

Occurrence Mostly in young sedimentary rocks, often clays, associated with bitumen. Frequently as small crystals around fumaroles on volcanoes. Sicily (large crystals, associated with selenite and calcite), Indonesia, USA (mainly in Louisiana and Texas, but also found around fumaroles in Yellowstone Park, Sulfur Bank mercury mine in California, and in many other states).

SULFIDES

Sphalerite ZnS Sulfide Group

Mohs' Hardness 3.5–4	Specific Gravity 3.9–4.1	Crystal System Isometric

Distinctive features Resinous luster and color, and often associated with galena, pyrite, quartz, calcite, barytes, and fluorite.
Color Dull yellow-brown to black, also greenish to white, but nearly colorless when pure.
Luster Resinous and adamantine.
Streak Pale brown to light yellow.
Transparency Transparent to translucent.
Cleavage Perfect on 110.
Fracture Conchoidal.

Tenacity Not applicable.
Forms Dodecahedra, massive to granular, sometimes amorphous.
Varieties None.
Uses Principal ore of zinc.
Occurrence Can occur in veins in most rocks, where it is associated with galena, pyrite, quartz, and calcite. Romania, Italy (Tuscany), Switzerland, Spain, UK, Sweden, Mexico, Canada, USA (Missouri, Colorado, Montana, Wisconsin, Idaho, and Kansas).

Left Sphalerite on galena

Chalcopyrite CuFeS$_2$ Sulfide Group

Mohs' Hardness 3.5–4	Specific Gravity 4.1–4.3	Crystal System Isometric

Distinctive features Similar to pyrite but deeper in color and often iridescent. Usually massive,

brittle, and soluble in nitric acid.
Color Tarnished brassy gold, often iridescent.

Luster Metallic.
Streak Green-black.
Transparency Opaque.
Cleavage Poor, variable on 201.
Fracture Uneven.
Tenacity Not applicable.
Forms Usually massive, sometimes rounded. Crystals less common than for pyrites.
Varieties None.
Uses Principal ore of copper.
Occurrence Metalliferous veins in granites, gneisses, and schists. Often associated with bornite, malachite, azurite, and quartz. Germany, Italy, France, UK, Spain, Sweden, Namibia, Australasia, South America, USA (New York State, Pennsylvania, Missouri, Colorado).

Cinnabar HgS Sulfide Group

Mohs' Hardness 2–2.5	Specific Gravity 8–8.2	Crystal System Hexagonal

Distinctive features Color and streak, high specific gravity, and its softness. When heated in a tube it yields globules of mercury metal which settle on the sides of the tube.
Color Cochineal red to brownish-red.
Luster Adamantine to dull.
Streak Scarlet.
Transparency Transparent to opaque.
Cleavage Prismatic, perfect on $10\bar{1}0$.
Fracture Uneven to subconchoidal.
Tenacity Not applicable.
Forms Rhombohedral to tabular in habit. Also granular and massive.
Varieties None.
Uses Only common, and therefore principal, ore

of mercury.
Occurrence Forms with pyrite and realgar, at hot springs, and around volcanic vents. Spain,

Italy, Serbia, the Czech Republic, Bavaria (good crystals), Russia, China, Peru, USA (California, Nevada, Utah, Oregon).

Galena PbS Sulfide Group

Mohs' Hardness 2.5–2.75	Specific Gravity 7.4–7.6	Crystal System Isometric

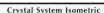

Distinctive features Cubic, cleavage, color, high specific gravity.
Color Lead gray, often silvery.
Luster Metallic, shining.
Streak Lead gray.
Transparency Opaque.
Cleavage Cubic, perfect on 100, 010, and 001.
Fracture Flat on cubic form to even.
Tenacity Not applicable.
Forms Mainly cubes, tabular, sometimes skeletal crystals.
Varieties None.

Uses Chief ore of lead and important source of silver.
Occurrence Widespread in beds and veins due to hydrothermal action of mineralizing fluids. Found in limestones, dolomites, granites, and other crystalline rocks, where it is often associated with sphalerite, pyrite, calcite, and quartz. France, Austria, UK, Australia, Chile, Peru, USA (extensive deposits in Missouri, Illinois, and Iowa, and also found in lesser quantities in many other states).

Molybdenite MoS$_2$ Sulfide Group

Mohs' Hardness 1–1.5	Specific Gravity 4.7–4.8	Crystal System Hexagonal

Distinctive features Soft, flexible, silvery, foliated scales, and has a greasy feel. When heated in a tube, it yields sulfurous fumes and a pale yellow sublimate.
Color Silvery lead gray.

Luster Metallic.
Streak Gray to greenish-gray.
Transparency Opaque.
Cleavage Perfect basal on 000.
Fracture Not applicable.
Tenacity Flexible, but not elastic.
Forms Tabular prisms, often short and tapering and often foliated or massive.
Varieties None.
Uses Principal ore of molybdenum.
Occurrence In granite pegmatites and quartz veins, also in syenites and gneisses. UK, Norway, Namibia, Australia (Queensland), USA (New Hampshire, Connecticut, Pennsylvania, and Washington State).

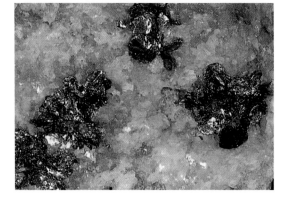

Orpiment As$_2$S$_3$ Sulfide Group

Mohs' Hardness 1.5–2	Specific Gravity 3.4–3.5	Crystal System Monoclinic

Distinctive features Lemon yellow, often tinged with fine streaks of orange, its luster and flexibility in thin plates. When heated in a closed tube, it yields a dark red liquid that becomes yellow when cold.
Note: Arsenic trisulfide is poisonous.

Color Lemon yellow to medium yellow.
Luster Pearly to resinous.
Streak Slightly paler than color.
Transparency Subtransparent to translucent.
Cleavage Perfect on 010 and striated.
Fracture Rough.
Tenacity Sectile.
Forms Massive and foliated, but the tiny crystals are difficult to see.
Varieties None.
Uses Pigment and for removing hair from animal skins.
Occurrence Often associated with the equally poisonous orange-red realgar, arsenic sulfide. The Czech Republic, Romania, Japan, USA (Utah, Nevada, Yellowstone Park).

Pyrite FeS₂ Sulfide Group

Mohs' Hardness 6–6.5	Specific Gravity 4.95–4.97	Crystal System Isometric

Distinctive features Glistening to metallic brassy gold cubic and pyritohedron crystals, and produces a greenish-black streak.
Color Pale brassy gold.
Luster Metallic to glistening.
Streak Greenish-black to brown-black.
Transparency Opaque.
Cleavage Poor on 100 and 111.
Fracture Usually uneven, sometimes conchoidal.
Tenacity Not applicable.
Forms Cubes, pyritohedrons. Often intergrown, massive, radiated, granular, globular, and stalactitic.
Varieties None.
Uses As source of gold and copper, which it contains in small amounts. Also to produce sulfur, sulfuric acid and iron sulfate.

Occurrence
Universal—the most common sulfide. The Czech Republic, Switzerland, Italy (large crystals up to 6 inches), Spain, UK, USA (New York, Pennsylvania, Illinois, Colorado, and lesser amounts in many other states).

Stibnite Sb₂S₃ Sulfide Group

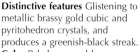

Mohs' Hardness 2	Specific Gravity 4.56–4.62	Crystal System Orthorhombic

Distinctive features Color, softness, cleavage. Also, when heated in a tube, it yields sulfur dioxide and fumes of antimony oxide, the latter condensing to form a white powder.
Color Steel gray to dull gray, often with a black, iridescent tarnish.
Luster Metallic; splendent on fresh crystal surfaces.
Streak Same as color.
Transparency Opaque.
Cleavage Perfect on 010, less on 001.
Fracture Small-scale subconchoidal.
Tenacity Somewhat sectile.
Forms Masses of radiating elongated crystals. Also massive and granular.

Varieties Metastibnite, which is an earthy, reddish deposit found at Steamboat Springs, Nevada.
Uses Principal source of antimony.
Occurrence Mostly in quartz veins in granites, but also in schists and limestones. Italy, Germany, Romania, Algeria, China, Borneo, Mexico, Peru, USA (California, Nevada—scarce in both states).

Arsenopyrite FeAsS to FeS₂.FeAs₂ Sulfide Group

Mohs' Hardness 5.5–6	Specific Gravity 5.9–6.2	Crystal System Orthorhombic

Distinctive features Color, streak. Also, when heated in an open tube, it gives off sulfurous fumes and produces a white sublimate of arsenic trioxide.
Color Silvery-tin white to iron gray.
Luster Metallic.
Streak Black to dark gray.
Transparency Opaque.
Cleavage Good on 110.
Fracture Uneven.
Tenacity Brittle.
Forms Prismatic crystals, often flattened. Granular.

Varieties None.
Uses Principal ore of arsenic.
Occurrence Associated with cassiterite, wolframite, sphalerite, and galena mineralized veins in granite and associated rocks. Also in limestones and dolomites, and frequently associated with gold. Austria, Germany, Switzerland, Sweden, UK, Bolivia, Canada, USA (New Hampshire, Connecticut, Montana, and Colorado).

Proustite 3Ag₂S.As₂S₃ Sulfide Group

Mohs' Hardness 2–2.5	Specific Gravity 5.57–5.64	Crystal System Hexagonal

Distinctive features Color, streak, and, when heated in a closed tube, it fuses, emits sulfurous fumes, and leaves a white sublimate of arsenic trioxide.
Color Dark red to vermilion.
Luster Adamantine.
Streak Same as color.
Transparency Transparent to translucent.
Cleavage Distinct rhombohedral, good on 10$\bar{1}$1.

Fracture Uneven to occasionally conchoidal.
Tenacity Brittle.
Forms None.
Varieties None.
Uses Mineral collections.
Occurrence In hydrothermal silver veins and associated with galena and sphalerite. France, Germany, the Czech Republic, Chile, Mexico, USA (though very rare).

Argentite Ag$_2$S Sulfide Group

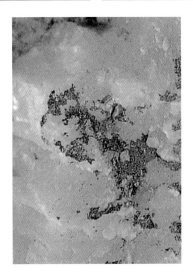

Mohs' Hardness 2–2.5	Specific Gravity 7.3	Crystal System Isometric

Distinctive features Fuses easily, frequently occurs with galena.
Color Gray-green.
Luster Metallic.
Streak Dark gray.
Transparency Opaque.
Cleavage Imperfect.
Fracture Conchoidal, sectile.
Tenacity Ductile, malleable.
Forms Branching crystals, distorted.
Varieties Also known as "silver glance" and argyrose.
Uses An important silver ore.
Occurrence Occurs in veins of hydrothermal origin. Crystals have been found in Norway, the Czech Republic, Bolivia, and Mexico. As a mineral deposit found in Australia, Canada, Chile, Peru, USA (Colorado, Nevada).

Chalcocite Cu$_2$S Sulfide Group

Mohs' Hardness 2.5–3	Specific Gravity 5.5–5.8	Crystal System Orthorhombic

Distinctive features Fusible, soluble in nitric acid.
Color Gray.
Luster Metallic.
Streak Gray.
Transparency Opaque.
Cleavage Indistinct, poor.
Fracture Conchoidal, uneven.
Tenacity Malleable.
Forms Granular, dull gray aggregate, crystal rare.
Varieties Also known as redruthite (named for Redruth in Cornwall, England) or "copper glance."
Uses Copper ore.
Occurrence Occurs in regions of secondary enrichment of primary copper ores. As well as England, crystals have also been found in Spain, Namibia, South Africa, Chile, Mexico, USA (Connecticut, Montana).

Pyrrhotite FeS Sulfide Group

Mohs' Hardness 3.5–4.5	Specific Gravity 4–6	Crystal System Hexagonal

Distinctive features Magnetic, gives off hydrogen sulfide fumes when dissolved in hydrochloric acid.

Color Bronze-yellow to bronze-red.
Luster Metallic.
Streak Dark gray.

Transparency Opaque.
Cleavage None.
Fracture Conchoidal, uneven.
Tenacity Brittle.
Forms Tabular or platy crystals, can be massive or granular.
Varieties Associated with copper, iron, and sulfur.
Uses By itself, has no use. Can be a source of cobalt, nickel, and platinum.
Occurrence Fairly common in mafic and ultramafic extrusive rocks, but also occurs in pegmatites, high temperature hydrothermal veins, and, occasionally, as a sedimentary deposit. Substantial deposits in Canada (Manitoba, Ontario). Quality crystals have been found in Brazil, Mexico, USA (Maine, New York State).

BORATES

Sinhalite MgA(BO₄) Borate Group

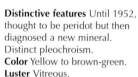

Mohs' Hardness 6.5	Specific Gravity 3.48	Crystal System Orthorhombic

Distinctive features Until 1952, thought to be peridot but then diagnosed a new mineral. Distinct pleochroism.
Color Yellow to brown-green.
Luster Vitreous.
Streak Yellow.
Transparency Transparent.
Cleavage None.
Fracture Conchoidal.
Tenacity Brittle.
Forms Grains, crystal.
Varieties None.
Uses Gemstone.
Occurrence Mainly gem gravels in Sri Lanka. Rarely found in Burma and Tanzania. Non-gem quality found in USA (Warren County, New York).

OXIDES

Corundum Al$_2$O$_3$ Oxide Group

Mohs' Hardness 9	Specific Gravity 3.95–4.1	Crystal System Hexagonal

Distinctive features Hardness, form, association with crystalline rocks and gneisses.
Color Common form brown to gray, but also white, red, blue, yellow.
Luster Adamantine to vitreous.
Streak White.
Transparency Transparent to translucent.
Cleavage None.
Fracture Conchoidal to uneven.
Tenacity Brittle.
Forms Steep bipyramidal, tabular, prismatic, rhombohedral crystals; also massive or granular.
Varieties Sapphire (blue) ruby (red), oriental topaz (yellow), oriental amethyst (purple), dull or opaque varieties of the mineral, emery (granular form with magnetite and ilmenite).
Uses Gemstones, when transparent, abrasives, and grinding powders.
Occurrence In crystalline rocks, schists, gneisses. Switzerland, Greece, Russian Urals, South Africa, Madagascar, India, Burma, Cambodia, Japan, Canada (Ontario), USA (New York State, New Jersey, Pennsylvania, North Carolina, Georgia, Montana).

Ruby AL$_2$O$_3$ Oxide Group

Mohs' Hardness 9.0	Specific Gravity 4.0	Crystal System Trigonal

Rubies are a form of corundum. Pure corundum is colorless and the gem color is caused by the presence of small amounts of chemical impurities. Small traces of chromium give rise to the rich red color of ruby—the name is derived from the Latin for red, *ruber*. If there is any brown hue in the stone it is due to the presence of iron impurities.

Ruby crystalizes in the trigonal crystal system, but the habit varies with the variety and locality, for example Burmese rubies are usually found as tabular hexagonal prisms terminated at both ends. Ruby has an uneven or conchoidal fracture. There is no true cleavage but a line of weakness or parting may be present. The luster is vitreous. The absorption spectrum is characterized by fine lines in the red, lines which cut out most of the yellow, most of the green and violet parts of the spectrum. When rubies are viewed through "crossed filters" (the stone is placed in a beam of light which has passed through a flask of blue copper sulfate solution and is then viewed through a Chelsea color filter), the chromium causes a luminescence that can be seen as a red glow.

The highest quality rubies come from the Mogok area of Burma. Written records of ruby mining go back as far as 1597, but legends tell of mining long before. Gems are also collected from river gravels. The color of the best Burmese stones is described as "pigeon's blood." Thailand provides most of the world's rubies, but they are a brownish-red and darker in color than the Burmese rubies. Rubies

from Tanzania are distinctive as they are found as short prismatic crystals in a bright green rock. Rubies have been found in mica shists in the Hunza Valley in Pakistan that are up to 2 inches in length. Small quantities are also found in Afghanistan, Australia, Brazil, Cambodia, Mysore in India, Malawi, Montana and North Carolina in the USA.

Rubies are faceted or cut *en cabochon*. Stones may have inclusions of the mineral rutile. These appear as short needlelike shapes arranged within the crystal

in lines parallel with the edges of the crystal. This may be seen as a sheen known as "silk" or cut *en cabochon* to show a six-pointed star.

Rubies were first made synthetically toward the end of the nineteenth century using the flame-fusion method. They soon became the first gems to be made in commercial quantities. Synthetic rubies have replaced the "jewel" rubies which were traditionally used as bearings in watches and precision instruments.

Sapphire AL₂0₃ Oxide Group

Mohs' Hardness 9.0	Specific Gravity 4.0	Crystal System Trigonal

The name sapphire is given to any color of corundum other than red, the red stones being rubies. Although sapphires are commonly thought of as being blue and the name is derived from the greek *sapphirus* for blue, they can be black, purple, violet, dark blue, bright blue, light blue, green, yellow, and orange. The blue colors are due to traces of titanium and iron, and the red hues are due to chromium.

As with ruby, sapphires crystalize in the trigonal crystal system and the form the crystals take depends on the variety and locality, for example Sri Lankan sapphires are usually found as bipyramids. Sapphires have an uneven or shell-like fracture, but no real cleavage. They have a vitreous luster.

Burmese sapphires are of excellent quality. The stones are found in a coarse yellow sand and often have black featherlike inclusions. Color is important in determining the origin of a stone; cornflower blue sapphires from Kashmir occur in pegmatite rock and as water-worn pebbles in river valleys. The colors of Sri Lankan sapphires include pale blue, violet, yellow, white, green, and pink, and the rare orange-pink sapphire called *padparadscha*, which comes from a Sinhalese word meaning "lotus-color." Blue, green, and yellow corundum is found in Queensland and New South Wales, Australia. Australian sapphires are usually rather dark blue and somewhat inky but there is an attractive greenish-yellow variety. Other localities include Brazil, Cambodia, Kenya, Malawi, Tanzania, Thailand, and Zimbabwe.

Sapphire is often parti-colored (one part is blue and the rest is colorless). The cutter places the clear part near the front of the gem and blue part toward the back so that the complete stone appears blue from the front. Stones are usually faceted as mixed cut gems. Star-stones are cut *en cabochon*.

Corundums are imitated by spinel, garnet, and glass. A garnet-topped doublet, with a blue glass base, and a garnet top may imitate sapphire. Most of the blue glasses and the blue doublets show strong red through the Chelsea color filter and can be distinguished from real sapphires which do not. A quartz cabochon with colored reflective pieces on its base may be used to imitate star corundum.

Chrysoberyl BeAl$_2$O$_4$ Oxide Group

Mohs' Hardness 8.5	Specific Gravity 3.68–3.78	Crystal System Orthorhombic

Distinctive features Weak pleochroism.
Color Greenish-yellow.
Luster Adamantine.
Streak White.
Transparency Transparent to opaque.
Cleavage Good.
Fracture Weak conchoidal.
Tenacity Brittle.
Forms Prismatic crystal, trillings.
Varieties Alexandrite, cat's-eye.
Uses Gemstone.
Occurrence The best alexandrites are found in mica schists in the Ural Mountains of Russia. Russian chrysoberyl has two-phase inclusions (a bubble within a liquid-filled cavity) and feathers. Larger crystals of chrysoberyl are found as water-worn pebbles in the gem gravels of Sri Lanka, but these are

generally not of such a good quality as those from Russia. Other localities include Burma (Mogok area), Brazil (states of Minas Gerais, Espirito Santos, Bahia), Zimbabwe, Madagascar, Zambia, Tanzania.

The mixed cut (brilliant-cut crown and trap-cut pavilion) is usually used for chrysoberyl. To show the cat's-eye, the stone must be cut *en cabochon*. Chrysoberyl cat's-eyes, not to be confused with quartz cat's-eyes, are greenish yellow or yellow, often with a cold, grayish tone. They contain a moving green light ray which, with the color, gives them their name.

Synthetic chrysoberyl, synthetic corundum, and synthetic spinel are made to imitate alexandrite and its color change.

Spinel MgAl$_2$O$_4$ Oxide Group

Mohs' Hardness 8.0	Specific Gravity: 3.6-3.7	Crystal System Isometric

Distinctive features Spinels are found in a number of different colors including shades of red, blue, violet, purple, and mauve. Dark green and brown iron-rich spinels are usually too dark to be used in jewelry. Black spinels have been found on the volcano Vesuvius in Italy. Star stones are also found occasionally. Iron-rich spinels are termed *ceylonites* and zinc-rich spinels are termed *gahnospinels*. The name spinel is probably derived from the Latin *spina*, meaning a thorn. Red spinel has been known as "Balas ruby" after a place in northern India where the stones were thought to be found. The highly precious "Black Prince's Ruby" (uncut) set in the front of the Imperial State Crown and the "Timur Ruby" (engraved) are both in the British crown jewels and are both spinels.

Color Various.
Luster Vitreous.
Streak White.
Transparency Transparent to opaque.
Cleavage None.
Fracture Conchoidal, uneven.
Tenacity Brittle.
Forms Cubic, octahedral.
Varieties Spinel is a collective name for a whole group of related minerals, only a few of which are of gem quality. Ceylonite and pleonaste are black.
Uses Gemstone.
Occurrence Spinel is generally found in association with corundum, usually in alluvial deposits such as those of Burma and Sri Lanka. Other localities include Sweden, Afghanistan, Thailand, Australia, Brazil, and the USA.

Spinels are fashioned in the mixed-cut or trap-cut styles although in the past octahedral crystals were sometimes set in jewelry without any faceting. The star stones when cut *en cabochon* show a four-rayed star.

Spinel is made synthetically. It is colored to imitate other gemstones such as aquamarine and zircon.

Taafeite $Mg_3Al_8BeO_{16}$ Oxide Group

| Mohs' Hardness 8.0 | Specific Gravity 3.62 | Crystal System Hexagonal |

Distinctive features An extremely rare mineral first discovered by Count Taafe as a cut stone in a Dublin jeweler's box. Only a few have been found since.
Color Violet, colorless, pale pink.
Luster Vitreous
Streak White.
Transparency Transparent.
Cleavage None.
Fracture Conchoidal.
Tenacity Brittle.
Forms Limited to alluvial grains.
Varieties None.
Uses Gemstone.
Occurrence Specimens found in Russia, Sri Lanka, China.

Axinite $Ca_2(Fe^{+2},Mn^{+2})Al_2Bsi_4O_{15}(OH)$ Oxide Group

| Mohs' Hardness 6.5–7 | Specific Gravity 3.36–3.66 | Crystal System Triclinic |

Distinctive features Strong pleochroism, pyro- and piexo-electric, crystals have sharp axlike edges.
Color Reddish-brown, yellow, colorless, blue, violet, or gray.
Luster Vitreous.
Streak White.
Transparency Transparent to translucent.
Cleavage Good.
Fracture Conchoidal.
Tenacity Brittle.
Forms Tabular, wedge-shape crystals.
Varieties None.
Uses Gemstone.
Occurrence Found in calcareous rocks altered by contact metamorphism. France (Pyrenees, Isère), Mexico (Baja California), Japan, USA (Colorado, Nevada, New Jersey).

Rutile TiO₂ Oxide Group

Mohs' Hardness 6–6.5	Specific Gravity 4.18–4.25	Crystal System Tetragonal

Distinctive features Bright metallic coppery to reddish-brown needlelike crystals in quartz crystals or as darker, compact masses in acid to intermediate crystalline rocks. Sometimes in limestones, where deposited by mineralizing fluids. Transparent varieties have adamantine luster, but many specimens are opaque. Produces a pale brown streak.
Color Coppery to reddish-brown.
Luster Metallic to adamantine.
Streak Pale brown.
Transparency Transparent to opaque.
Cleavage Distinct, on 110 and 100.
Fracture Subconchoidal to uneven.

Tenacity Brittle.
Forms Often found as prismatic acicular crystals in quartz. Occasionally compact to massive.
Varieties Ordinary rutile is brown-red to black, iron-rich rutile is black, while chromium-rich rutile is green.
Uses Ore of titanium and manufacture of items where strength is of great importance.
Occurrence In acid to intermediate crystalline rocks. Austria, Switzerland, France, Norway, Australia, Brazil, USA (Vermont, Massachusetts, Connecticut, New York State, Virginia, Georgia, North Carolina, Arkansas).

Cassiterite SnO₂.I Oxide Group

Mohs' Hardness 6–7	Specific Gravity 6.4–7.1	Crystal System Tetragonal

Distinctive features Hardness, color, form, and specific gravity.
Color Brown to black.
Luster Brilliant.
Streak White to brownish.
Transparency Nearly transparent to opaque.
Cleavage Poor on 100.
Fracture Subconchoidal to rough.
Tenacity Brittle.
Forms Dumpy pyramids and prismatic.
Varieties Tin stone, which is crystalline and massive, wood tin, which is botryoidal and reniform with a fibrous structure, toad's eye, which is the same as wood tin, but on a smaller scale, and stream tin, which is cassiterite in the form of sand, admixed with

other mineral and rock grains.
Uses Principal ore of tin.
Occurrence Mostly in granitic rocks and associated pegmatites. Often associated with fluorite, apatite, topaz, and wolframite deposited by mineralizing fluids. England, Eastern Europe, Congo, Malaysia, Indonesia, Bolivia, Mexico, USA (California, South Carolina, South Dakota, New Hampshire, Maine, New Mexico, Texas).

Chromite $FeCr_2O_4$ to $FeO.Cr_2O_3$ (Oxide Group)

Mohs' Hardness 5.5	Specific Gravity 4.1–4.9	Crystal System Isometric

Distinctive features Streak, feebly magnetic.
Color Black.
Luster Submetallic.
Streak Brown.
Transparency Opaque.
Cleavage None.
Fracture Uneven to rough.
Tenacity Brittle.
Forms Octahedral. Massive to granular.
Varieties None.

Uses Chromium ore, for hardening steel, chrome plating, and chromium pigments.
Occurrence In peridotites and serpentine and often associated with magnetite. The Urals, Austria, Germany, France, UK, South Africa, Iran, Canada (Newfoundland), USA (New Jersey, Pennsylvania, North Carolina, California).

Pyrolusite MnO_2 Oxide Group

Mohs' Hardness 2–2.5	Specific Gravity 4.73–4.86	Crystal System Orthorhombic

Distinctive features Hardness and color of streak.
Color Iron black to dark steel gray; occasionally bluish.
Luster Metallic.
Streak Same as color.
Transparency Opaque.
Cleavage Perfect on 100 and 011.
Fracture Rough.
Tenacity Brittle.
Forms Commonly dendritic, granular to massive.
Varieties Crystals, massive, and the very pure form, which is

called polianite.
Uses Ore of manganese, for coloring glass, in the preparation of chlorine, bromine, and oxygen.
Occurrence Concentrated as a secondary ore deposit by circulating fluids, often in clays and siltstones. Germany, the Urals, India, Cuba, Brazil, USA (Arkansas, Georgia, Virginia, Minnesota, Tennessee, and lesser amounts in other states).

Vesuvianite Ca_{10} $(Mg,Fe)_2Al_4[(OH)_4/(SiO_4)_5/(Si_2O_7)_2]$ Oxide Group

Mohs' Hardness 6.5	Specific Gravity 3.27–3.45	Crystal System Orthorhombic

Distinctive features Also known as idiocrase. Weak pleochroism, indissoluble in acid.
Color Olive green, yellow-brown, blue.
Luster Vitreous to greasy.
Streak White.
Transparency Translucent.
Cleavage Indistinct.
Fracture Fracture.
Tenacity Brittle.
Forms Prismatic, columnar, massive.
Varieties Californite, cyprine, wilnite, xanthite.
Uses Gemstone.
Occurrence Forms in impure limestones altered by contact metamorphism. First found on Mount Vesuvius in Italy. Found in Switzerland, Russia, Kenya, Sri Lanka, Pakistan, Brazil, Mexico, USA (California).

Magnetite $Fe''Fe'''_2O_4$. to $FeO.Fe_2O_3$ Oxide Group

Mohs' Hardness 5.5–6.5	Specific Gravity 5.17–5.18	Crystal System Isometric

Distinctive features Heavy and magnetic, often with north and south poles.
Color Black.
Luster Metallic.
Streak Black.
Transparency Opaque.
Cleavage Indistinct.
Fracture Uneven.
Tenacity Brittle.
Forms Octahedral, massive to fine granular.
Varieties Lodestone, which is strongly magnetic and has north and south poles.
Uses Iron ore.
Occurrence Found in most igneous rocks, particularly those of basic composition, black beach sands, serpentines, and metamorphic rocks. Sweden and Norway (largest deposits in the world), Siberia, Australia, Cuba, Brazil, Canada (Ontario, Quebec), USA (New York State, New Jersey, Pennsylvania, Arkansas, Utah).

Hematite Fe₂O₃ Oxide Group

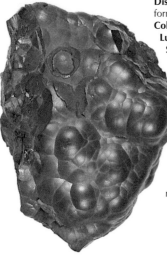

Mohs' Hardness 5.5–6.5	Specific Gravity 4.9–5.3	Crystal System Hexagonal (rhombohedral)

Distinctive features Streak, color, form, density.
Color Metallic gray to earthy red.
Luster Metallic to splendent.
Streak Bright red to Indian red.
Transparency Opaque.
Cleavage None.
Fracture Uneven to subconchoidal.
Tenacity Brittle, but elastic in thin plates.
Forms Tabular to thick crystals.
Varieties Specularite, which has splendent tabular crystals, often in brilliant masses, pencil ore, which is a fibrous compact form, often used in jewelry, kidney ore, which has botryoidal masses resembling kidneys, clay iron-stone, which has deep red-brown compact masses, often in sedimentary rocks.
Uses Principal ore of iron.
Occurrence Ubiquitous in formation and occurrence. The Urals in Russia, Romania, Austria, Germany, Switzerland, France, Italy, UK, Ascension Island, Brazil, Canada (Nova Scotia, Newfoundland), USA (Michigan, Wisconsin, Minnesota, Wyoming, New York State, Colorado).

Uraninite UO₂ Oxide Group

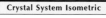

Mohs' Hardness 5–6	Specific Gravity 7.5–10	Crystal System Isometric

Luster Submetallic, greasy.
Streak Black, brownish.
Transparency Opaque.
Cleavage Indistinct.
Fracture Conchoidal to uneven.
Tenacity Brittle.
Forms Crystal uncommon; usually massive, botryoidal, or granular.
Varieties Massive form known as pitchblende.
Uses Main source of uranium and radium.
Occurrence Found in some igneous rocks, such as pegmatites and granites, and in stratified sedimentary rocks, such as conglomerate and sandstone. France, Namibia, South Africa, Australia, Canada, USA (Arizona, Colorado, Utah).

Distinctive features Also known as pitchblende. Pierre and Marie Curie first identified polonium, redium, and helium from a sample of pitchblende. Radioactive, infusible, will dissolve slowly in nitric acid.
Color Black, brownish.

HYDROXIDES

Bauxite $Al_2O_3.2H_2O$ Hydroxide Group

Mohs' Hardness Not applicable	Specific Gravity 2.5	Crystal System: Amorphous

Distinctive features Massive, red to reddish-yellow, earthy, and amorphous.
Color Shades of red to yellow, occasionally white.
Luster Earthy.
Streak Reddish.
Transparency Opaque.
Cleavage None.
Fracture Earthy.
Tenacity Not applicable.
Forms Mostly in reddish, earthy-like masses, but sometimes occurs as fine grains.
Varieties Concretions of grains, clay, or earthy-like masses.
Uses Principally ore of aluminum and in ceramics.
Occurrence Formed by weathering of aluminum rocks under tropical conditions and deposited as a colloid. France, Germany, Romania, Italy, Venezuela, USA (Arkansas, Georgia, Alabama, Missouri).

Limonite $2Fe_2O_3.3H_2O$ Hydroxide Group

Mohs' Hardness 5–5.5	Specific Gravity 3.5–4	Crystal System Amorphous

Distinctive features Ochreous yellow, earthy, amorphous.
Color Deep ochreous yellow to brown and black.
Luster Earthy, dull.
Streak Ochreous yellow.
Transparency Opaque.
Cleavage None.
Fracture Earthy.
Tenacity Not applicable.
Forms Compact to stalactitic and botryoidal ochreous earthy masses.
Varieties Bog ore, which occurs in bogs where it petrifies plant material, clay-ironstone, which has concretions and nodules and is mostly found in sandstone rocks.
Uses Pigments and iron ore.
Occurrence Deposited near the surface after weathering of iron-rich minerals. Worldwide, but particularly in Canada (Nova Scotia), USA (ubiquitous).

BORATES

Borates are formed when metallic elements combine with the borate radical $(BO_3)^{-3}$. As well as borax (see below), the group includes colemanite, kernite, and ulexite.

Borax $Na_2B_4O_5(OH)_4.8H_2O$ Borate Group

Mohs' Hardness 2–2.5	Specific Gravity 1.7–1.74	Crystal System Monoclinic

Distinctive features An evaporite with close similarities to halides. Has a bittersweet taste, will turn flame yellow, and, as it dries, will turn white.
Color Gray, greenish, blue.
Luster Silky.
Streak White.
Transparency Transparent to opaque.

Cleavage Perfect.
Fracture Conchoidal.
Tenacity Sectile.
Forms Prismatic.
Uses As a cleaning agent, in the manufacture of high temperature glass, and as a flux in soldering, brazing, and welding. Also used as a source of boron, which has the ability to absorb neutrons and

is used in the control rods employed in nuclear reactors.
Occurrence In ancient times, borax was taken from the salt lakes of Tibet. Today the main deposit is in the USA in Death Valley, California, with smaller deposits in Turkey and Argentina.

HALIDES

Usually soft with a pronounced crystalline structure, halides should be treated with care because they are also evaporites which will deliquesce if exposed to water or even damp air. They are compounds of metals and halogens (the elements chlorine, fluorine, bromine, and iodine).

Because they can dissolve so readily they can sometimes be distinguished by taste; halite, for instance, tastes salty and the less common sylvite bitter. Other evaporite minerals such as gypsum, dolomite, and anhydrite are often found in association with halides.

Halite NaCl Halide Group

Mohs' Hardness 2.5	Specific Gravity 2.1–2.6	Crystal System Isometric

Distinctive features Taste—it is the natural form of table salt—solubility, cleavage. *Note:* Specimens will absorb atmospheric water and deliquesce if not kept in a sealed container.
Color Colorless, white to yellowish-brown or shades of gray-blue.
Luster Vitreous.
Streak Same as color.

Transparency Transparent to translucent.
Cleavage Cubic, perfect on 100.
Fracture Conchoidal.
Tenacity Brittle.
Forms Cubes, often with sunken crystal faces. Massive, granular, and compact.
Varieties None.
Uses Principal source of common salt, but also in

preparation of sodium compounds, glass, and soap.
Occurrence Worldwide as a main constituent of seawater. Commonly stratified up to 33 yards in thickness in sedimentary rocks. Under pressure, the salt may flow upward to produce huge salt domes of the surface. Southeast Russia, Poland, Austria, Germany, Switzerland, France, UK, Iran, India, Peru, Colombia, Canada (Ontario), USA (New York State, Wyoming, Michigan, Ohio, Louisiana, Kansas, Arizona, Nevada).

Fluorite CaF Halide Group

Mohs' Hardness 4	Specific Gravity 3.01–3.25	Crystal System Isometric

Distinctive features Excellent cubic form, cleavage, and sometimes banded. The crystals may be coated with other minerals, including quartz and pyrite. Fluorite derives its name from the fact that it fluoresces under ultraviolet light (see opposite page).

Color Very variable. The pure form is colorless, but it also comes in all shades of blue, yellow, green, as well as brown, violet, and pink. The colors are often banded.

Luster Vitreous.

Streak White.

Transparency Transparent to subtransparent.

Cleavage Perfect octahedral.

Fracture Conchoidal to flat.

Tenacity Brittle.

Forms Cubes, often with beveled edges, and granular; massive and compact forms often show excellent color banding.

Varieties Blue John (see below).

Uses As a flux in the steel industry, for enameling, opal glass, manufacturing hydrofluoric acid, for ornaments and, rarely, faceted for collectors.

Occurrence Fluorite occurs mostly in mineralized veins associated with galena, sphalerite, calcite, and quartz, especially in limestones. It is also found in granites in the form of minute crystals. Fluorite from each mine has a characteristic color. It is found in the UK, France, Italy, Germany, Austria, Switzerland, Norway, Poland, the Czech Republic, Canada (Ontario), USA (New Hampshire, Illinois, Connecticut, Virginia, Kentucky, Missouri, Colorado).

As stated above, fluorite gets its name from the fact that it

Varieties

Blue John

colors it produces are generally much less striking.

The variety of fluorite named Blue John is made up of curved bands of blue, violet, and purple, which may be so dark as to appear black. The purple color is thought to be due to the inclusion of manganese or possibly oil (crude petroleum). It has a fibrous to columnar form. Blue John is inert under ultraviolet light. It is more important ornamentally than the crystals, and has been carved into vases and other decorative objects since Roman times. The only source of this variety of fluorite is the lead mine at Castleton in Derbyshire, England.

Synthetic fluorite has been made, including some pink in color, imitating the pink octahedral crystals that are found in a mine near Chamonix, France. Because fluorite has a hardness of 4 on Mohs' scale, it is regarded as too soft to be used in jewelry. The perfect octahedral cleavage makes cutting difficult, but some has been faceted for collectors, usually in the trap-cut style.

fluoresces under ultraviolet light. Most fluorite gives a sky blue to violet glow under longwave ultraviolet light. Brown fluorite crystals from Clay Center, Ohio, are known to glow white and have a yellow afterglow. This is said to be due to the inclusion of petroleum or bituminous compounds. Although some fluorite does glow under shortwave ultraviolet light, the

Above
A highly decorative fluorite vase.

Right
The pure form of fluorite is colorless, but samples such as this from the UK owe their color to traces of impurities.

CARBONATES

Malachite Cu₂CO₃(OH)₂ Carbonate Group

Mohs' Hardness 4	Specific Gravity 3.8	Crystal System Monoclinic

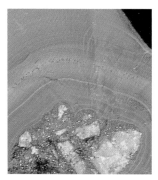

Luster Vitreous to adamantine.
Streak Pale green.
Transparency Translucent to opaque.
Cleavage Perfect.
Fracture Uneven, hackly.
Forms Crystals acicular or prismatic, more usually stalactitic, botryoidal masses.
Varieties Usually intergrown with azurite.
Uses Ornamental.
Occurrence Much of the older malachite used in jewelry making was from copper mines in the Ural Mountains in Russia. Malachite suitable for cutting is also found in Queensland, New South Wales, and South

Distinctive features Soluble in dilute hydrochloric acid, vibrant color.
Color Rich green.

Australia, where it is found with azurite. Other localities of malachite include England (Cornwall), Chile, USA (Arizona), the copper-mining areas of Africa, including Namibia, Zaire, Zambia, and Zimbabwe.

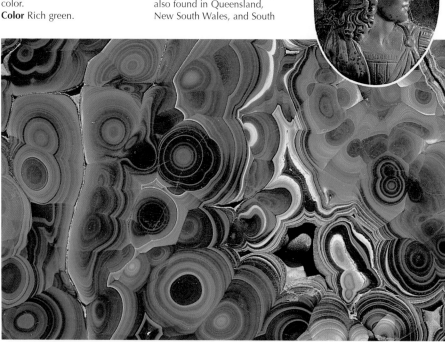

Azurite 2CuCO₃.Cu(OH)₂ Carbonate Group

Mohs' Hardness 3.5–4	Specific Gravity 3.8–3.9	Crystal System Monoclinic

Distinctive features Vivid blue crystals in association with malachite and reacts to nitric acid (take care when doing this).
Color Dark, vivid blue to cerulean blue.
Luster Vitreous to adamantine.
Streak Pale blue.
Transparency Transparent to translucent.
Cleavage Excellent on 021.
Fracture Conchoidal.
Tenacity Brittle.

Forms Varied: slender prismatic crystals to granular, massive, columnar or earthy.
Varieties None.
Uses As ore of copper and in mineral collections.
Occurrence Associated with oxidized copper ores, invariably in association with malachite. Siberia, Greece, Romania, France, Scandinavia, Namibia, Australia, USA (Arizona, New Mexico).

Like malachite **(see opposite)**, azurite is formed where copper-bearing rocks have been altered by water seeping into them. The two minerals are often found together, and many specimens are a mix of the two.

Calcite CaCO₃ Carbonate Group

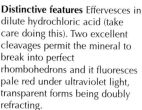

Mohs' Hardness 3	Specific Gravity 2.7	Crystal System Hexagonal

Distinctive features Effervesces in dilute hydrochloric acid (take care doing this). Two excellent cleavages permit the mineral to break into perfect rhombohedrons and it fluoresces pale red under ultraviolet light, transparent forms being doubly refracting.
Color Colorless to white. Also any combination of colors, due to impurities, even to black.
Luster Vitreous to earthy.
Streak White to gray.
Transparency Transparent to opaque.
Cleavage Rhombohedral perfect on $10\bar{1}1$.
Fracture Difficult to obtain because of excellent cleavage.
Tenacity Brittle.
Forms Nail-head spa and dog-tooth spa.
Varieties Iceland spa, which is transparent and doubly refracting. Calcite is the main component of limestone, and varieties form in them—massive, oolitic limestone, chalk, tufa, stalactites and stalagmites, and marble.
Uses Many, including cement manufacture, making building

blocks, ornamental, furnace flux, polarizing Nicol prisms, whitewash, agriculture.
Occurrence Worldwide in limestone rocks, but particularly in Austria, Germany, France, UK, Iceland, Ireland, Mexico, USA (New York State, Ohio, Michigan, Illinois, Missouri, North Dakota, Montana, Arizona).

Varieties

Iceland spa showing double refraction

Dolomite CaMg(CO₃)₂ to CaCO₃.MgCO₃ Carbonate Group

Mohs' Hardness 3.5–4	Specific Gravity 3	Crystal System Hexagonal (rhombohedral)

Distinctive features White to pale brownish saddle-shaped crystals that react to dilute, warm hydrochloric acid (care is needed when doing this).
Color White when pure, otherwise brownish to reddish-brown or greenish to red, gray, and black.
Luster Vitreous to pearly.
Streak Same as color.
Transparency Translucent (the transparent form is rare).
Cleavage Rhombohedral, perfect on 10$\bar{1}$1.
Fracture Subconchoidal.
Tenacity Brittle.
Forms Rhombohedrons or curved, saddle-like crystals. Granular to massive (often full of tiny cracks).
Varieties None.
Uses An important building material, which is used as a structural and ornamental stone, and for producing building blocks and special cements. It is used in the manufacture of magnesia for refractories, as a metallurgical flux for the iron and steel industries, as well as being used in the chemical industry as a source of magnesium.
Occurrence Massive dolomite is formed by replacement of calcium in massive limestones by magnesium (hence synonymous name of magnesium limestone). England, Spain, Italy, Switzerland, Germany, Austria, the Czech Republic, southern Africa, Brazil (Bahia), Mexico, Canada (Quebec), USA (Vermont, New York State, New Jersey, North Carolina, Missouri).

Left An aggregate of dolomite crystals from Tsumeb, southern Africa.

Rhodochrosite MnCO₃ Carbonate Group

Mohs' Hardness 3.5–4.5	Specific Gravity 3.5–3.6	Crystal System Hexagonal

Distinctive features Rose-red colored rhombohedral crystals in mineral veins, where it occurs as a secondary mineral.

Color Pale rose-red to dark red, though yellowish-gray forms are known.
Luster Vitreous to pearly.
Streak White.
Transparency Transparent to translucent.
Cleavage Rhombohedral, perfect on 10$\bar{1}$1.
Fracture Uneven.
Tenacity Brittle.
Forms Rhombohedral, but also massive, compact, granular, and botryoidal.
Varieties None.
Uses Mineral collections.
Occurrence As a secondary mineral associated with lead and copper veins rich in manganese. Rather rare mineral. Romania, UK, Germany, USA (Connecticut, New Jersey, Michigan, Montana, Colorado).

Cerussite PbCO₃ Carbonate Group

Mohs' Hardness 3–3.5	Specific Gravity 6.5–6.6	Crystal System Orthorhombic

Distinctive features White, striated elongated prismatic crystals, often in small stellate groups. Reacts to nitric acid (take care doing this).
Color Mostly white, but may be greenish or dark bluish-gray.
Luster Adamantine.
Streak Colorless.
Transparency Translucent to, rarely, transparent.
Cleavage Distinct prismatic, good on 110 and 021.
Fracture Conchoidal (though this is difficult to see).

Tenacity Brittle.
Forms Tabular to elongated prismatic crystals, often in stellar-shaped groups. Occasionally stalactitic.
Varieties None.
Uses Lead ore.
Occurrence In oxidized zones of lead-bearing veins, where lead ores have reacted with carbonate-rich water. Siberia, Austria, Germany, France, Scotland, Tunisia, Namibia, Australia, USA (Pennsylvania, Missouri, Colorado, Arizona, New Mexico).

SILICATES

Dioptase $CuSiO_2(OH)_2$ Silicate Group

Mohs' Hardness 5	Specific Gravity 3.3	Crystal Structure Hexagonal

Distinctive features Deep emerald green, short prismatic crystals, and found in association with deposits of copper sulfides. A somewhat rare mineral.
Color Deep to medium emerald.
Luster Vitreous.
Streak Green.
Transparency Transparent to translucent.
Cleavage Perfect on 10Ī1.
Fracture Conchoidal, but difficult to see because the crystals are either too small or too valuable to break.

Tenacity Brittle.
Forms Short, prismatic, six-sided crystals. Also massive or in granular clusters.
Varieties None.
Uses Much-prized by mineral collectors.
Occurrence In upper, oxidized zones of copper ore deposits, where excellent (but rare) crystals occur in drusy cavities. Russia, the Congo, Chile, USA (Arizona).

Enstatite $Mg_2Si_2O_6$ Silicate Group, Pyroxene subgroup

Mohs' Hardness 5.5	Specific Gravity 3.27	Crystal System Orthorhombic

Distinctive features Infusible, indissoluble in acid, pyroxene.
Color Brown.
Luster Adamantine.
Streak Colorless/gray.
Transparency Transparent to translucent.
Cleavage Good.
Fracture Conchoidal.
Tenacity Brittle.
Forms Prisms, gem quality usually rolled pebbles.
Varieties None.
Uses Gemstone.
Occurrence Crystals of enstatite are found as prisms, but gem-quality enstatite is usually found as rolled pebbles. Enstatite of a good green color is found with diamonds in the blue ground of the South African mines, especially the Kimberley mine.

Brownish-green specimens are found in Austria, Norway, the Mogok area of Burma, Sri Lanka, and in California.

Bronzite is a dark iron-rich enstatite which comes from Austria and can be cut *en cabochon* to show the cat's-eye effect. Some Sri Lankan gray enstatite is chatoyant.

Diopside CaMgSi$_2$O$_6$ Silicate Group, Pyroxene Subgroup

Mohs' Hardness 5	Specific Gravity 3.29	Crystal System Monoclinic

Distinctive features Indissoluble in acid.
Color Bottle green.
Luster Vitreous.
Streak White-gray.
Transparency Transparent to almost opaque.
Cleavage Good.
Fracture Uneven, rough.
Tenacity Brittle.
Forms Prismatic crystals, massive, lamellar, granular, columnar.
Varieties Violan (dark violet-blue). Star which has been on the market since 1964 and comes from southern India.
Uses Gemstone.
Occurrence Diopside that contains chromium is called chrome diopside. The best specimens are bright green and found in the blue ground of the Kimberley diamond mines of South Africa. Gem-quality chrome diopside is also found in the gem gravels of Sri Lanka, Siberia, and the Hunza region of Pakistan. The Hunza specimens are often large crystals, almost emerald in color. They may contain fibrous inclusions which give the crystals a cloudy appearance, but these can be cut *en cabochon* to give an attractive stone. The chrome diopside from Burma is chatoyant. Smoky yellow crystals are found in Canada while small bright green crystals are found in California.

Massive specimens (without crystal shape) of violane diopside are polished as beads or used for inlay work. Transparent stones may be faceted, while those with inclusions are cut *en cabochon* to show the cat's-eye effect.

Sphene CaTiSiO₅ Silicate Group

Mohs' Hardness 5.5	Specific Gravity 3.53	Crystal System Monoclinic

Distinctive features Soluble in sulfuric acid. High "fire" and birefringence.
Color Brown, yellow, green, red, and black. Can vary within one crystal.
Luster Adamantine.
Streak White.
Transparency Transparent to almost opaque.
Cleavage Distinct.
Fracture Conchoidal.
Tenacity Brittle.
Forms Wedge-shape.
Varieties None except color. Titanite is the correct mineralogical name.
Uses Gemstone. Important ore of titanium.
Occurrence Major localities for sphene are the Austrian Tyrol and Swiss Grisons, and also Canada and Madagascar. Other sources include Burma, Mexico (Baja California), Brazil and Sri Lanka.

Sphene is usually cut as brilliant or mixed cut gems to show the "fire" to its best effect.

Benitoite BaTiSi₃O₉ Silicate Group

Mohs' Hardness 6–6.5	Specific Gravity 3.65–3.68	Crystal System Hexagonal

Distinctive features Fluoresces blue under shortwave ultraviolet light, strong dispersion, obvious dichroism.
Color Blue, pink, purple, white.
Luster Vitreous.
Streak Colorless.
Transparency Transparent to translucent.
Cleavage Indistinct.
Fracture Conchoidal to uneven.

Tenacity Brittle.
Forms Pyramidal, tabular.
Varieties None.
Uses Gemstone.
Occurrence Benitoite is very rare and is only found in California.
Blue Benitoite has been faceted for collectors. Colorless crystals of benitoite are not uncommon but are not considered worth cutting.

Zircon ZrSiO₄ Silicate Group

Mohs' Hardness 7.5	Specific Gravity 4.5–5	Crystal System Tetragonal

Distinctive features Usually pale to deep brown short prisms, with pyramidal terminations. Mostly small crystals with an adamantine luster.
Color Various shades of brown, to blue, green, or colorless.
Luster Adamantine.
Streak Colorless.
Transparency Transparent to opaque.
Cleavage Poor on 110.
Fracture Conchoidal. Often difficult to see because of small crystal size.
Tenacity Brittle.
Forms Short prisms with pyramidal terminations.
Varieties Hyacinth, which is red to orange.
Uses Gemstone, with colorless forms being used as imitation diamonds.
Occurrence Important accessory mineral in acid igneous rocks. Because of its hardness and resistance to weathering, it also occurs in sandstones, especially those bearing gold. Worldwide, mostly associated with coarsely

crystalline granitic rocks. Much gem-quality zircon is found in the gem gravels of Sri Lanka, in the Mogok area of Burma, and in Thailand. The main zircon gem localities in Thailand are the Champasak, Pailin, and Kha districts. Rough zircon from Kha is heat-treated to give blue, golden, and colorless stones. Well-formed red crystals are found in France, brown crystals in Norway, and near-white rolled pebbles have been found in Tanzania. Gem-quality zircon is also found in Australia.

Above Zircon comes in a variety of colors, and is not just the familiar colorless gem that is used to imitate diamonds. It can also be heat-treated to give different colors.

Zircon is faceted, usually as round brilliants. Although it is moderately hard, the facet edges of zircon are easily chipped when worn as jewelry.

Synthetic blue spinel is used to imitate blue zircon, and colored glass is used to imitate other colors. Most vivid blue, golden, or colorless zircons are heat-treated brown zircons.

Hemimorphite $Zn_4Si_2O_7(OH)_2.H_2O$ Silicate Group

Mohs' Hardness 4.5–5	Specific Gravity 3.4–3.5	Crystal System Orthorhombic

Distinctive features Soluble in acid, gives off water when heated in a test tube. Also known as calamine in the USA (and see smithsonite entry, page 84).
Color White, blue, greenish.
Luster Vitreous, silky.
Streak Colorless.
Transparency Transparent to translucent.
Cleavage Perfect.
Fracture Uneven to conchoidal.
Tenacity Brittle.
Forms Platex crystals with different, or hemimorphic, ends.
Varieties Crystal rare, massive, granular, botryoidal, and stalactitic.
Uses Zinc ore, gemstone, and ornamental.
Occurrence Found where veins of zinc have been altered by oxidation. Commonly occurs in mineral veins with other minerals, such as anglesite, aurichalcite, calcite, cerussite, galena, smithsonite, and sphalerite. Found in Algeria, Greece, Italy, Namibia, Mexico, USA (Colorado, Montana, New Jersey).

Scapolite $(Na,Ca,K)_4Al_3(Al,Si)_3Si_6O_{24}(Cl,F,OH,CO_3,SO_4)$ Silicate Group

Mohs' Hardness 6	Specific Gravity 2.6–2.7	Crystal System Tetragonal

Distinctive features Soluble in hydrochloric acid, strong pleochroism.
Color White, blue, green, yellow, brown.
Luster Resinous.
Streak Colorless.
Transparency Transparent to translucent.
Cleavage Distinct.
Fracture Uneven.
Tenacity Brittle.
Forms Prismatic crystals, granular, massive.
Varieties Meionite, marialite.
Uses Gemstone.
Occurrence Gem material was first found in the Mogok area of Burma as fibrous white, pink, or violet stones. The pink and violet stones have strong pleochroism, showing dark blue and lavender blue, and can be cut *en cabochon* to show the cat's-eye effect. Yellow stones have been found in Madagascar and Brazil. These show strong pleochroism; the colors are three shades of yellow. An opaque massive yellow variety of scapolite is found in Quebec and Ontario, Canada, which emits a brilliant yellow fluorescence under longwave ultraviolet light, and may be cut *en cabochon*. Colorless, purple, and gem-quality yellow scapolite has been found in Kenya.

The Burmese scapolite is cut *en cabochon* to show the cat's-eye effect, while the Brazilian yellow scapolite is usually presented faceted.

Smithsonite ZnCO₃ Silicate Group

Mohs' Hardness 4–5	Specific Gravity 4.3–4.5	Crystal System Hexagonal

Distinctive features Also known as calamine in the UK (but see hemimorphite entry, page 83),

and dry-bone ore. Soluble in hydrochloric acid.
Color Gray, white, green, brown.

Luster Vitreous.
Streak White.
Transparency Transparent to translucent.
Cleavage Uneven.
Fracture Conchoidal.
Tenacity Brittle.
Forms Crystal (trigonal) rare, reniform, massive, botryoidal, spongelike, resembling dry bones.
Uses Zinc ore, ornamental.
Occurrence Forms in oxidized copper-zinc deposits. Associated with azurite, cerussite, hemimorphite, malachite, and pyromorphite. Austria, UK, Greece, Sardinia, Spain, Turkey, Russia, Namibia, Australia, USA (Arkansas, Colorado, New Mexico).

Rhodonite MnSiO₃ Silicate Group

Mohs' Hardness 5.5–6.5	Specific Gravity 3.6	Crystal System Triclinic

Distinctive features Distinctive pink tabular crystals, often associated with rhodochrosite or tetrahedrite in metamorphic rocks.
Color Rose-pink to red and, rarely, green-yellow.
Luster Vitreous.
Streak White.

Transparency Usually translucent, though transparent forms do sometimes occur.
Cleavage Perfect.
Fracture Uneven to conchoidal.
Tenacity Brittle.
Forms Usually as clusters of large tabular crystals.
Varieties None.

Uses Ornamental.
Occurrence In manganese ores associated with rhodochrosite or tetrahedrite. The Urals in Russia, Romania, Sweden, Australia, Mexico, USA (Massachusetts and New Jersey).

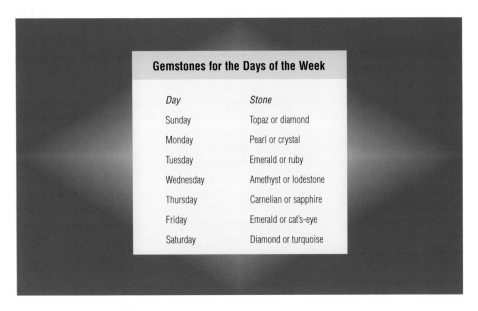

Gemstones for the Days of the Week

Day	Stone
Sunday	Topaz or diamond
Monday	Pearl or crystal
Tuesday	Emerald or ruby
Wednesday	Amethyst or lodestone
Thursday	Carnelian or sapphire
Friday	Emerald or cat's-eye
Saturday	Diamond or turquoise

Danburite Ca($B_2Si_2O_8$) Silicate Group

Mohs' Hardness 7–7.5	Specific Gravity 2.97–3.02	Crystal System Orthorhombic

Distinctive features Weak pleochroism, boron in the crystal will color a flame green.
Color Colorless, pale yellow, pink.
Luster Vitreous, greasy.
Streak White.
Transparency Transparent.
Cleavage Uneven.
Fracture Conchoidal.
Tenacity Brittle.
Forms Prismatic.
Varieties None.
Uses Of marginal value as a gemstone.
Occurrence Named for Danbury, Connecticut, where the crystal was first found. Deposits also occur in the Swiss and Italian Alps, Madagascar, Japan, and Mexico.

Serpentine Mg$_6$[(OH)$_8$Si$_4$O$_{10}$] Silicate Group

Mohs' Hardness 2.5	Specific Gravity 2.58–2.59	Crystal System Monoclinic

Distinctive features Sensitive to acids.
Color Green, yellow.
Luster Greasy, silky.
Streak White.
Transparency Transparent to opaque.
Cleavage Perfect.
Fracture Conchoidal.
Tenacity Splintery, tough.
Forms Two aggregate structures: leafy antigorite and fibrous chrysotile.

Varieties The bowenite variety, which is translucent green, is sometimes used as an alternative to jade, because it has a similar appearance, and may be referred to as "new jade." Bowenite is named for Dr Bowen, who originally misidentified bowenite as nephrite jade. Williamsite is another variety of serpentine. Oil-green in color, it is softer than bowenite and contains black inclusions.

Uses Decorative and ornamental.
Occurrence Occurs as dikes, lenses, and stocks. Formed by the serpentinization of rocks, mainly peridotite. Occurs commonly in folded metamorphic rocks, most likely from altered olivine-rich intrusions. UK, France, Austria, Germany, Italy, South Africa, and USA.

Olivine (Mgfe)₂SiO₄ Silicate Group

Mohs' Hardness 6.5–7	Specific Gravity 3.34	Crystal System Orthorhombic

Distinctive features Called peridot when the forsterite olivine is used as a gem, and sometimes chrysolite. Distinctive absorption spectrum with three broad lines in the blue caused by the presence of iron. High double refraction.

Color Green, yellow-green, brownish.

Luster Greasy.

Streak Colorless.

Transparency Transparent to translucent.

Cleavage Imperfect.

Fracture Small conchoidal.

Tenacity Brittle. Can burst under great stress and is thus sometimes called metal-foiled.

Forms Vertically striated flattened prisms, massive, compact, granular.

Uses Gemstone.

Occurrence The most important source of peridot was St John's Island, but the island is no longer accessible for collecting. Gem-quality stones are found in the Mogok area of Burma. Crystals and rolled pebbles have been found in Norway, Australia, and Brazil. Peridot from New Mexico and Arizona has been found in sands and even in ant-hills. Other localities include the diamondiferous "pipes" of South Africa. Pebbles are found on the beaches of Hawaii. Peridot has been found as far afield as Antarctica and it has even been found in meteorites.

Peridot is usually cut in the trap-cut style. Oval, pendeloque, round, and mixed cuts are also used. Because of its softness, peridot is fashioned into brooches, pendants, and earrings, but it is seldom used as a gemstone in rings or bracelets.

Glass and composite stones including garnet topped doublets and synthetic spinel composites (using green-colored cement to join two pieces of spinel) are used to imitate peridot but these should be recognizable by the fact that they lack the greasy luster.

Andalusite Al₂OSiO₄ Silicate Group

Mohs' Hardness 7.5	Specific Gravity 3.1	Crystal System Orthorhombic

Distinctive features Elongated glassy prisms in slates, hornfels, and schists of contact metamorphism zones associated with granite intrusions. Also

found in gneisses and schists in regionally metamorphosed zones.
Color Clear to white, but also pale red, brown, and green.
Luster Vitreous.
Streak Colorless.
Transparency Transparent to opaque.
Cleavage Distinct prismatic, perfect on 110, poor on 100.
Fracture Uneven.
Tenacity Brittle.
Forms As elongated prisms—square forms not so common.
Varieties Chiastolite, which has fat, elongated crystals with an internal pale or colored cross running along the length of each one.
Uses Gemstone, when clear.
Occurrence In zones of contact metamorphism surrounding granite masses. Also in gneisses

and schists resulting from regional metamorphism. Gem-quality andalusite is found as dull-green water-worn pebbles in Sri Lankan gem gravels, and in stream beds or on slopes of hills under clays and gravel in Brazil. Other localities include Russia, Australia, Canada (Quebec), and USA (California, Maine, Massachusetts, Pennsylvania). Good examples of the chiastolite are found in Zimbabwe and Burma. Other localities for chiastolite include France, Spain, Australia, Bolivia, Chile, USA.

Good quality crystals, especially the greenish or reddish varieties, are faceted into gemstones. Chiastolite "cross-stones" are popular in the Pyrenees of France where they are worn as amulets and charms.

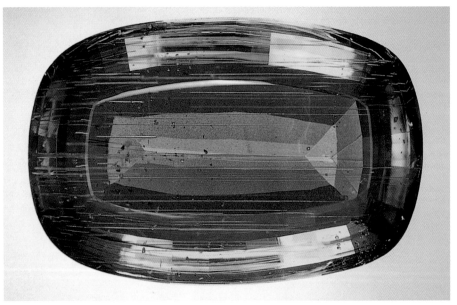

Kyanite Al₂OSiO₄ Silicate Group

Mohs' Hardness 4(C axis) 7(B axis)	Specific Gravity 4	Crystal System Triclinic

Distinctive features Translucent, pale blue, lath-shaped crystals. Hardness along length is less than across crystal. Often associated with staurolite in schists.
Color Usually pale cerulean blue, but can also be white, gray, or green.
Luster Vitreous to pearly.

Streak White.
Transparency Translucent to transparent.
Cleavage Perfect on 100.
Fracture Not applicable.
Tenacity Brittle.
Forms Long, bladed or lath-shaped crystals.
Varieties None.

Uses In refractory materials for furnaces, and jewelry.
Occurrence In mica schists resulting from regional metamorphism, often in association with staurolite, garnet, and corundum. The European Alps, Urals in Russia and USA (North Carolina).

Phenacite Be₂SiO₄ Silicate Group

Mohs' Hardness 7.5–8	Specific Gravity 2.95–3	Crystal System Hexagonal

Distinctive features Also spelt phenakite. Definite pleochroism, infusible, and indissoluble in acid.
Color Colorless, white, yellow, or pink-tinted.
Luster Vitreous, greasy when polished.
Streak White.
Transparency Transparent.
Cleavage Distinct.
Fracture Conchoidal.
Tenacity Brittle.
Forms Trigonal, short columnar.
Varieties None.
Uses Gemstone.
Occurrence Occurs in hydrothermal veins and granitic igneous rocks, including pegmatites. Also in schists, when it is associated with topaz, beryl, and chrysoberyl, apatite, and quartz. Belarus, Brazil, Mexico, USA (Colorado).

Sillimanite Al_2SiO_5 Silicate Group

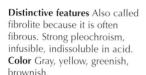

Mohs' Hardness 7.5	Specific Gravity 3.25	Crystal System Orthorhombic

Distinctive features Also called fibrolite because it is often fibrous. Strong pleochroism, infusible, indissoluble in acid.
Color Gray, yellow, greenish, brownish.
Luster Vitreous to silky.
Streak Colorless/white.
Transparency Transparent to translucent.
Cleavage Perfect.
Fracture Uneven.
Tenacity Brittle.
Forms Elongated, prismatic crystals.
Uses Gemstone.
Occurrence Forms in metamorphic rocks and some igneous rocks. Burma, Sri Lanka, USA (Idaho) as massive fibrous, water-worn pebbles).

Leucite $KAlSi_2O_6$ Silicate Group

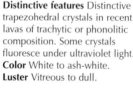

Mohs' Hardness 5–5.6	Specific Gravity 2.5	Crystal System Isometric

Distinctive features Distinctive trapezohedral crystals in recent lavas of trachytic or phonolitic composition. Some crystals fluoresce under ultraviolet light.
Color White to ash-white.
Luster Vitreous to dull.

Streak Colorless.
Transparency Usually opaque, sometimes translucent.
Cleavage Poor on 110.
Fracture Conchoidal.
Tenacity Brittle.
Forms Trapezohedral crystals.
Varieties None.
Uses Mineral collections.
Occurrence In potassium-rich, silica-poor, igneous lavas, such as syenites and trachytes. Worldwide, but particularly in Italy, Canada (British Columbia), USA (New Jersey, Arkansas, Wyoming).

Hiddenite LiAlSi$_2$O$_6$ Silicate Group, variety of Spodumene

Mohs' Hardness 6–7	Specific Gravity 3.16–3.2	Crystal System Monoclinic

Distinctive features Green variety of spodumene, named for W.E. Hidden, owner of the North Carolina mine where it was discovered. Indissoluble in acid, colors a flame red because of its lithium content.
Color Green.
Luster Vitreous.
Streak White.
Transparency Translucent.
Cleavage Perfect.
Fracture Uneven.
Tenacity Brittle.
Forms Crystals long and unevenly terminated, platy.
Uses Mineral collections, gemstone.
Occurrence Deposits occur in granite pegmatite. Gem-quality crystals in North Carolina; less attractive, paler crystals in Burma, Madagascar, Brazil, USA (California, North Carolina).

Kunzite LialSi$_2$O$_6$ Silicate Group, variety of Spodumene

Mohs' Hardness 6–7	Specific Gravity 3.16–3.2	Crystal System Monoclinic

Distinctive features The pink-brown coloring, caused by manganese, fades in light.
Color Pink/brown.
Luster Vitreous.
Streak White.
Transparency Translucent.
Cleavage Perfect.
Fracture Uneven.
Tenacity Brittle.
Forms Prismatic, tabular, can be large.
Uses Gemstone, source of lithium.
Occurrence Deposits occur in granite pegmatite. Madagascar, Brazil, USA (California, Connecticut, Maine).

Microcline $KAlSi_3O_8$ Silicate Group

Mohs' Hardness 6	Specific Gravity 2.55	Crystal System Triclinic

Distinctive features Pale turquoise to white, slightly streaked crystals. Similar to orthoclase in appearance, but with slightly lower specific gravity.
Color Pale turquoise to whitish-yellow, sometimes pale brick red.
Luster Vitreous.
Streak Colorless.
Transparency Usually translucent, rarely transparent.
Cleavage Perfect on 001.
Fracture Uneven.
Tenacity Brittle.

Forms Prismatic orthorhombic (like orthoclase), also massive to granular.
Varieties None.
Uses Jewelry, ornamental, in porcelain manufacture.
Occurrence Abundant in acid igneous rocks, such as granite. Good crystals may be obtained from granite pegmatites. Worldwide, but particularly Italy, Scandinavia, the Urals in Russia, Madagascar, USA (Pennsylvania, Delaware, Colorado).

Jade $NaAl(Si_2O_6)$ Silicate Group

Mohs' Hardness 6.5–7	Specific Gravity 3.4	Crystal System Monoclinic

Distinctive features Extreme tenacity meant that in prehistoric times it could be used as a tool and has thus been called "ax-stone." Indissoluble in acid.
Color Green, white, gray, bluish.
Luster Greasy.
Streak Colorless.
Transparency Translucent.
Cleavage Good.
Fracture Splintery.
Tenacity Very strong.
Forms Rare as a crystal.
Varieties Jadeite, nephrite (see pages 93–94). High quality synthetic jade has diminished its importance.
Uses Ornamental, gemstone.
Occurrence Burma, Tibet, Guatemala, China, Japan, USA (California).

Jadeite NaAl(Si$_2$O$_6$) Silicate Group

Mohs' Hardness 6.5–7	Specific Gravity 3.3–3.5	Crystal System Monoclinic

Jadeite is the rarer "jade." It is found in a large variety of colors, but it is the dark emerald green ("imperial green") that is the most prized in jewelry. White, pink, brown, red, orange, yellow, mauve (due to manganese), blue, violet, black, shades of green and mottled green, and white jadeites also occur. The presence of iron tends to give a dull green jadeite.

Jadeite is found as a mass of interlocking granular crystals. This causes a dimpled effect when polished. It is less tough than nephrite jade. Jadeite has a characteristic absorption spectrum with a strong band in the blue and a pattern of weaker bands. The white, mauve, yellow, and pale green stones show a whitish glow under longwave ultraviolet light and a strong violet-colored glow under X-rays, while the darker jadeite is inert. Green jadeite shows green under the Chelsea color filter.

Myanmar (formerly Burma) is the most important source of jadeite. Burmese jadeite is found in metamorphic rocks and also as alluvial boulders. The boulders have a brown skin which is due to weathering. Boulders found in California since the 1930s are white, pale green, dark green, and bluish- green, but they are semi-opaque and not of such good quality as the Burmese material. Green jadeite is found in Japan, but it is not of gem quality.

Jadeite is used mainly for carvings. Small pieces may be used to make beads, cabochons, ring stones, brooches, and drop earrings. The boulder material with a brown skin can be used to make cameos or snuff bottles which show both the skin and the internal color in a single piece.

Jadeite has been imitated by bowenite which is a variety of serpentine. Bowenite is softer than jadeite and can be distinguished by the fact that it can easily be scratched with a knife. Jadeite has also been imitated by prehnite, feldspar, aventurine quartz, chrysoprase, stained serpentine, and green-colored lead glass. "Transvaal jade" is a massive green grossular garnet which can be recognized by its orange fluorescence under X-rays and its higher density than jadeite.

Nephrite $Ca_2(Mg,Fe)_5[(OH,F)/Si_4O_{11}]_2$ Silicate Group

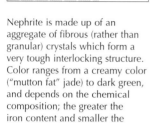

Mohs' Hardness 6.5	Specific Gravity 2.9–3.1	Crystal System Monoclinic

Nephrite is made up of an aggregate of fibrous (rather than granular) crystals which form a very tough interlocking structure. Color ranges from a creamy color ("mutton fat" jade) to dark green, and depends on the chemical composition; the greater the iron content and smaller the magnesium content, the darker the stone.

Nephrite has a distinct absorption spectrum with a doublet in the red and a sharp line in the green. It shows no luminescence under ultraviolet light and looks green through the Chelsea color filter.

Nephrite is found in eastern Turkestan. Most of the early Chinese jade carvings are of nephrite which was probably imported from Central Asia. It was not until the eighteenth century that jadeite from Burma was introduced. Siberian nephrite is found as dark green boulders which may have black spots. New Zealand nephrite is found in talc-serpentine rocks on South Island and also on the D'Urville island between North and South Island. The dark green nephrite is found as pebbles in glacial deposits and used by Maoris to fashion ornaments and flattened clubs called *meres*. Considerable amounts of black nephrite are produced in South Australia. European localities include northern Italy, the Harz mountains of Germany, and also

Poland where nephrite is a creamy white to sand color with green patches. In Switzerland nephrite deposits were used by early lake dwellers. Nephrite has also been found in Brazil and Taiwan and some good quality dark green nephrite has been found in Zimbabwe. Large boulders of yellow-green to dark green nephrite have been found in Canada. American nephrite is found in several states, including California, in a variety of colors mainly as alluvial deposits.

Nephrite is mainly carved, although some Alaskan nephrite and some from the Rocky Mountains of the USA can be cut *en cabochon* to show the cat's-eye effect.

Phlogopite K(Mg,Fe)$_3$(Si$_3$Al)O$_{10}$(OH)$_2$ Silicate Group

| Mohs' Hardness 3 | Specific Gravity 2.8–3 | Crystal System Monoclinic |

Distinctive features Shiny, coppery brown, patchy black, platy mineral. The plates are flexible and easily prised off with a knife point or pin. Flakes often show a starlike figure in transmitted light.
Color Coppery-brown to yellowish brown, with much darker patches.
Luster Pearly and sometimes slightly metallic.
Streak Colorless.
Transparency Transparent to subtransparent.
Cleavage Basal, perfect on 001.
Fracture Bends without breaking.
Tenacity Flexible, elastic.
Forms Tabular, scaly masses. Often seen as small flakes in acid igneous rocks.

Varieties None.
Uses Mineral collections.
Occurrence A product of metamorphism. Occurs in serpentine, granular limestones,

and dolomites. Romania, Switzerland, Italy, Scandinavia, Finland, Ceylon, Madagascar, Canada (Ontario, Quebec), USA (New York State, New Jersey).

Zoisite Ca$_2$Al$_3$[OH(SiO$_4$)$_3$] Silicate Group

| Mohs' Hardness 6.5 | Specific Gravity 3.35 | Crystal System Orthorhombic |

Distinctive features Distinct pleochroism. Will turn blue when heated.
Color Gray, yellow, green, blue.
Luster Vitreous.
Streak White.
Transparency Translucent.
Cleavage Perfect.
Fracture Uneven.
Tenacity Brittle.
Forms Crystals flattened acicular but can be fibrous-curved.
Varieties Best quality gemstones are called tanzanite; thulite is a massive pink variety.
Uses Gemstone, ornamental.
Occurrence In numerous rocks, including granites

and metamorphosed sediments. Tanzanite in Tanzania, thulite in Norway, the Austrian Tyrol, Western Australia, USA (North Carolina).

Prehnite $Ca_2Al_2Si_3O_{10}(OH)_2$ Silicate Group

Mohs' Hardness 6–6.5	Specific Gravity 2.9	Crystal System Orthorhombic

Distinctive features Pale green botryoidal or reniform masses of small tabular crystals. Often stalactitic or in radiating clusters.
Color Pale green to whitish-gray, the color fading on exposure to air.
Luster Vitreous.
Streak Colorless.
Transparency Usually translucent, rarely subtransparent.
Cleavage Not applicable.
Fracture Uneven to rough.
Tenacity Brittle.
Forms Tabular, often barrel-shaped crystals; often globular or in radiating clusters.

Uses Mineral collections.
Occurrence Mostly as a secondary mineral in basic igneous rocks and gneisses. Austria, Italy, Germany, France, UK, South Africa, USA.

Stilbite $Ca,Na_2,K_2)Al_2Si_7O_{18}.7H_2O$ Silicate Group

Mohs' Hardness 3.5–4	Specific Gravity 2	Crystal System Monoclinic

Distinctive features Waisted, tabular, white crystals filling cracks or lining cavities in basaltic lavas.
Color White to brownish-red.
Luster Vitreous to silky.
Streak Colorless.
Transparency Transparent to translucent.
Cleavage Perfect on 010.
Fracture Uneven.
Tenacity Brittle.
Forms Tabular crystals compounded into sheaflike aggregates, giving them a waisted appearance.
Varieties None.
Uses Mineral collections.

Occurrence Filling or lining cracks or cavities in basaltic lavas. UK, India, Iceland, Canada (Nova Scotia), USA (New Jersey).

Iolite Mg$_2$Al$_3$(AlSi$_5$O$_{18}$) Silicate Group

Mohs' Hardness 7	Specific Gravity 2.57–2.66	Crystal System Orthorhombic

Distinctive features Also known as cordierite and dichroite. Strong pleochroism.
Color Blue, violet, brown.
Luster Greasy, vitreous.
Streak White
Transparency Transparent.
Cleavage Good.
Fracture Conchoidal, uneven.
Tenacity Brittle.
Forms Pseudo-hexagonal prismatic twins.
Varieties Trade name for sapphire-blue cordierite is "water sapphire."
Uses Gemstone.
Physical Properties and Occurrence The optical and physical values of iolite vary due to the complexity of the composition. Gem-quality iolite is sapphire blue in color.

Iolite was called cordierite by mineralogists, named for the French geologist P.L.A. Cordier. The name iolite is derived from the Greek word for violet. As stated, iolite can be distinguished by its strong pleochroism; the three colors seen are brownish-yellow, light blue, and dark blue. The best blue color is seen when the crystal is viewed down the length of the prism. This physical property gives the stone its third name—dichroite.

Iolite may have various inclusions. The Sri Lankan specimens can contain so many thin platelets of the minerals hematite and goethite that they give the stone a red color. These stones have been named "bloodshot iolite."

Most gem-quality iolite is found as water-worn pebbles in gem gravels in Sri Lanka and Burma. Other localities for gem material include Madagascar, India, and Canada. Good iolite may be found in Namibia, Tanzania, and Brazil.

Above Iolite often takes on a violet-gray coloration, seen in this specimen from Brazil.

Most iolite is faceted, although gray iolite, which looks rather like gray jadeite, makes a decorative stone for carving.

Staurolite $(Fe,Mg)_2(AlFe)_9O_6(SiO)_4(O,OH)_2$ Silicate Group

| Mohs' Hardness 7–7.5 | Specific Gravity 3.6–3.8 | Crystal System Orthorhombic |

Distinctive features Mostly opaque to deep red stumpy prisms or cruciform twins in mica schists resulting from regional metamorphism. Often associated with kyanite, garnet, and quartz. Crystal surfaces often rough.
Color Deep wine red to brown or yellow.
Luster Resinous to poorly vitreous.
Streak White.
Transparency Mostly opaque, but sometimes translucent.
Cleavage Distinct, good on 010.
Fracture Subconchoidal, but this is difficult to see because the crystals are small.

Tenacity Brittle.
Forms Stumpy or flattened prismatic crystals and cruciform twins.
Varieties None.
Uses Rarely as a gemstone.
Occurrence In schists of regionally metamorphosed zones. Associated with kyanite, garnet, quartz, and tourmaline. Worldwide, but particularly in Switzerland, France, USA (New Hampshire, Massachusetts, Virginia, Ducktown Tennessee, Montana).

Biotite $K(Fe,Mg)_2(Si_3Al)0_{10}(OH)_2$ Silicate Group

| Mohs' Hardness 2.4–3.1 | Specific Gravity 2.6–3.0 | Crystal System Monoclinic |

Distinctive features Shiny black tabular scales, which are flexible and can be easily prised off with a knife or pin.

Color Black to greenish-black and brown.
Luster Splendent to submetallic.
Streak White.
Transparency Transparent to opaque.
Cleavage Basal, perfect on 001.
Fracture Tends to bend before breaking.
Tenacity Flexible, elastic.
Forms Usually tabular.
Varieties None.
Uses Mineral collections.
Occurrence Important component of most igneous rocks, from granite through gabbro, and their fine-grained equivalents. Found in granite pegmatites as large booklike masses. Worldwide.

Epidote (or Pistacite) Ca$_2$Fe(Al$_2$O)(OH)(Si$_2$O$_7$)(SiO$_4$) Silicate Group

Mohs' Hardness 6–7	Specific Gravity 3.3–3.5	Crystal System Monoclinic

Streak None.
Transparency Subtransparent to opaque (transparent varieties rare).
Cleavage Perfect on 001.
Fracture Uneven.
Tenacity Brittle.
Forms Elongated and striated clusters of prismatic crystals. Also massive.
Varieties Crystals, fibrous, massive. Withamite, which is bright red to pale yellow, and chrome epidote, which is emerald green to lemon yellow.
Uses Mineral collections.
Occurrence In contact-metamorphic zones, in regionally metamorphosed rocks, such as gneisses and schists. Worldwide, but particularly France, Norway, the Urals in Russia, USA (Connecticut, Colorado, California, Alaska).

Distinctive features Deep green to black, elongated and striated, prismatic crystals occurring in fibrous or granular masses in contact-metamorphosed limestone.
Color Emerald green to pistachio green to reddish or yellow.
Luster Vitreous to resinous.

Augite (Ca,Mg,Fe,Ti,Al)$_2$(Si,Al)$_2$O$_6$ Silicate Group

Mohs' Hardness 5–6	Specific Gravity 3.2–3.6	Crystal System Monoclinic

Distinctive features Dark color, crystalline shape, rock association, 90 degree cleavage.
Color Green to brownish-black.
Luster Vitreous to resinous.
Streak White to gray to greenish.
Transparency Transparent to opaque.
Cleavage Perfect on 110 at 90 degrees.
Fracture Conchoidal to uneven.
Tenacity Not applicable.

Forms Fat, prismatic crystals, sometimes tabular on 100.
Varieties Aegirine-augite, which is green to yellow, and fassaite, which is deep green.
Uses As important rock-forming mineral in nature.
Occurrence Worldwide in most basic igneous rocks, but ankaramite often yields large specimens up to 3 inches.

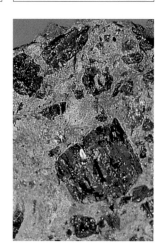

Hornblende $(Ca,Na,K)_{2-3}(Mg,Fe,Al)_5 (SiAl)_8O_{22}(OH,F)_2$
Silicate Group

Mohs' Hardness 5–6	Specific Gravity 3–3.5	Crystal System Monoclinic

Distinctive features Common mineral in igneous rocks, where it occurs as black to dark green stubby, prismatic crystals, although elongated forms are not uncommon. Distinguished in basal section from augite by its two cleaves that intersect at 120 degrees.
Color Black to green-black and dark brown.
Luster Vitreous, but often dull.
Streak Colorless.
Transparency Opaque. Occasionally subtransparent.
Cleavage Perfect on 110 directions. Intersect at 120 degrees.
Fracture Subconchoidal.
Tenacity Brittle.

Forms Stubby, prismatic crystals. Fibrous, granular, and massive.
Varieties Hornblende is the most common member of the amphibole group of minerals. Other forms in the group include common hornblende, which is black; basaltic hornblende which is deep green; riebeckite, which is dark blue-black, and asbestos, which is a fibrous-flaxy form in various colors.
Uses Mineral collections.
Occurrence An important component of many igneous rocks. Indeed, the classification of these rocks is based on the presence or absence of hornblende. Worldwide in igneous and metamorphic rocks.

Sodalite $Na_8(Al_6Si_6O_2)Cl_4$ Silicate Group

Mohs' Hardness 5.5–6	Specific Gravity 2.3	Crystal System Isometric

Distinctive features Usually found as lavender blue, dodecahedral crystals or masses in phonolitic lavas.
Color Lavender blue to greenish-yellow.
Luster Vitreous.
Streak Colorless.
Transparency Transparent to translucent.
Cleavage Poor, parallel to dodecahedral faces.

Fracture Uneven, sometimes conchoidal.
Tenacity Brittle.
Forms Dodecahedral crystals.
Varieties None.
Uses Mineral collections.
Occurrence In intermediate, fine-grained igneous rocks, such as phonolites. Austria, Italy, Norway, Greenland, Canada (Quebec, British Columbia), USA (Maine, and Massachusetts).

Topaz $Al_2(SiO_4)(OH,F)_2$ Silicate Group

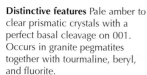

Mohs' Hardness 8	Specific Gravity 3.5–3.6	Crystal System Orthorhombic

Distinctive features Pale amber to clear prismatic crystals with a perfect basal cleavage on 001. Occurs in granite pegmatites together with tourmaline, beryl, and fluorite.
Color Pale honey-yellow to pale orange-yellow, clear with hint of blue or colorless. A pale green and pink form is known.
Luster Vitreous.
Streak Colorless.
Transparency Transparent to subtransparent.
Cleavage Basal, perfect on 001.
Fracture Subconchoidal to uneven.
Tenacity Brittle.
Forms Stumpy prismatic crystals, often with striated faces along their length.
Varieties None.
Uses Gemstone.
Occurrence Acid igneous rocks, such as granite, where crystals may occur in pegmatite or druses. Often associated with fluorite, cassiterite, and beryl. *See below for countries.* Much is found as water-worn pebbles in alluvial deposits. Sherry-brown topaz is found in the state of Minas Gerais, Brazil, as detached crystals embedded in a clay and can be heat-treated to give attractive pink stones. Blue and white topaz crystals and rolled pebbles are also found in Brazil. Topaz with a slight blue color is usually irradiated with gamma rays to darken its color and make a more attractive stone. Colorless, pale blue, reddish, and yellow crystals are found in the USA, particularly in the Pike's Peak region of Colorado. Blue,

Above Crystal, carving, and heat-treated blue topaz.

colorless, and pale brown topaz from Tasmania and Queensland and New South Wales, Australia, are found as rolled pebbles with few flaws or as crystals. Other localities include Germany, the Urals in Russia, many of the countries of Africa, Sri Lanka, Burma, Nigeria, Japan. In the USA (Maine, New Hampshire, Connecticut, Texas, Virginia, Utah, California). Non gem-quality topaz is found in Northern Ireland, the Cairngorm mountains of Scotland, and St Michael's Mount and Lundy Island off the Cornish and Devon coasts of England.

Topaz is often cut as oval or pendeloque (drop-shaped) stones using the mixed-cut style. Dark colored topaz may be cut in the trap-cut style. Pale pink topaz may be backed by red-colored foil in a closed setting to give the appearance of a stronger colored stone.

Natural and synthetic corundum may have colors similar to topaz but these can be distinguished by their different refractive indices.

Kornerupine Mg$_4$Al$_6$[(O,OH)$_2$/BO$_4$/(SiO$_4$)$_4$] Silicate Group

Mohs' Hardness 6.5	Specific Gravity 3.32	Crystal System Orthorhombic

Distinctive features Also called prismatine. Strong pleochroism.
Color Green, green-brown.
Luster Vitreous.
Streak White.
Transparency Transparent.
Cleavage Good.
Fracture Conchoidal.
Tenacity Brittle.
Forms Long prismatic.
Varieties None.
Uses Gemstone.
Occurrence Scarce in Greenland and not of gem quality; gem-quality stones found in Madagascar, Sri Lanka, Burma (Mogok area), Kenya, Tanzania.

Mica KAl$_2$(AlSi$_3$)O$_{10}$(OH,F)$_2$ Silicate Group

Mohs' Hardness 2–3	Specific Gravity 2.7–3.1	Crystal System Monoclinic (looks hexagonal)

Distinctive features Elastic, platy, indissoluble in acid, heat resistant.
Color Colorless to pale yellow.
Luster Pearly.
Streak White.
Transparency Transparent in thin layers.

Cleavage Perfect.
Fracture Even.
Tenacity Flexible.
Forms Poorly crystalized, generally in irregular plates.
Varieties Many, mainly white

mica muscovite with potassium, and black mica biotite with iron.
Uses Various industrial.
Occurrence In weathered granite. Germany, Austria, Norway, Russia, India, Australia.

Vermiculite (Mgfe,Al)$_3$(Al,Si)$_4$O$_{10}$(OH)$_2$.4H$_2$O Silicate Group

Mohs' Hardness 2–3	Specific Gravity 2.4–2.7	Crystal System Monoclinic

Distinctive features Expands dramatically when heated (up to times 20 at 572°F).
Color Honey.
Luster Vitreous.
Streak Pale yellow.
Transparency Translucent.
Cleavage Perfect.
Fracture Uneven.
Tenacity Brittle.
Forms Clay, scaly, aggregate.
Varieties Several types, similar to mica.
Uses Industrial, especially as an alternative insulating material to asbestos.
Occurrence Formed from the alteration of biotite and

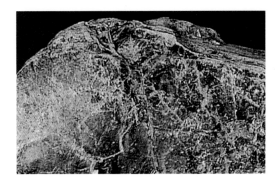

phlogopite. Largest deposits are in South Africa; other masses in Australia, Argentina, Canada,

USA (Massachusetts, Montana, North Carolina).

Montmorillonite (Na,Ca)$_{0.3}$(Al,Mg)$_2$Si$_4$O$_{10}$(OH)$_2$ .nH$_2$O Silicate Group

Mohs' Hardness 1	Specific Gravity 1.2–2.7	Crystal System Monoclinic

Distinctive features Chief constituent of the clay mineral bentonite. Absorbs water—especially water that has a high alkaline value—and swells accordingly. Will become semisolid when left undisturbed but pumpable again when agitated, being thixotropic.
Color Gray, beige, or white.
Forms Microcrystalline. Forms earthy masses which are greasy to the touch and crumble easily.
Uses The liquefied clay is used in the oil drilling and construction industries, because of its ability to suspend solids. It can also seal the pores of formations which normally accept fluids. Montmorillonite is also used as a purifying medium and as a filler in the manufacture of paper and rubber.
Occurrence It is formed either in

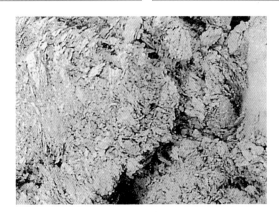

a hydrothermal environment, where volcanic ash has been altered, or in a sedimentary tropical environment, where feldspars have been altered. In large masses in France (Montmorillon—hence the name),

Above The montmorillonite shown here is swelling rapidly, on being placed in water. This example is from Wyoming.

Germany, Japan, USA (Alabama, California, Florida, Wyoming).

Talc $Mg_3(OH)_2[Si_4O_{10}]$ Silicate Group

Mohs' Hardness 1	Specific Gravity 2.58–2.83	Crystal System Monoclinic

Streak White.
Transparency Translucent to opaque.
Cleavage Perfect.
Fracture Uneven.
Tenacity Flexible.
Forms Crystals rare, generally in foliated aggregates.
Varieties In massive form, known as soapstone.
Uses Industrial, tailor's chalk, talcum powder.
Occurrence Formed by the alteration of dolomites and ultrabasic igneous rocks. The world's largest talc mine is in the French Pyrenees, where high quality talc is selectively mined by hand for just six months of the year. Smaller deposits occur in Austria, India, South Africa, Korea, Australia, Canada.

Distinctive features A secondary mineral formed by the metamorphic alteration of a number of magnesium silicates. Indissoluble in acid, almost infusible.
Color Gray.
Luster Greasy to pearly.

Bismuth Bi Native Metal and Nonmetal Group *(but see below)*

Mohs' Hardness 2–2.5	Specific Gravity 9.7–9.83	Crystal System Hexagonal

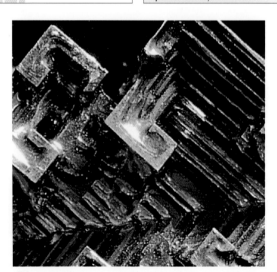

Distinctive features This native element is usually associated with silicate as bismuthinite, hence its inclusion within the silicate group.
Color Gray, multicolored.
Luster Metallic.
Streak Gray.
Transparency Opaque.
Cleavage Perfect basal.
Fracture Uneven.
Tenacity Brittle.
Forms Crystal very rare, feathery aggregates, massive.
Varieties Bismuthinite (Bi_2S_3).
Uses Alloys, lubrication, medicines, cosmetics.
Occurrence Forms in hydrothermal veins, and pegmatites. Bolivia. Found as an associate mineral with lead, cobalt, and silver in Germany, Norway, Canada.

ARSENIDES (SILICATES)

Nickeline NiAs Silicate Group, subgroup Arsenide

Mohs' Hardness 5–5.5	Specific Gravity 7.5–7.8	Crystal Structure Hexagonal

Distinctive features Also called niccolite. Crystals very rare. Fuses easily, giving off strong garlic-like aroma. Soluble in nitric acid, producing a green solution.
Color Copper-red, gray, brownish-black.
Luster Metallic.
Streak Brown/black.
Transparency Opaque.
Cleavage Uneven.
Fracture Conchoidal.
Tenacity Brittle.
Forms Massive, reniform, columnar.
Varieties Rotnickelkies, kupfernickel, copper nickel.
Uses Nickel ore.
Occurrence Found in hydrothermal veins and in norites. Associated with cobalt,

nickel, and silver ores. Crystals in Germany; large masses in

Germany, Russia, South Africa, Japan, Argentina, Canada.

CHROMATES (SILICATES)

Crocoite $PbCrO_4$ Silicate Group, subgroup Chromate

Mohs' Hardness 2.5–3	Specific Gravity 5.9–6.1	Crystal Structure Monoclinic

Distinctive features Pinkish-red elongated prismatic crystals, often in masses.
Color Shades of pinkish-red to bright saffron-coppery pink.
Luster Adamantine to vitreous.
Streak Yellowish orange.
Transparency Transparent.
Cleavage Distinct prismatic, good on 110.
Fracture Uneven, sometimes conchoidal.
Tenacity Sectile.

Forms Elongated, prismatic crystals. Also columnar or granular.
Varieties None.
Uses Mineral collections.
Occurrence Secondary minerals deposited by mineralizing waters that have leached lead from adjacent veins. The Urals in Russia, Romania, Tasmania, Philippines, USA (Arizona, California).

FELDSPARS (SILICATES)

Left Orthoclase is one of the most common feldspars, forming large masses like this in granites and pegmatites. The small gray crystals in this specimen are quartz. The word orthoclase comes from the Greek for "straight break," and it has almost perfect right-angle cleavage.

Below Moonstones are feldspars. You can see how much difference polishing makes.

The feldspars are a family of minerals covering a wide range. Feldspathoids have a similar chemical makeup but contain less silicate. Between them feldspar, which means "in every field," and feldspathoids are the most common type of mineral.

There are two main types of feldspar: orthoclase and plagioclase. Each has different chemical properties. They range in color from milky white to pink, green, and almost black, but the streak is always white. They are found in many rock types. Granite is rich in feldspar, which often shows up as quite large, well-formed crystals shaped like the ends of matchboxes. In the pegmatites which often form veins, feldspar crystals may be bigger, and there may be large masses of pink orthoclase feldspar. Pegmatites are often the source of the semiprecious gemstone moonstone, which has

a ghostly sheen due to the chemicals it contains, rather like the light reflected from the moon. Feldspars also occur in many metamorphic rocks such as gneiss, and the type of sandstone called arkose.

Among the various forms of feldspar is amazonstone, a blue-green colored feldspar which often occurs as striking crystals. Its color comes from tiny amounts of water and lead in the mineral's structure. Amazonstone has been used for thousands of years for jewelry and ornaments. Labradorite is an amazing, dark blue feldspar with a glittering surface of rainbow colors that change as the mineral is angled differently at the light. This effect is caused by minute rutile and magnetite crystals within the labradorite.

Orthoclase K(AlSi₃O₈) Silicate Group, subgroup Feldspar

Mohs' Hardness 6	Specific Gravity 2.57	Crystal System Monoclinic

Distinctive features Speckled, creamy white typical crystal form and two cleavages at 90 degrees.
Color White to mostly creamy white. Often pinkish red.
Luster Vitreous to pearly.
Streak White.
Transparency Mostly subtransparent, rarely transparent.
Cleavage Perfect on 001, good on 010.
Fracture Uneven.
Tenacity Brittle.
Forms Prismatic orthorhombic, twins common. Also massive, granular, and cryptocrystalline.
Varieties Adularia, which is a transparent form, and sanidine, which is a glassy, high-temperature form common in acid lavas.
Uses In the manufacture of porcelain, jewelry.
Occurrence Abundant and important rock-forming mineral of acid igneous rocks, schists, and gneisses. Good crystals occur in granitic pegmatites. Worldwide, but particularly in Switzerland, Italy, France, UK, Madagascar, Ceylon, USA (New England, Pennsylvania, Arkansas, Colorado, Texas, Nevada, and California).

Moonstone KAlSi₃O₈ Silicate Group, subgroup Feldspar

Mohs' Hardness 6–6.5	Specific Gravity 2.56–2.62	Crystal System Monoclinic

Distinctive features A variety of orthoclase which has a blue schiller caused by the reflection of light from the internal structure of alternate layers of albite and orthoclase feldspar. Thicker layers give a less attractive white schiller. Luminescence is usually bluish under longwave ultraviolet light and a weak orange under shortwave ultraviolet light, with a whitish to violet glow under X-rays, which may help distinguish moonstone from its imitations.
Color Colorless, yellow, with iridescent pale sheen of blue or pink.
Luster Vitreous to silky.
Streak White.
Transparency Semitransparent.
Cleavage Perfect.
Fracture Uneven, conchoidal.
Tenacity Brittle.
Forms Massive.
Varieties Moonstone cat's-eye

is also known.
Uses Gemstone.
Occurrence Occurs in pegmatites and in placers. Each locality may have characteristic inclusions. Sri Lankan moonstone usually has straight lathlike "stress cracks" which run parallel to the vertical axis of the crystal and from which there are branching cracks which appear to taper off. They may look like centipedes or other insects. Sri Lankan moonstone, with a white or blue "flash," is found in dikes or in water-worn pebbles in the gem gravels. Indian moonstone is characterized by the variations in body color from white to reddish brown, or plum-blue, and even green. Other localities include Madagascar, Burma, Tanzania, Australia, Brazil, USA (Colorado, Indiana, New Mexico, North Carolina, Pennsylvania, Virginia, and Wisconsin).

To show the sheen of moonstone to its best advantage, the stone should be cut *en cabochon* with the base of the cabochon parallel to the plane of the layers.

Heat is used to give synthetic white spinels a schiller to imitate moonstone. White chalcedony may also be cut *en cabochon* to imitate moonstone and may show a blue moon effect.

Amazonite KAlSi$_3$O$_8$ Silicate Group, subgroup Feldspar

Mohs' Hardness 6–6.5	Specific Gravity 2.56–2.58	Crystal System Triclinic

Distinctive features A green variety of microcline with similar composition to moonstone (see page 107).
Color Greenish.
Luster Vitreous.
Streak White.
Transparency Translucent, opaque.
Cleavage Perfect.

Fracture Uneven.
Tenacity Brittle.
Forms Prismatic.
Uses Gemstone.
Occurrence Occurs in metamorphic, intrusive, and pegmatic rocks. Best quality stones come from India; other sources are Russia, Madagascar, Tanzania,

the Sahara Desert, southern Africa, Canada (Ontario), USA (Virginia, Colorado).

Adularia KAlS$_3$O$_8$ Silicate Group, subgroup Feldspar

Mohs' Hardness 6	Specific Gravity 2.56	Crystal System Monoclinic

Distinctive features Bladed to prismatic, white to transparent crystals with a pearly appearance.

Occurs in crystalline schists.
Color Clear to white.
Luster Pearly.

Streak White.
Transparency Transparent to translucent.
Cleavage Perfect on 001, good on 010.
Fracture Uneven.
Tenacity Brittle.
Forms Bladed to prismatic crystals with elongated 110 faces.
Varieties None.
Uses Mineral collections.
Occurrence Adularia is the purest form of orthoclase, found in granites, granitic gneisses, and schists. It occurs in open druses and pegmatite veins, where it is associated with other granite minerals. Switzerland, Austria, Italy.

Plagioclase NaAlSi$_3$O$_8$ to CaAl$_2$Si$_2$O$_8$ Silicate Group, subgroup Feldspar

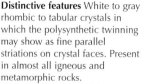

Mohs' Hardness 6	Specific Gravity 2.6–2.7	Crystal System Triclinic

Distinctive features White to gray rhombic to tabular crystals in which the polysynthetic twinning may show as fine parallel striations on crystal faces. Present in almost all igneous and metamorphic rocks.
Color White to grayish-blue or reddish.
Luster Vitreous to pearly.
Streak Colorless.
Transparency Mostly translucent, but some forms are transparent.
Cleavage Perfect basal on 001, 010 at 90 degrees.
Fracture Uneven.
Tenacity Brittle.
Forms Tabular.
Varieties Albite, olioclave, andesine, labradorite, bytownite, and anorthite. A continuous compositional series from sodium-rich albite to calcium anorthite in which varieties can be distinguished only by specialized testing.
Uses In porcelain manufacture, jewelry.
Occurrence Abundant and important rock-forming mineral of nearly all igneous rocks, but good crystals are only found in pegmatites and similar cavities and veins. Worldwide.

Sunstone (Ca,Na)[(Al,Si)$_2$Si$_2$O$_8$] Silicate Group, subgroup Feldspar

Mohs' Hardness 6–6.5	Specific Gravity 2.64	Crystal System Triclinic

Distinctive features Also known as aventurine feldspar, sunstone is a type of oligoclase feldspar. Inert under ultraviolet light but shows a whitish glow when irradiated with X-rays.
Color Orange, red-brown, with a red, or more rarely a green or blue, glitter caused by light interference on tiny hematite or goethite platelets.
Luster Vitreous.
Streak White.
Transparency Translucent, opaque.
Cleavage Perfect.
Fracture Grainy.
Tenacity Brittle.
Forms Massive.
Uses Gemstone.

Occurrence Deposits found in Norway, Siberia, southern India, Madagascar, Canada (Ontario), USA (Maine, New Mexico, New York, North Carolina, Pennsylvania, Virginia).
Used with flat surfaces or cut *en cabochon*.

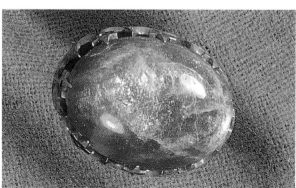

Labradorite NaAlSi$_3$O$_8$ to 50 percent CaAl$_2$Si$_2$O$_8$ 70 to 50 percent
Silicate Group, subgroup Feldspar

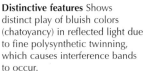

Mohs' Hardness 6.3	Specific Gravity 2.6	Crystal System Triclinic

Distinctive features Shows distinct play of bluish colors (chatoyancy) in reflected light due to fine polysynthetic twinning, which causes interference bands to occur.
Color Medium to dull gray.
Luster Satin to pearly.
Streak Colorless.
Transparency Translucent to transparent.
Cleavage Perfect basal on 001.
Fracture Uneven, sometimes conchoidal.
Tenacity Brittle.
Forms Mostly granular with large crystals.

Varieties A member of the continuous series in the plagioclase feldspars.
Uses Ornamental masonry when it occurs as a monominerallic rock.
Occurrence Mostly in basic to intermediate igneous rocks, such as diorite, gabbro, andesite, and basalt. Associated with augite and hornblende. Worldwide, but particularly in Scandinavia, Italy, Romania, Greenland, Canada (Labrador, Ontario, Quebec), and USA (New York State).

BERYL (SILICATES)

This striking mineral is well known for its wonderful, transparent, colored crystals. These are long and six-sided, sometimes with rather flat pyramids at the top. Beryl varies in color from rich green (emerald) to blue-green (aquamarine), yellow (heliodor), and pink (morganite). It has a white streak. The crystals often have thin grooves (striations) running along them. Crystals up to 18 feet long have been found in Colombia. A gigantic specimen from Madagascar weighed 36 tons.

Emerald is green beryl and was mined by the Aztecs in Mexico and Incas in Peru over 500 years ago. Long before this, both Roman and Greek civilizations used beryl for decoration, and emerald was mined in Egypt 3,500 years ago. The oldest Egyptian emerald mines were

rediscovered by the French adventurer Cailliaud in 1816. Then in 1900 Cleopatra's mines near the Red Sea were found. Cleopatra is said to have had an emerald engraved with her portrait.

Beryl is found in a variety of rocks, especially the igneous

rocks granite and pegmatite. It also occurs in metamorphic schist and gneiss, particularly in cavities, called vug, along with other crystals.

Below A very pale green variety of beryl, this crystal was found in Africa.

Emerald Be$_3$Al$_2$Si$_6$O$_{18}$ Silicate Group, subgroup Beryl

Mohs' Hardness 7.5	Specific Gravity 2.71	Crystal System Hexagonal

Emerald is the best known variety of beryl and is green in color. The color is due to a trace of chromium and usually some iron. The name emerald is derived from the Greek *smaragdus*, which in turn was derived from an earlier Persian word meaning a green mineral. Cleopatra's emerald mine by the Red Sea in Egypt dates back to about 2000BC and was probably the source of most of the emerald used in ancient jewelry.

Emerald crystalizes as hexagonal prisms with two flat terminations. Occasionally, small pyramidal faces bevel the junction of the flat (basal) face and the prism faces. There is poor cleavage parallel to the basal plane. The luster is vitreous.

Emerald has distinct dichroism, showing blue-green and yellow-green. Most emeralds show bright red through the Chelsea color filter. In South African and Indian stones this fluorescence is dulled by the presence of iron, and they may show green through the filter.

The world's finest emeralds are from the Chivor and Muzo mines in Colombia. The crystals are found in cracks or pockets within the rock. Chivor stones usually show a strong red under the Chelsea color filter and a red fluorescence under ultraviolet light. Three-phase inclusions are typical. Beautiful yellowish-green emeralds, often with three-phase inclusions (containing sodium chloride—common salt), are found in the Muzo mines. The color of emerald and the inclusions within it may give clues as to its source. Emeralds from the Bahia and Minas Gerais regions of Brazil are of a pale yellowish-green color and are colored by chromium. They are fairly clear but may contain two-phase inclusions. Emeralds are found in the Ekaterinburg region of Russia, but the larger stones are generally cloudy. Australian emeralds are mainly pale, badly flawed, and often embedded in other minerals. The larger emerald crystals found in South Africa are also usually cloudy or flawed, and typically contain brown mica plate inclusions. Zimbabwean emeralds from the Sandawana area are a superb green; they are commonly zoned and have inclusions of tremolite needles or rods. Indian emeralds vary in quality and have characteristic "comma" inclusions (rectangular cavities containing both a liquid and a bubble of gas).

Other localities include the Habachtal area of Austria, Norway, Pakistan, Tanzania, Zambia and the USA.

The best quality emeralds are cut in the trap-cut or step-cut style, also known as the emerald cut. Emerald that is flawed but has a good color may be carved. Poor quality flawed emeralds are cut *en cabochon* or as beads. Almost all emeralds are oiled to fill cracks and improve their appearance.

Composites, such as garnet-topped doublets, *soudé* emeralds, composites using quartz, or spinel, or glass are used to imitate emerald. Sometimes pale emeralds are painted or foiled on the back to improve their color. Crackled quartz dyed green is sometimes called "Indian emerald." Most imitations of emerald show green through the Chelsea color filter.

Synthetic emeralds were first produced just before the Second World War, and have since been made in commercial quantities in the USA and elsewhere. Early synthetic emeralds show a red color through the Chelsea color filter that is far brighter than that from natural emerald.

Aquamarine $Be_3Al_2Si_6O_{18}$ Silicate Group, subgroup Beryl

Mohs' Hardness 7.5	Specific Gravity 2.69	Crystal System Hexagonal

Aquamarine is a blue-green variety of beryl. The best quality aquamarine has a sky-blue color. The name aquamarine means sea water.

Hexagonal crystals of aquamarine are often large and flawless. They may be striated, making them like a ribbed cylinder, and tapered due to erosion. Luster is vitreous and there is a weak basal cleavage.

Aquamarine is dichroic, showing colorless and deep blue. The absorption spectrum is weak and there is no luminescence. A strong greenish-blue color is seen through the Chelsea color filter. Some aquamarines show chatoyancy (the cat's-eye effect) when cut en cabochon.

The best known locality for gem quality aquamarine is Minas Gerais, Brazil, where crystals have been weathered out from pegmatites and are found as alluvial deposits in a layer of brown gravel called cascalho. The Russian Urals are also known for their fine aquamarine. There are said to be 50 sources of beryl, including aquamarine, on the island of Madagascar. Aquamarine is found in Burma but is not common in Sri Lanka. Other localities include Northern Ireland, Norway, Namibia, Tanzania, Zimbabwe, India, China, Argentina, and the USA.

The cutter normally uses a trap-cut on aquamarine because of the pale color. The size of the stone is kept large enough to give a fairly strong color and the table facet is cut parallel to the length of the prismatic crystals to get maximum color. The blue color is usually enhanced by heat treatment.

Aquamarine is imitated by synthetic spinel colored with cobalt. The imitation can be recognized because it appears bright red through the Chelsea color filter (instead of green). Pale blue glass imitating aquamarine is easily recognized as it is only singly refractive, whereas aquamarine is doubly refractive.

Topaz may look similar to aquamarine, but the refractometer will show the higher refractive index readings of topaz.

Morganite $Be_3Al_2Si_6O_{18}$ Silicate Group, subgroup Beryl

Mohs' Hardness 7.5	Specific Gravity 2.8	Crystal System Hexagonal

The pink, rose, and peach colors of morganite are due to manganese. Morganite is heat treated to drive off any yellow tinge and so enhance the color. It is named for J.P. Morgan, an American banker and gem enthusiast. Morganite is usually found as tabular prisms. It is dichroic, the two colors being pink and a deeper bluish-pink. There is no characteristic absorption spectrum, and luminescence under ultraviolet light is weak. Under X-rays there is an intense red glow.

A pure pink morganite is found in Minas Gerais, Brazil and also in Madagascar. Pale rose-colored beryl is found around San Diego, California. Deposits also occur in Mozambique, Namibia, and Zimbabwe.

Morganite is usually faceted as trap-cut stones in order to give a strong color. Morganite is imitated by pink topaz, kunzite, natural and synthetic pink sapphire, and spinel. Garnet-topped doublets and pastes are also made in a pink color.

Heliodor $Be_3Al_2Si_6O_{18}$ Silicate Group, subgroup Beryl

Mohs' Hardness 7.5	Specific Gravity 2.68	Crystal System Hexagonal

Heliodor varies in color from a pale yellow to a rich golden color. The name heliodor is derived from the Greek meaning sun and gift. Its physical properties are like those of aquamarine. The absorption spectrum is weak and the presence of iron, which gives rise to the golden-yellow color, dulls any luminescence. Although many heliodors, morganites, and aquamarines are virtually flawless, inclusions in the form of slender, parallel tubes can occur which reduces the stones' transparency and luster.

Yellow beryls are found in all the aquamarine localities, particularly Madagascar, Brazil, and Namibia. They are also found in Connecticut. The trap cut is the most usual cut for yellow beryls because they need the depth to give a strong color.

Bixbite Be$_3$Al$_2$Si$_6$O$_{18}$ Silicate Group, subgroup Beryl

Mohs' Hardness 7.5–8	Specific Gravity 2.65–2.75	Crystal System Hexagonal

Due to its rarity, distinctive color, and the publicity surrounding its recent discovery, bixbite—also known as red beryl—is a relatively highly valued semiprecious gemstone. While commanding a high market price, bixbite has not as yet been commercially imitated or produced synthetically. Unlike the other beryl group crystals which are found in or near pegmatic veins, bixbites are found in effusive magmatic rhyolite rocks.

Bixbite has a strong, ruby red, violet, or strawberry red hue. The crystals, which tend to be small, always contain numerous inclusions and more often than not internal flaws.

Bixbite crystals are only found in the USA (New Mexico and Utah).

Other Varieties of Beryl

Dark Brown beryl has a bronzy sheen, which is due to inclusions of the mineral ilmenite. It shows a star when cut *en cabochon*. This type of beryl is found at Minas Gerais, Brazil.

Confusion can easily arise with further varieties because of the different approach made by gemologists and mineralogists. All beryls have the same chemical constitution, and thus to the mineralogist are the same. Since however the colors and birefringence (the difference between the refractive indices of a doubly refractive jewel like beryl) vary, different beryls are important to jewelers who tend to give further classifications to beryls, mainly by color.

TOURMALINES (SILICATES)

This mineral probably has the greatest color range of any gemstone and many of the different color types have their own names. The nineteenth-century philosopher John Ruskin described the chemistry of tourmaline as "more like a medieval doctor's prescription than the making of a respectable mineral." Varieties include red and pink (rubellite), blue (indicolite), emerald green (Brazilian emerald), colorless (achroite), brown (dravite), violet (siberite), yellow, green, and black (schorl). Tourmaline may also be particolored, showing two colors in the one stone. A type with a pink center and green surround is referred to as "watermelon" tourmaline.

The crystals are usually long thin prisms that are vertically striated. They show a characteristic rounded triangular section when viewed down their length. The terminations at either end of a crystal are differently shaped. Tourmaline has an uneven fracture and very poor cleavage. Luster is vitreous, and transparency varies from transparent to opaque. The refractive indices are different for each color. Birefringence is high and a doubling of the back facets should be apparent in cut stones. Diochroism is more obvious in the darker stones with two shades of the body color visible in the principal optical directions. The absorption spectrum is usually too weak to be used for identification and luminescence is not distinctive. Inclusions are black patches or threadlike fluid-filled cavities which may sometimes be cut en cabochon to show a cat's-eye.

When a tourmaline, apart from the black and dark colored iron-rich varieties, is heated, it becomes electrically charged. One end of the crystal becomes positively charged and the other negatively charged, and the crystal may attract small pieces of paper or dust toward one end. Because dust is attracted, tourmaline in a jeweler's window display will appear dusty sooner than most other gemstones. When pressure is applied to tourmaline it also becomes charged; this property is used in some depth-recording equipment.

The Ural Mountains of Russia have well-known gem-quality tourmaline localities. These are blue or red and are found in yellow clays formed from weathered granites. Much gem-quality tourmaline comes from pegmatic rocks in Madagascar.

Red varieties are the most popular and colorless the most rare, but all colors are found there. Sri Lanka has yellow and brown colored tourmalines which are found in alluvial deposits. Fine red tourmaline is found in Burma. Tourmaline from Brazil is green, blue, or red, and many of the crystals are particolored. Bright green tourmaline crystals colored by chromium (and sometimes vanadium) have been found in Tanzania. Dark green tourmaline crystals from Namibia are usually lightened by heating.

The mixed cut (step-cut pavilion and brilliant-cut crown) and the trap cut ore used for fashioning most tourmaline. Flawed tourmaline is used to make beads and may be carved as small figurines. The black schorl tourmaline has been used for mourning jewelry.

Tourmaline Na(Mg,Fe,Mn,Li,Al)$_3$Al(Si$_6$O$_{18}$) (BO$_3$)$_3$.(OH,F)$_4$
Silicate Group

Mohs' Hardness 7–7.5	Specific Gravity 3.02–3.26	Crystal System Hexagonal

Distinctive features Elongated, well striated, prismatic crystals in granites and pegmatites. Color varies widely.
Color Mostly black, but also dark brown, violet, green, and pink and some forms are bicolored pinkish-red and green.
Luster Vitreous, sometimes resinous.
Streak Colorless.
Transparency Transparent to opaque.
Cleavage All very poor.
Fracture Poor conchoidal, uneven.
Tenacity Brittle.
Forms Parallel elongated or acicular prisms, sometimes radiating. Also massive and as scattered grains in granites.
Varieties See opposite.
Uses As gemstones, when perfectly transparent.
Occurrence In schists, pegmatites, and granites and gneisses, where it has crystalized from late-stage mineralizing fluids and gases. The Urals in Siberia, Germany, Greenland, the Czech Republic, Switzerland, UK, Ceylon, Brazil, South Africa, Madagascar, Zimbabwe, Mozambique, Kenya, Burma, USA (Maine, Connecticut, California).

Varieties

Rubellite

Dravite

Indicolite

Green tourmaline

GARNETS (SILICATES)

Garnet is the name of a group of silicates with various amounts of magnesium, iron, or calcium. The garnets can be divided into two series, the pyrope-almandine series ("pyralspite" series) and the uvarovite-grossularite-andralite series ("ugrandite" series). Within each series there is a continuous change in physical and optical characteristics from one end to the other.

Garnet $XAl_2Si_3O_{12}$ (where $X=Ca_3,Mg_3,Fe_3,Mn_3,$ Fe_2,Cr_2)
Silicate Group, subgroup Garnet

Mohs' Hardness 6.5–7.2	Specific Gravity 3–4	Crystal System Isometric

Distinctive features Crystal shape, color, rock association.
Color Deep red to pale yellowish-red, black, deep or bright green.
Luster Resinous to glassy.
Streak White.
Transparency Transparent to translucent to opaque.
Cleavage None.
Fracture Uneven and occasionally subconchoidal.
Tenacity Brittle.
Forms Dodecahedron and trapezohedrons.

Varieties Grossularite, which is pale green through amber to deep brown, pyrope, which is blood red to black, almandine, which is brownish red to black, spessartite, which is dark red to brownish red, andradite, which is shades of red, yellow, green, brown, and black, and uvarovite, which is emerald green (rare).
Uses Gemstone.
Occurrence Widespread in many rocks some of the best crystals are from schist, serpentines, metamorphosed limestones, gneisses, and granite pegmatites. Worldwide, but grossularite is very common in schists and metamorphosed limestones, pyrope in South Africa, almandine in USA (New York State), spessartite in Germany and Italy, androdite in Sweden, Germany, the Urals and USA (New Jersey), uvarovite in the Urals in Russia, Canada (Quebec), Spain, Scandinavia, West Africa.

Grossular Garnet Ca₃Al₂(SiO₄)₃ Silicate Group, subgroup Garnet

Mohs' Hardness 7–7.5	Specific Gravity 3.65	Crystal System Isometric

characteristic inclusions that look like swirls, giving a treacle-like appearance. Pure grossular is colorless. "Transvaal jade" is a massive variety from South Africa, and may be green, gray, blue, or pink.
Uses Gemstones.
Occurrence Occurs in a variety of metamorphic rocks, although most commonly in marble. Hessonite is found in the gem gravels of Sri Lanka, and in Russia, Brazil, Canada, and the USA. Green grossular garnet occurs in Tanzania and Kenya, and has been called "tsarvorite."

Grossular garnets may be faceted or cut en cabochon. "Transvaal jade," which contains specks of magnetite, makes an attractive stone when carved.

Distinctive features Insoluble in acids.
Color Varies greatly. Can be green, yellowish-green, yellow, brown, red, orange, reddish brown, pink, white, gray, black.
Luster Vitreous or resinous.
Streak White
Transparency Transparent to nearly opaque.
Cleavage None.
Fracture Uneven to conchoidal.
Tenacity Brittle.
Forms Dodecahedral or trapezohedral crystals; also granular, compact, or massive.
Varieties Hessonite is yellowish brown to orange-red with

Andradite Ca₃Al₂(SiO₄)₃ Silicate Group, subgroup Garnet

Mohs' Hardness 6.5	Specific Gravity 3.85	Crystal System Isometric

Andradite garnet has two varieties that have been used in jewelry. One is opaque black melanite, which has popularly been used for mourning jewelry. The other is green demantoid garnet, the color of which is due to the presence of chromium. Melanite crystals are usually dodecahedra or icositetrahedra, or a mixture of both.

Demantoid is a rare variety of andradite. It has a higher dispersion than diamond, but the vivid green color masks this property. It is relatively soft and so is not commonly used in jewelry. Demantoid garnet looks red through the Chelsea color filter and has a characteristic

absorption spectrum with a strong band in the red which is due to iron. It is inert under ultraviolet light and X-rays. Inclusions are groups of radiating asbestos fibers which look like "horse-tails." Demantoid is the only green mineral that has these horse-tails.

The main source for gem-quality demantoid is the Ural Mountains. It is also found in Zaire and Korea, although these are not of such good quality. Melanite is found in Italy and the Haute-Pyrenees of France. Topazolite is the name given to yellow andradite garnet.

Andradite garnet is faceted for use in jewelry.

Almandine Ca₃Al₂(SiO₄)₃ Silicate Group, subgroup Garnet

Mohs' Hardness 6.5–7.5	Specific Gravity 3.95–4.2	Crystal System Isometric

Brightly colored almandine crystals, which are free of inclusions and internal cracks, are sometimes cut into gemstones. Almandine is often ground and used as a medium-hard abrasive in polishing paper and cloth. Almandine crystals, which are usually well formed, are common in medium-grade metamorphic or contact metamorphic environments.

Almandine crystals have a red color but often contain a deep, violet-red tint. Although cut crystals have a brilliant luster, their transparency is often marred, even in clear stones, by an excessive depth of color. In an effort to lighten the stone, the underside of such gems are often hollowed out. Unlike rubies, the

deep-red color does not lighten in natural light. The crystal splinters and fuses easily, but is insoluble in acids.

Almandine is found in large quantities in sand deposits in Sri Lanka, with lesser deposits occurring in the Czech Republic, Norway, Afghanistan, India,

Above The very deep color of this almandine sample from the USA is typical of these crystals.

Madagascar, Tanzania, Brazil, Greenland, USA (Alaska, California, Colorado, Connecticut, Idaho, Michigan, Pennsylvania, South Dakota).

Rhodolite Ca₃Al₂(SiO₄)₃ Silicate Group, subgroup Garnet

Mohs' Hardness 6.5–7.5	Specific Gravity 3.74–3.94	Crystal System Isometric

Rhodolite is not the most common of the red garnets, but it is the most valuable. It is formed in plutonic and ultramafic rocks, but, due to its resistance to weathering, the crystals are usually found in alluvial secondary deposits or in arenaceous rocks.

The name rhodolite is derived rom the Greek word *rhodon* meaning rose colored, and *lithos* meaning stone. The crystal itself can vary in color from pinkish-red through rose-red and pale violet. The cut crystal displays a strong luster and a good transparency. Rhodolite is distinguished from similar-colored crystals of the corundum group by its lack of pleochroism or fluorescence.

Rhodolite crystals are found in Sri Lanka, Tanzania, Zambia, Zimbabwe, Brazil, and the USA (North Carolina).

Above The example of rhodolite from the USA demonstrates the strong luster of these gemstones.

Spessartine Ca$_3$Al$_2$(SiO$_4$)$_3$ Silicate Group, subgroup Garnet

Mohs' Hardness 7	Specific Gravity 4.16	Crystal System Isometric

The name is derived from the Spessart district of Germany, where the crystals were once found. Petrologists, who study the origin and structure of rocks, refer to the rock itself as spessartite, but the gems are referred to as spessartine.

Spessartine garnets are orange-pink, orange-red, red-brown, or brownish-yellow in color. They have a characteristic absorption spectrum which is partly due to the presence of manganese. Spessartine is inert under ultraviolet light and X-rays. There are characteristic lacelike or featherlike inclusions which can only be detected by experts. Hessonite garnet is similar in color but has quite different inclusions which give it a treacly appearance.

Gem-quality examples are rare. Most of the crystals found in Germany and Italy are too small to be used in jewelry, but good examples are found in Australia (New South Wales), Burma, Madagascar, Norway, and the USA (Virginia and California). Some gem-quality spessartine is found in Brazil, but the majority of it is too dark to be of use in jewelry.

Spessartine may be faceted or cut *en cabochon*.

Uvarovite Ca$_3$Al$_2$(SiO$_4$) Silicate Group, subgroup Garnet

Mohs' Hardness 6.5–7.2	Specific Gravity 3–4	Crystal System Isometric

Distinctive features Crystal shape, color, rock association.
Color Emerald green.
Luster Resinous to glossy.
Streak White.
Transparency Transparent to translucent to opaque.
Cleavage None.
Fracture Uneven and occasionally subconchoidal.
Tenacity Brittle.
Forms Dodecahedron and trapezohedrons.
Uses Gemstone.
Occurrence Spain, Scandinavia, the Urals in Russia, West Africa, Canada (Quebec).

Pyrope $Ca_3Al_2(SiO_4)_3$ Silicate Group, subgroup Garnet

Mohs' Hardness 7–7.5	Specific Gravity 3.7–3.9	Crystal System Isometric

Pyrope gets its name from the Greek word *pyropos*, meaning fiery. It is also known as Cape ruby. It is a moderately valuable semiprecious gemstone, with the darkest crystals being the most common.

Pyrope is usually red. It is colored by iron, and sometimes also by chromium. Pyrope does not fluoresce under ultraviolet light due to its iron content, but red spinel, which is similar, does. Pyrope is moderately magnetic and this can also be used to separate it from red spinel. The pyrope absorption spectrum is characterized by three dark bands. The bright red stones from the Czech Republic, Kimberley in South Africa, and Arizona have a typical chromium spectrum with a narrow doublet in the red and a broad band. Pyrope rarely has inclusions. When they are present they are usually small rounded crystals with irregular outlines.

Pyrope from the Czech Republic is found in conglomerates, volcanic rocks, and in various alluvials, but rarely as good crystals. Most pyrope now used is found in the diamond mines of South Africa. Russian pyrope is also of good quality. Other localities include Burma, Tanzania, Australia, Argentina, and Brazil.

Most pyrope is faceted for

Above Gem-quality pyrope crystals from alluvial deposits in the Czech Republic.

setting in jewelry and was particularly popular in the nineteenth century.

QUARTZ (SILICATES)

Quartz is one of the most common minerals, found in many rocks. The shiny gray crystals in granite are quartz. So are the grains in sandstone. The metamorphic rock, metaquartzite, is almost entirely quartz. Because it is so hard, quartz is left behind in river gravels and on pebble beaches. Look for milky white or glassy pebbles that cannot be scratched with a knife blade.

Crystals of quartz are common and are hexagonal, often pyramidal on the top. Look for them in rock cavities, especially where there are faults or mineral veins. The crystals grow out into the hollows in the rocks. Big crystals up to 3 feet long are most likely to be found in cavities in volcanic rocks such as lava and basalt. Some kinds of quartz, such as rock crystal, are as clear as water—the Roman scholar Pliny the Elder thought clear quartz was ice frozen too hard to melt. Others are colored by different minerals: small amounts of iron make amethysts purple, and very small amounts of manganese or titanium give the pink in rose quartz. Whatever its color, a quartz streak is always white.

Electrical Properties of Quartz

Quartz exhibits a piezoelectric effect, which means that an electric charge can be induced to the crystal when pressure is applied to the crystal in certain directions. In 1922 W. G. Cady found that the electrically vibrating crystals could be used as a means of measuring and controlling the frequencies of radio waves. Since then many other uses of this property have been found, including the use of quartz in clocks and watches, underwater signalling and detecting apparatus, and as lenses in microscopes, which also takes advantage of the fact that quartz is transparent to ultraviolet rays.

Above Look for quartz in mountainous regions, where hard metamorphic rocks may have crystalline quartz veins running through them.

Left The rounded grains visible in the piece of sandstone are quartz—which makes up 80 percent of the rock's structure. The quartz was originally formed in another rock such as granite, and then detached by rain and ice, and carried by the wind to be deposited as layers of sand.

Quartz SiO₂ Silicate Group, subgroup Quartz

Mohs' Hardness 7	Specific Gravity 2.65–2.66	Crystal System Hexagonal

Distinctive features Shape, rock association, hardness.
Color Colorless when pure, but otherwise white, yellow, red, brown, green, blue, black.
Luster Vitreous
Streak White.
Transparency Transparent to opaque.
Cleavage Not seen.
Fracture Conchoidal.
Tenacity Brittle.
Forms Prismatic and terminated by rhombohedrons that look like hexagonal pyramids
Varieties Rock crystal, which is clear and glasslike; amethyst, which is purple; rose quartz, which is rose; citrine, which is yellow; smoky, which is dark brown; chalcedony, which is waxlike; plasma, which is green; agate, which is banded colors; flint, which is opaque black-brown, and jasper, which can be various colors.
Uses Manufacture of glass and porcelain, ornamental, jewelry, abrasives, sand in mortar, sandstone in building.
Occurrence Universal, mainly as sand. Smoky quartz is mainly found in the Swiss Alps, amethyst in the Alps, Brazil, USA (Maine, Virginia, and Arkansas).

Above This is an unusually large crystal of cairngorm, over 3 inches long, found in the mountains of Scotland. Such large crystals can only grow where there are large cavities in the rocks.

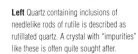

Left Quartz containing inclusions of needlelike rods of rutile is described as rutillated quartz. A crystal with "impurities" like these is often quite sought after.

Above Many types of quartz, including amethyst, rock crystal, and cairngorm stones, are used in jewelry.

Rock Crystal SiO$_2$ Silicate Group, subgroup Quartz

Mohs' Hardness 7	Specific Gravity 2.65	Crystal System Trigonal

The name quartz comes from the Greek for ice, since it was once believed that the crystals were forever frozen by a process of extreme cold. Although quite common, rock crystal, also known as colorless quartz, is often carved into *objets d'art* or fashioned into jewelry. In the past it has been used for optical and piezoelectrical purposes; synthetic crystals are now generally used for this purpose. Rock crystal is crystalized directly from magma, in pegmatites, and in low-temperature hydrothermal regions.

Rock crystal is colorless, transparent, and—unlike glass—is birefringent. It is distinguishable from ordinary glass by its absence of air bubbles, and from lead-glass by its hardness (7 compared to 5).

Quartz is one of the most commonly occurring minerals in the Earth's crust (12 percent by volume). Brazil has produced some spectacular crystals which have weighed in excess of 4 tons.

Left A rock crystal showing an internal ghost crystal.

Citrine SiO$_2$ Silicate Group, subgroup Quartz

Mohs' Hardness 7	Specific Gravity 2.65	Crystal System Trigonal

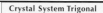

Left The citrine crystal is a heat-treated amethyst, mined in Brazil.

citrine crystals take the form of prisms with pyramid ends.

Citrine is rare, but does occur in France, Madagascar, Brazil, and the USA in Colorado.

Faceted cuts are used for fine transparent citrines, while the remaining varieties are cut as cabochons.

Natural yellow citrine is rare and most commercial stones are actually heat-treated amethysts. Some heat-treated stones have a red tint and show no pleochroism. Citrine is used to imitate the more expensive gemstone, topaz.

The distinctive color of citrine is due to the presence of iron, and varies from pure yellow, dull yellow, honey, or brownish-yellow. Citrine is dichroic but has no characteristic absorption spectrum or fluorescence. The crystals will turn white if heated and dark brown if exposed to X-rays. As with amethysts, citrines are often parti-colored. Cut crystals have a good luster. Larger

Amethyst SiO_2 Silicate Group, subgroup Quartz

Mohs' Hardness 7	Specific Gravity 2.65	Crystal System Trigonal

been the main source of reddish-colored amethyst. Other good sources include Germany, Namibia, Western Australia and Zambia. Brazilian and Uruguayan amethyst is found in cavities in igneous rocks. Amethyst is found in a number of states in the USA, with large crystals from North Carolina and Maine. Violet-colored amethyst is found in Canada and many geodes containing amethyst are found in the Deccan trap area of India. Good quality amethyst comes from the Sri Lankan gem gravels.

Crystals of amethyst are cut in the mixed-cut style or the trap-cut style, and are often fashioned into beads.

Synthetic corundum and glass can be made in a color to imitate amethyst. Pale amethyst has been mounted in a closed setting with paint or foil behind the stone to enhance the color.

Below These Brazilian amethysts have grown inside a geode, a common place for these crystals to form.

Amethyst varies in color from pale violet to dark purple and may be parti-colored with clear or yellow quartz. The tips of the crystals are often darkest and may grade to colorless quartz. Amethyst is found lining hollow cavities in rocks.

Amethyst changes color with heat, and stones from different localities show different color changes to brown, yellow, and sometimes green. However, these changes are unpredictable and the color may fade. Amethyst has distinct dichroism, showing a bluish purple and a reddish purple. This distinguishes it from heat-treated stones which do not show any dichroism. Amethyst does not have a characteristic absorption spectrum. Inclusions are usually featherlike, or may resemble a thumb print or tiger stripes.

The Ural Mountains of Russia have

Brown Quartz SiO$_2$ Silicate Group, subgroup Quartz

Mohs' Hardness 7	Specific Gravity 2.65	Crystal System Trigonal

Brown quartz varies in color from yellow-brown cairngorm, named for the Cairngorm mountains in the Scottish Highlands, to the almost black quartz sometimes called morion. Morion can he heat treated to lighten its color and make a more attractive stone.

Brown quartz is found as hexagonal prisms. It has no characteristic absorption spectrum or luminescence under ultraviolet light or X-rays. Brown quartz may have inclusions of the mineral rutile (titanium oxide). These are long needlelike crystals which may be seen easily without magnification. The inclusions may add to the beauty and interest of the stone.

The main localities for brown quartz are in the Swiss Alps. Other localities include Spain, Japan, and Australia.

Brown quartz is often faceted for gemstones or carved for *objets d'art*. Most of the cairngorm variety of brown quartz is Brazilian amethyst that has been heat treated to give the brown color.

Smoky Quartz SiO$_2$ Silicate Group, subgroup Quartz

Mohs' Hardness 7	Specific Gravity 2.65	Crystal System Hexagonal

Smoky quartz, also known as smoky topaz, with its intricate patterns, is often cut into gemstones or *objets d'art*. Crystals weighing up to 670 pounds have been found in hydrothermal veins in Brazil. Its distinctive smoky characteristic is probably due to rock crystal being subjected to natural radiation.

Smoky quartz is named for its smoky color. It can be brown, black, or smoky gray. When heated to 572–752°F crystals turn yellow then white. Quality crystals will often contain rutile inclusions.

Smoky quartz is found worldwide. Quality crystals have been found in Alpine fissures, Madagascar, and in Brazil. Good crystals have also been found at Pike's Peak, Colorado.

Above This sample of smoky quartz was found in Cornwall, England.

Rose Quartz SiO₂ Silicate Group, subgroup Quartz

Mohs' Hardness 7	Specific Gravity 2.65	Crystal System Trigonal

Rose quartz varies in color from pale whitish-pink to dark rose pink. Magnesium and titanium have both been suggested as the impurity which causes the color. Transparent rose quartz is very rare and the stones are usually rather cloudy. The crystals are brittle and often cracked. The stones tend to lose their color when heated and turn black when exposed to radiation. Dichroism is apparent in the darker colored stones.

Quality rose quartz is found in Madagascar, Brazil, and the USA in California and Maine.

Some rose quartz contains tiny rutile needles which cause a star effect. This is best seen when the stone is cut *en cabochon* and light is directed up through the stone. Rose quartz may be faceted although it is more usually fashioned as cabochons, beads, or carved for ornaments.

Milky Quartz SiO₂ Silicate Group, subgroup Quartz

Mohs' Hardness 7	Specific Gravity 2.65	Crystal System Trigonal

Milky quartz is of variable opacity, white, and may be layered or striped with milky bands. The distinctive coloration of milky quartz is due to inclusions of numerous bubbles of gas and liquid in the crystal.

Milky quartz is found in pegmatites and hydrothermal veins; it is still not known exactly how the crystal forms. This variety of quartz is one of the most common materials found in the Earth's surface. Massive crystals have been found in Siberia. Other localities include central Europe, Madagascar, Namibia, Brazil, and the USA.

Milky quartz is rarely cut as a gemstone, and is most often cut into beads or ornaments. It may contain grains of gold and is usually cut *en cabochon* to show these.

Tiger's-eye SiO₂ Silicate Group, subgroup Quartz

Mohs' Hardness 7	Specific Gravity 2.64–2.71	Crystal System Hexagonal

Tiger's-eye is one of a group (which includes Quartz Cat's-eye and Hawk's-eye, see below), formed from fine fibrous quartz aggregates. Tiger's-eye is often used for carving boxes and other ornamental items as these will display its attractive markings to their full advantage. The characteristic golden-brown color forms when the blue crocidolite asbestos (a type of hornblende) is broken down to leave a residue of iron oxides.

Tiger's-eye crystals vary in color from gold-yellow to gold-brown stripes against an almost black background. The fibers making up the stripes are concentrated into semiparallel groupings.

The most important tiger's-eye deposit occurs in South Africa but it is also found in India, Burma, Western Australia, and the USA (California).

Quartz Cat's-eye SiO₂ Silicate Group, subgroup Quartz

Mohs' Hardness 7	Specific Gravity 2.65	Crystal System Trigonal

Quartz Cat's-eye is one of a group formed from fibrous quartz aggregates (see tiger's-eye above). It is semitransparent and the fibers are clearly visible. It becomes greenish-gray or green when ground. Like tiger's-eye, hawk's-eye forms when blue crocidolite asbestos is replaced by quartz. Unlike tiger's-eye, hawk's-eye retains the original blue color of asbestos.

Quartz cat's-eye is found in Germany, India, Sri Lanka, and Burma. Like tiger's-eye, hawk's-eye is mainly found in South Africa, but other localities include Burma, India, Australia, and the USA.

Aventurine Quartz SiO₂ Silicate Group, subgroup Quartz

Mohs' Hardness 7	Specific Gravity 2.65	Crystal System Trigonal

Aventurine quartz is named for a type of glass discovered in Italy at the beginning of the eighteenth century. It was called *a ventura* because the glass was discovered "by accident" or "luck."

Aventurine quartz contains mica plates which give it a sheen, with spangles of different colors.

Green aventurine quartz contains green mica. Other aventurine quartz include the brownish-red stones, which contain cubes of the mineral pyrite. Other varieties of aventurine include bluish-white and bluish-green material.

The main localities for good quality aventurine include Siberia, India, Tanzania, and Brazil.

Aventurine is used for ornamental objects and may also be cut *en cabochon*.

Carnelian SiO₂ Silicate Group, subgroup Quartz

Mohs' Hardness 7	Specific Gravity 2.6	Crystal System Trigonal

Carnelian, also known as cornelian, is the translucent red variety of chalcedony. The red color comes from the presence of iron oxides.

Carnelian is found as rolled pebbles in Egypt, India, China, and Brazil. Other localities include Scotland, Germany, Japan, Colombia, and the USA.

Carnelian is carved or cut and polished *en cabochon*.

Most commercial carnelian is stained chalcedony.

Chalcedony SiO₂ Silicate Group, subgroup Quartz

Mohs' Hardness 7	Specific Gravity 2.6	Crystal System Trigonal

Chalcedony is a variety of quartz with a crystalline structure that is so small it can only be seen with the use of a microscope (microcrystalline). The word chalcedony covers a group of quartzes, including all agates, carnelian, and chrysoprase, which form from thin layers of tiny quartz fibers. Pure chalcedony, however, has its own distinct properties. Chalcedony itself is translucent and has a white or bluish color, but it may be colored green by chromium. The banding of chalcedony cannot be seen without a microscope. Under ultraviolet light the luminescence of chalcedony varies from bluish-white to yellowish-green.

Good quality chalcedony is found in Brazil, India, Madagascar and Uruguay.
The fibrous structure gives chalcedony its toughness and makes it ideal for carving, particularly popular in Germany. Chalcedony is porous and may be dyed with a variety of metallic salts.

Sard, Sardonyx, and Onyx SiO₂ Silicate Group, subgroup Quartz

Mohs' Hardness 7	Specific Gravity 2.6	Crystal System Trigonal

Sard is the brownish-red variety of chalcedony. Sardonyx has straight bands of white, together with bands of brownish red sard. Onyx is made up of black and white bands. It is similar to agate except that the bands are straight.
Localities include Brazil and Uruguay.
Sard, sardonyx, and onyx are carved and polished for use as beads and cameos.
Black onyx has almost always been stained. Natural black onyx is rare and so it is produced by chemically treating agate.

Agate—Introduction

Agate is well known for its concentric bands of color, created by traces of iron and manganese. In fact, agate is just banded chalcedony. If cut into thin slices, the bands show up as light glows through. The natural colors of agate vary and may be red, white, blue, gray, brown, or black. Many agates sold in gem stores, however, are dyed or stained artificially, and the most expensive rough agates are those which can be easily colored. The chemical composition of agate is the same as quartz, but agate has a different physical structure. Instead of forming as large crystals, it is made of minute fibers and crystals, visible only with a microscope. Onyx is the variety of agate with straight layers. Fortification agate has angular, concentric bands. Moss agate has greenish branched veins. Jasper agate is red. Thunder eggs have star-shaped patterns.

Above Inclusions of chlorite make moss agate look like the green coating of moss that sometimes grows on walls and trees.

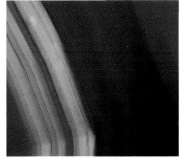

Left The lovely bands on this red agate are the result of artificial staining. Most agates can be stained very well to make jewelry. Staining agate is a very ancient practice. Onyx is now stained by soaking agate in sugar solution then heating it in sulfuric acid to brown and harden the sugar particles.

Agate SiO_2 Silicate Group, subgroup Quartz

Mohs' Hardness 7	Specific Gravity 2.6	Crystal System Hexagonal

Distinctive features Translucent, strongly banded, white to gray-blue to orange-red, waxy mineral in rock cavities.
Color Variable: white to gray, whitish-blue, orange to red, gray, and black.
Luster Waxy.
Streak None.
Transparency Mostly translucent, but transparent forms occur.
Cleavage None.
Fracture Conchoidal, with very sharp edges.
Tenacity Brittle.
Forms Cryptocrystalline silica filling geodes.

Varieties Can grade into opal or chalcedony.
Uses Mineral collections.
Occurrence Found filling rock cavities as a secondary mineral deposited by silica-rich water. Often found in metamorphic zones surrounding granite intrusions, but can also occur in sediments. Worldwide.

Crocidolite Na(Al,Fe)(SiO₃)₂ with (Mg,Fe)SiO₃ Silicate Group

Mohs' Hardness 6	Specific Gravity 3	Crystal System Monoclinic

Distinctive features Glistening fibrous to hairlike blue to green crystals.
Color Medium to pale blue to medium green.
Luster Silky.
Streak Bluish.
Transparency Transparent.
Cleavage Perfect on 110.
Fracture Uneven.
Tenacity Brittle to flexible.
Forms Fibrous masses to thin, prismatic crystals
Varieties Synonymous with blue asbestos. When replaced by quartz, it forms the mineral tiger's-eye, hence its inclusion here.

Uses Mineral collections.
Occurrence In veins and pegmatites in granites and syenites. South Africa, Austria, France, UK, South Africa, Bolivia, USA (Massachusetts).

Chrysoprase SiO₂ Silicate Group, subgroup Quartz

Mohs' Hardness 7	Specific Gravity 2.6	Crystal System Trigonal

Chrysoprase is a form of chalcedony. It is translucent and apple green.

Most early chrysoprase came from Bohemia. A more recent source is Marlborough in Queensland, Australia.

It is usually cut *en cabochon*, as beads, which are thought to date from Greek and Roman times. Like other rare gemstones, chrysoprase is imitated. These imitations include glass and stained agate.

Opal SiO_2nH_2O Silicate Group

Mohs' Hardness 6	Specific Gravity 2.1	Crystal System Amorphous

There are four types of opal commonly used in jewelry: white, black, fire, and water opal. Opals are also classified as either common or precious stones; only the precious stones display iridescence. The name opal is thought to come from the Sanskrit word for precious stone—*upala*.

Opal is one of the few noncrystalline, or poorly crystalline, gemstones. It is a hardened jelly made up of silica and water. It is found filling cavities in rocks, as stalagmites, or replacing organic matter such as shell and bone. It has an uneven or conchoidal fracture. White opal has a light-colored body color with a good play of color, showing all the spectral colors (see page 134). Black opal has a dark body color (black, blue, green, or gray) and a good play of color. Fire opal is a transparent yellow, orange, or red stone which may show a play of color. Water opal is a clear and colorless stone with flashes of color. The play of color, or iridescence, is due to the interference of white light on minute silica spheres in the structure of opal (see page 134).

Opal used by the Romans came from the area that is now the Czech Republic where white opal was found in volcanic lava and mined from tunnels dug deep into the mountains. Guatemala, Honduras, and Mexico are opal localities, but since the discovery of precious opal in Queensland, Australia, they have become less important. The first type of opal to be found in Australia was boulder opal, used in cameo carving.

Opal also occurs in sedimentary and igneous rocks in veins, as lumps, or in pipes, and may replace organic matter forming opalized fossils of shellfish or dinosaur bones, such as those found at White Cliffs, New South Wales. At Lightning Ridge in New South Wales, isolated nodules of black opal are found. Precious white opal is found at Coober Pedy in South Australia. Other localities include South Africa,

Zimbabwe, Brazil, and the USA.

Fire opals are usually faceted, but other opals are cut *en cabochon* or carved. Opal has been imitated in several ways; one method is to place chips of colored plastic and opal behind a hollow-backed cabochon of rock crystal. Another is to cement iridescent shell to the back of a flat-based cabochon of rock crystal. Gilson has manufactured "created" opals from silica spheres.

The Play of Color in Opal

The flashes of color seen in precious opal are called the play of color. For hundreds of years theories have been put forward to explain the reasons for this phenomenon, but it is only recently that laboratory equipment has been sufficiently advanced to give the true story. Baier in Germany and Sanders in Australia both examined the structure of opal using an electron microscope which is able to magnify the structure more than 1,000 times. They saw that areas of precious opal were made up of regularly arranged rows of silica spheres of similar size. Where the spheres are not similar there is no play of color and the opal is referred to as common opal, milky opal, or "potch." The play of color is due to diffraction of light by the spheres. The colors seen depend on the size of the spheres. Larger spheres give red, yellow, green, blue, and white, while smaller spheres may give only blue flashes of color.

PHOSPHATES

Lapis Lazuli (Na,Ca)$_{7-8}$(Al,Si)$_{12}$O$_{24}$[SO$_4$,Cl$_2$(OH)$_2$] Phosphate Group

Mohs' Hardness 5.5	Specific Gravity 2.7–2.9	Crystal System Isometric

The color of lapis lazuli varies from greenish-blue to a rich purple-blue. Dark intense blue is the most prized color. The rock was powdered for the pigment ultramarine, but since 1828 the pigment has been made synthetically. The name lapis lazuli is derived from the Persian word *lazhward*, meaning blue.

Under longwave ultraviolet light orange spots or streaks can be seen. These are more pronounced in the material from Chile than that from Afghanistan. Lapis lazuli shows a bright whitish glow under longwave ultraviolet light and dull orange spots or streaks under shortwave ultraviolet light and X-rays.

Lapis lazuli has been mined in Afghanistan for over 6,000 years. The mines were described by Marco Polo in 1271. Light blue boulders of lapis lazuli are found in rivers on the southern end of Lake Baikal, Russia. A paler-colored lapis lazuli is mined in the Chilean Andes. A very dark lapis lazuli was found in the Colorado Rockies in rocks formed by contact metamorphism; it

contains pyrite but lacks the textures and hardness of good lapis. Other localities include California, Myanmar (formerly Burma), Angola, Pakistan, and Canada. Canadian lapis lazuli is blue-gray, with patches of bright blue and white, and contains pyrite, but is not used as a gem material as it is porous and does not take a good polish.

Lapis lazuli is an opaque

mineral and is therefore usually cut *en cabochon* or used as seal stones, beads, small carved objects and inlay material.

Lapis lazuli has been imitated by blue-stained jasper ("Swiss lapis"), which can be recognized by its lack of pyrite inclusions. Imitations are also made using glass with copper inclusions and by coloring synthetic spinel blue by cobalt. Crushed lapis lazuli with included pyrite is bonded with plastic and some is dyed, but these are recognizable as nail varnish will remove the dye.

A Gilson "created" lapis lazuli was produced in the mid 1970s. Although the color is similar, the density is lower, and the porosity higher than true lapis lazuli. The pyrite inclusions also appear far too regularly arranged. Imitations can all be recognized by their lack of a whitish glow under longwave ultraviolet light.

Turquoise $CaAl_6(PO_4)_4(OH)_8.4H_2O$ Phosphate Group

Mohs' Hardness 5–6	Specific Gravity 2.6–2.8	Crystal System Triclinic

Turquoise mining has been carried out in or near Egypt since 3000BC. The name is derived from the French *pierre turquoise* (*tourques* in Old French) possibly because the Persian (Iranian) material was imported to Europe via Turkey.

Distinctive features Cerulean blue to pale bluish-green nodular masses, or as seams in weathered lavas and pegmatites.

Color Bright cerulean blue to pale, bluish-green.

Luster Waxy.

Streak White to pale green.

Transparency Mostly opaque.

Cleavage None.

Fracture Small-scale conchoidal.

Tenacity Brittle.

Forms Botryoidal or reniform, stalactitic. Massive, small seams, or fine grains.

Varieties None.

Uses Jewelry, ornamental.

Occurrence As small veins and masses in altered lavas or pegmatites and often associated with limonite and chalcedony. Cornwall in England, France, Germany, Siberia, Egypt, Iran, Tibet, Australia (Victoria and Queensland), Chile, USA (Arizona, California, Nevada, Colorado, New Mexico, Virginia).

Turquoise forms as a porous blue cryptocrystalline aggregate and is found as encrustations, nodules, or botryoidal masses, or in veins within rocks in arid regions. It has been found as distinct crystals but only in Virginia. The blue color is due to copper and/or iron. It may fade with excess sunlight and alter to a green color, possibly due to dehydration. American turquoise is more porous than Iranian turquoise, and fades and alters more rapidly.

Turquoise is semitranslucent, and the absorption spectrum has a characteristic pattern of weak bands. Under longwave ultraviolet light, turquoise appears a greenish-yellow to bright blue. It is inert under shortwave ultraviolet light, whereas some imitations of turquoise show a strong blue color. Gilson "created" turquoise appears a dull blue under both longwave and shortwave ultraviolet light.

The best turquoise is the sky-blue turquoise from Iran. In Tibet it is the green turquoise that is more highly prized. The Sinai peninsula of Egypt is the most historically important source, and is the origin of many of the early pieces. The ancient Aztecs and Incas used turquoise for ornaments and artifacts which came from mines in New Mexico. Other localities in the USA include the Mohave (Mojave) desert, Colorado, which has quality compact turquoise of a good color, and Nevada, and Arizona. The turquoise from the USA is lighter in color and more porous and chalky than that of Iran and Mexico.

Turquoise has a waxlike luster and takes a good polish. It is carved, cut *en cabochon*, or cut flat for inlay work. It may be engraved and inlaid with gold. Natural minerals which resemble turquoise include lazulite, wardite, and odontolite (blue-colored fossil tooth or bone). Stained howlite, stained limestone, and marble are also used as imitations. Turquoise was one of the earliest gems to be imitated. Imitations have been made from glass, which can usually be distinguished by inclusions of small bubbles or pit marks on the surface, and also from enamel or stained chalcedony. In the USA small pieces of friable turquoise are bonded by resin to make them usable in jewelry, but some fade or turn green with time. A Gilson "created" turquoise was manufactured in 1972 in France. Microscopic examination shows that the structure is made of blue angular pieces on a white background, which is quite different than turquoise.

Variscite (or Utahlite) Al(PO₄).2H₂O Phosphate Group

| Mohs' Hardness 4–5 | Specific Gravity 2.4–2.6 | Crystal System Orthorhombic |

Distinctive features Often confused with turquoise. Infusible, soluble in acid only if heated first.
Color Pale yellow-green.
Luster Vitreous, waxy.
Streak White.
Transparency Transparent to translucent.
Cleavage None.
Fracture Conchoidal.
Tenacity Brittle.
Forms Massive and concretionary habits, and as crusts or veins, pseudo-octahedral crystals rare.
Uses Ornamental.
Occurrence Forms where phosphate-rich water has altered aluminum-rich rocks. UK, Austria, Bolivia, USA (Arkansas, Nevada, and nodules over 3½ feet in diameter have been found in Utah—hence the alternative name).

Brazilianite NaAl₃[(OH)₂/PO₄]₂ Phosphate Group

| Mohs' Hardness 5.5 | Specific Gravity 2.98–2.99 | Crystal System Monoclinic |

Distinctive features A rare and beautiful crystal, much prized by jewelers and collectors.
Color Yellow, yellow-green.
Luster Vitreous.
Streak White.
Transparency Transparent, translucent.
Cleavage Good.
Fracture Small conchoidal.
Tenacity Brittle.
Forms Monoclinic, short prisms.
Uses Gemstone.
Occurrence As the name suggests, Brazil is the major source and, until recently, the only one. Now also USA (New Hampshire).

Apatite Ca$_5$(PO$_4$)$_3$(F,Cl,OH) Phosphate Group

Mohs' Hardness 5	Specific Gravity 3.17–3.23	Crystal System Hexagonal

Distinctive features Soluble in hydrochloric acid. Some crystals lose their color when heated; others fluoresce a bright yellow under ultraviolet light. Characteristic absorption spectrum has intense narrow lines due to rare-earth elements, especially yellow apatite.

Color Usually green, but may be colorless, yellow, blue, or violet.

Luster Vitreous to subresinous.

Streak White.

Transparency Transparent to translucent.

Cleavage Poor.

Fracture Conchoidal to uneven.

Tenacity Brittle.

Forms Tabular or prismatic crystals, also massive, compact, or granular.

Varieties Spanish apatite is sometimes called "asparagus stone," because it is yellowish-green.

Uses Gemstones.

Occurrence Forms in igneous rocks and metamorphosed limestones. Worldwide. Spain (see above), and the Czech Republic. Norway has bluish-green stones and India sea-green. Gem-quality material comes from Burma, with blue Burmese apatite being strong dichroic, showing blue and colorless. Sri Lankan apatite comes in various colors; also Madagascar. Blue, yellow, and green stones are found in Brazil, Mexico has yellow stones, Canada a deep rich green variety, and the USA a violet variety.

Fibrous blue crystals from Burma and Sri Lanka show the cat's-eye effect when cut *en cabochon*. A massive apatite variety, which is sky-blue in color, has been polished as an ornamental stone. Apatite is faceted for collectors, but has a hardness of only five on Mohs' scale and so is easily scratched.

Pyromorphite Pb$_5$(PO$_4$,AsO$_4$)$_3$CL Phosphate Group

Mohs' Hardness 3.5–4	Specific Gravity 7	Crystal System Hexagonal

Distinctive features Small, yellowish-green, hexagonal, prismatic crystals filling rock cavities in mineralized zones rich in lead.
Color Pale yellowish-green usually, but also various shades of brown and yellow.
Luster Resinous.
Streak White to pale yellow.
Transparency Subtransparent to translucent.
Cleavage None.
Fracture Irregular.

Tenacity Brittle.
Forms Six-sided prismatic or tabular crystals. Sometimes botryoidal, fibrous, or granular.
Varieties According to form, e.g. fibrous pyromorphite.
Uses Source of lead.
Occurrence A sporadic secondary mineral in lead mineralized zones. Germany, France, Spain, UK, Australia, USA (Pennsylvania, North Carolina, and Idaho).

Mimetite 3Pb$_3$As$_2$O$_8$.PbCl$_2$ Phosphate Group

Mohs' Hardness 3.5	Specific Gravity 7	Crystal System Hexagonal

Distinctive features Small, yellow to brownish-orange hexagonal crystals with flat (0001) terminations found in areas where there are lead-rich metalliferous veins.
Color Yellow to yellowish-brown to orange and, rarely, white.
Luster Resinous.
Streak White.
Transparency Translucent, occasionally transparent.
Cleavage Poor on 10Ī1.
Fracture Subconchoidal, but difficult to see because of small size of the crystals.
Tenacity Brittle.
Forms Usually six-sided prismatic crystals, but sometimes as mammillated or globular forms

encrusting rocks.
Varieties Campylite, which has yellowish-brown-red crystals—found only in UK.
Uses Source of lead.
Occurrence Associated with lead carbonates and limonite in areas of lead-rich veins. Austria, Siberia, the Czech Republic, Germany, UK, France, Africa, Mexico, USA (Pennsylvania, Utah).

Vanadinite Pb$_5$(VO$_4$)$_3$Cl Phosphate Group

Mohs' Hardness 2.7–3	Specific Gravity 6.5–7	Crystal System Hexagonal

Distinctive features Hexagonal prismatic red to straw-colored crystals associated with areas of secondary lead deposits.
Color Various shades of red to yellowish-brown.
Luster Resinous to adamantine.
Streak White to yellow.
Transparency Subtransparent (darker colors are opaque).
Cleavage None.
Fracture Uneven.
Tenacity Brittle.
Forms Six-sided prismatic crystals. The 0001th face is often hollow. Also found as rock encrustations.
Varieties None.
Uses Source of vanadium and lead.
Occurrence Rather a rare mineral, found in areas of secondary lead deposits. The Urals in Russia, Austria, UK, Zaire, Mexico, Argentina, USA (Arizona, New Mexico, and South Dakota).

SULFATES

Celestite SrSO$_4$ Sulfate Group

Mohs' Hardness 3–3.5	Specific Gravity 9	Crystal System Orthorhombic

Distinctive features Also known as celestine.
Color White to greenish, and brown, and bluish.
Luster Vitreous.
Streak White.
Transparency Transparent to translucent.
Cleavage Perfect.
Fracture Uneven.
Tenacity Brittle.
Forms Crystals tabular, prism. Massive, fibrous, granular, and nodular.
Uses Principle source of strontium, which is used in fireworks and signal flare manufacture because it produces a bright crimson color when powdered and burned. It is also used as an additive to battery lead and in the manufacture of rubber and paint. Other uses are found for it in the nuclear industry, in sugar beet refining, and in the preparation of

iridescent glass and porcelain.
Occurrence Forms in hydrothermal veins with such minerals as quartz and calcite. Also in sedimentary rocks, like limestones. Found in some basic igneous rocks and some evaporite deposits. Crystals of exceptional quality have been found in England, Sicily, Tunisia, Madagascar, and in the USA at Put-in-Bay and Strontian Island on Lake Erie.

Gypsum CaSO₄·2H₂O Sulfate Group

Mohs' Hardness 1.5–2	Specific Gravity 2.3	Crystal System Monoclinic

Distinctive features Soft enough to be scratched by a fingernail. When it is heated in an open tube, it gives off water. There is no reaction to acid.
Color White to pale gray and shades of pinkish-red.
Luster Pearly to glistening, or dull and earthy.
Streak White.
Transparency Transparent to opaque.
Cleavage Excellent on 010.
Fracture Conchoidal, sometimes fibrous.
Tenacity Crumbly.
Forms Massive, flat, or elongated, generally prismatic, crystals.
Varieties Selenite, which has transparent, distinct, bladed crystals, satin spa, which has pearly, fibrous masses, and alabaster, which is fine-grained and slightly colored.
Uses Medical (source of plaster of Paris), for manufacturing wall plaster used in building trade, ornamental carvings made from alabaster.
Occurrence As beds, sometimes massive, in sedimentary rocks, such as limestones, shales, and clays. UK, France, Russia, USA (New York State, Kentucky, Michigan, Kansas, North Dakota, and Utah).

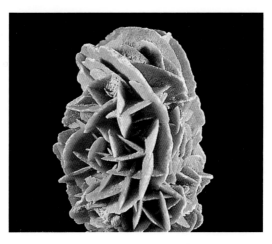

Varieties

Satin Spa

Selenite

Barytes BaSO$_4$ Sulfate Group

Mohs' Hardness 3–3.5	Specific Gravity 4.4–4.6	Crystal System Orthorhombic

Distinctive features High density, pale greenish-white to pale brownish tabular crystals. Also appears as desert roses of radiating pale brown crystals. Hardness.
Color White to greenish-white, or pale brownish-red.
Luster Vitreous to resinous.
Streak White.
Transparency Transparent to opaque.
Cleavage Perfect on 001 and 110.
Fracture Uneven.
Tenacity Brittle.
Forms Often occurs as groups of tabular or bladed crystals. Also massive, encrusting, banded, mammillary, and fibrous.
Varieties None.
Uses Barium ore, for refining sugar, for drilling mud in the oil industry, for medical barium meals for X-ray, as pigment, in the paper industry.
Occurrence In veins and beds associated with ores of lead, copper, zinc, and iron. Common gangue mineral in metalliferous veins. It is associated with fluorite, quartz, calcite, dolomite, and stibnite. France, Spain, England, Romania, the Czech Republic, USA (Connecticut, New York State, Pennsylvania, Michigan, and North Dakota).

TUNGSTATES

Scheelite CaWO$_4$ Tungstate Group

Mohs' Hardness 4.5–5	Specific Gravity 5.9–6.1	Crystal System Tetragonal

Distinctive features Soluble in acid, fusible with difficulty. Bluish-white fluorescence under shortwave ultraviolet light.
Color Colorless, white, gray, pale yellow, reddish.
Luster Adamantine, vitreous.
Streak White.
Transparency Transparent to translucent.
Cleavage Distinct.
Fracture Subconchoidal.
Tenacity Brittle.
Forms Pseudo-octahedral or dipyramidal crystals, also massive, granular, or columnar.
Uses Important source of tungsten.
Occurrence Found in quartz veins of granitic pegmatites, often in association with such minerals as arsenopyrite and cassiterite. Important deposits for industry in Burma, Malaysia, China, Japan, Australia, Bolivia, and the USA.

Wolframite (Fe,Mn)WO$_4$ Tungstate Group

Mohs' Hardness 4–4.5	Specific Gravity 7	Crystal System Monoclinic

Distinctive features Well-formed, tabular or prismatic, silvery black crystals in metalliferous sulfide and pegmatite veins in granites.
Color Black to very dark gray.
Luster Submetallic.
Streak Black.
Transparency Opaque.
Cleavage Good on 010.
Fracture Uneven to rough.
Tenacity Brittle.
Forms Mostly as tabular crystals, but prismatic forms also occur.
Varieties None.
Uses Source of tungsten.
Occurrence In metalliferous veins, cavities, and pegmatites in granites, where it is associated with cassiterite and copper ores. Worldwide: UK, Portugal, Myanmar (formerly Burma), China, Malaya, Australia, Bolivia, USA (Colorado, New Mexico, Nevada, Connecticut).

Wulfenite Pb(MoO$_4$,WO$_4$) Tungstate Group

Mohs' Hardness 2.5–3	Specific Gravity 6.5–8	Crystal System Tetragonal

Distinctive features Usually as thin, tabular brownish-yellow to orange crystals, associated with lead ore deposits.
Color Bright orange to brownish-yellow to brown.
Luster Resinous to adamantine.
Streak White.
Transparency Subtransparent to translucent.
Cleavage Distinct pyramidal, good on 111.
Fracture Subconchoidal, but very difficult to see with the naked eye.
Tenacity Brittle.
Forms Usually thin, square, tabular to octahedral or prismatic crystals, but granular and compact forms also occur.

Varieties None.
Uses Molybdenum ore.
Occurrence A secondary mineral, found in upper (oxidized) zones rich in lead ore deposits. Former Yugoslavia, Eastern Europe, Austria, Morocco, Congo, Australia, Mexico, USA (Massachusetts, Pennsylvania, New Mexico, Arizona, and Nevada).

HYDRATES

Brucite Mg(OH)$_2$ Hydrate Group

Mohs' Hardness 2.5	Specific Gravity 2.3–2.5	Crystal System Hexagonal

Distinctive features An associated mineral of asbestos, brucite is named for A. Bruce, an American mineralogist who first identified the mineral. It is infusible, and soluble in hydrochloric acid with no effervescence.
Color Colorless, white, pale green, bluish, gray, and occasionally pink. When it contains manganese, yellow to brown.

Luster Waxy, vitreous, to pearly. Fibrous varieties are silky.
Streak White.
Transparency Transparent, translucent.
Cleavage Perfect.
Fracture Uneven.
Tenacity Brittle.
Forms Broad, tabular crystals. Can be massive, foliated, fibrous (nemalite), and granular.
Varieties Nemalite is the fibrous

form of brucite.
Uses Widely used as a refractory material, in the extraction of magnesia, and as a source of metallic magnesium and its salts.
Occurrence Forms in metamorphosed limestones, in schists, and in serpentinites. Also found as an alteration product in the final stages of metamorphic incident.

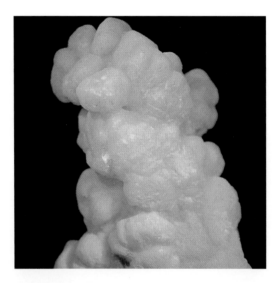

Above An example of a botryoidal mass of brucite, this specimen was found in Africa.

NATURAL GLASS

Tektites Natural Glass

Mohs' Hardness 5	Specific Gravity 2.34–2.39	Crystal System Amorphous

Tektites are natural glasses of unknown origin. They are transparent green, greenish brown, or brown in color, and have a bobbly or craggy surface. One theory suggests that the characteristic shape of tektites is due to the fact that they were still molten as they traveled through the atmosphere from outer space. Alternatively, tektites may be the scattered drops of molten rock thrown out by the impact of a large meteorite. The name comes from the Greek word *tektos* meaning molten.

Moldavites are a type of tektite named for the river in the Czech Republic, where these glassy pieces were first found in 1787. Pieces of tektite from other localities have also been named for the place where they were found. For example, billitonites from Billiton Island, now called Belitung, in Indonesia, australites from Australia, and georgiaites from Georgia in the USA.

Moldavites have been faceted as gemstones and look similar to the bottle green mineral peridot. They contain round or torpedo-shaped bubbles, and are easily distinguished from the swirls in paste (glass) since there are no crystalline inclusions as there are in volcanic obsidian. Other forms of tektites are carved into small decorative objects.

ORGANICS

Minerals by definition are inorganic, and crystals are formed by inorganic chemical reactions. However there are organic materials which are like minerals and which can be encountered in similar circumstances, particularly where organic material has become fossilized. There follow a few examples of mineral-like organic materials.

Amber Organics

Mohs' Hardness 2.5	Specific Gravity 1.08

much redder than the Baltic variety, and is harder and denser. Sicilian amber is called simetite for the name of the river along which it is found. Amber is also found in the Dominican Republic, Romania, the Czech Republic, Germany, Canada, and the USA.

Left Insects trapped in amber when it was still a sticky resin have been beautifully preserved.

Amber is a fossil resin thought to have come from pine trees. The Greek name for amber was *electron*, because rubbing it produces a negative charge which attracts small particles.

Amber is transparent to translucent and has a greasy luster. Its color is typically yellow or brown but it may have a red or white tinge. Amber is often cloudy, due to air spaces. Heating cloudy material in oil fills the air spaces and clears the amber. Insects, for example flies, pieces of moss, lichens, and pine needles can be found trapped in amber, which was once a soft,

sticky resin. Pyrite crystals and calcite have also been seen as inclusions in amber.

The main localities for amber are along the Samland Coast near Kaliningrad, Russia. Pit amber is obtained by open-pit mining. The amber is separated from the soft sandy deposits using strong jets of water. Sea amber, which has been washed out from the seabed, floats on water and is carried by the tides and currents to the shorelines of the Baltic, Norway, Denmark, and England. The variety from the Baltic is called succinite. The Burmese variety (burmite), found in clayey soil, is

Jet Organics

Mohs' Hardness 2.5–4	Specific Gravity 1.3–1.35

Jet is a variety of coal. It is a fossil wood which formed when wood rotted in stagnant water and was then flattened by the pressure of burial over millions of years. It smells like coal when burnt or when touched with a hot needle. Some jet may induce electricity when rubbed, and for this reason it is sometimes known as "black amber." The name is derived from the Old French *jyet* or *jaiet* after a place on the Mediterranean coast where the Romans obtained some of their jet.

There is evidence that jet was mined as early as 1400BC, and during the Roman occupation of the British Isles jet was shipped to Rome. It was a popular gem during Victorian times when it was used for mourning jewelry and the town of Whitby on the Yorkshire coast, England, received much of its income from the jet industry at this time. Jet for use in

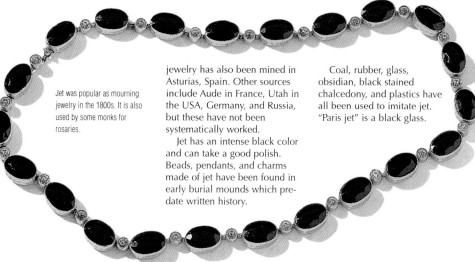

Jet was popular as mourning jewelry in the 1800s. It is also used by some monks for rosaries.

jewelry has also been mined in Asturias, Spain. Other sources include Aude in France, Utah in the USA, Germany, and Russia, but these have not been systematically worked.

Jet has an intense black color and can take a good polish. Beads, pendants, and charms made of jet have been found in early burial mounds which pre-date written history.

Coal, rubber, glass, obsidian, black stained chalcedony, and plastics have all been used to imitate jet. "Paris jet" is a black glass.

Pearl Organics

Mohs' Hardness 3.5	Specific Gravity 2.6–2.78

Any shelled mollusc can produce pearls, but only those animals which have a shell with a pearly (nacreous) lining can form lustrous pearls worth using as ornamentation. The animals which produce the pearls most used in jewelry are molluscs of the *Pinctada* type and all live in seawater. Other seawater molluscs that produce pearls include the giant conch (*Strombus gigas*) and giant clam (*Tridacna gigas*). "Scotch pearls" are found in freshwater molluscs in Scottish rivers.

Blister pearls form when a piece of grit or other irritant gets between the shell and the soft outer body parts of the mollusc (mantle). The mollusc secretes nacre to ease the irritation. The bulge or blister that this forms can be scraped off the shell and used in jewelry. Blister pearls are mounted so that the nonnacreous base is hidden.

True pearls are formed by encystation and are termed "cyst" pearls. The mollusc is unable to cover the irritant against the shell and instead it envelops it within the mantle. The irritant forms a dent in the mantle which becomes a sac surrounding the irritant. During the next stage the sac separates from the mantle and a cyst is formed. The nacre-secreting cells of the pearl sac continue to secrete nacre around the irritant and those concentric layers gradually build up to form the pearl.

The luster of pearls is known as the "orient of pearl." It is due to the optical effects of diffraction and interference. Light is diffracted by the irregular overlapping crystals of aragonite that make up the pearl, and there is interference at the platelets.

Freshwater pearls are fished from rivers in Europe and the USA. Seawater pearls are fished from the Persian Gulf, the Gulf of Manaar in the Indian Ocean, the Red Sea, to the northwest of the Australian coast, and from the Gulfs of California and Florida. The color and surface texture of the pearls is partly dependent upon the type of shellfish and local conditions.

Coral Organics

Mohs' Hardness 3.5	Specific Gravity 2.6–2.7

Coral polyps are marine organisms related to sea anemones. They have a hollow cylindrical body, with a ring of tentacles around the mouth, and secrete an external chalky or horny skeleton. Red, pink, white, and blue corals are made of calcium carbonate, while black and golden corals are formed of a horny substance called conchiolin. The polyps usually exist in large colonies and form the united, branching masses we know as coral. The coral grows as the polyps ingest small animals and plants, and secrete more of the skeleton-forming substances. Japanese precious coral is red, pink, or white. Red coral (*Corallium rubrum*) and white coral (*Oculinacea vaseuclosa*) have been fashioned for ornamentation. Black coral, known as "Akabar" or "King's coral," (*Antipathes spiralis*), and blue coral, known as "Akori" coral, (*Allopara subirolcea*), are two other varieties. All corals have the distinctive, delicate graining of stripes or spots as a result of the skeletal structure.

Most coral types prefer warm temperatures and are therefore restricted to the warm waters of the world including the Italian and African Mediterranean coasts, where red and pink corals are found, the Red Sea, and the waters off Malaysia and Japan. Black and golden coral are found off Hawaii, Australia, and the West Indies.

Coral is cut *en cabochon* or carved and fashioned into beads, small carved objects, and cameos.

Coral has been imitated by stained vegetable ivory, mixtures of rubber and the mineral gypsum, stained bone, glass, porcelain, and plastic.

Gilson "created" coral is manufactured in a laboratory by crushing and staining the mineral calcite. It has a similar color, luster, and general appearance to coral, but can be distinguished using a hand lens; the Gilson "created" coral appears quite homogenous in contrast to the true coral, which has a "wood-grain" structure.

Tortoiseshell Organics

Mohs' Hardness 2.5	Specific Gravity 1.29

Tortoiseshell is not the shell from a tortoise, but the carapace (shield) of a sea turtle called the Hawksbill turtle. It is made of a protein which is similar to that in animal horns, claws, and nails. The shell has a rich brown mottling on a warm translucent yellow background. Under a microscope the mottling can be seen as spherical spots of color. It can be distinguished from imitations such as plastic which appears as patches or swathes of color rather than dots or spots when viewed with a microscope. Tortoiseshell also gives off a characteristic smell of burning hair when touched with a hot needle.

The Hawksbill turtle is found in the seas of Indonesia.

To fashion the shells they must first be flattened, using low heat, and the ridges removed by scraping. Sheets can be pressed together using heat, being careful not to overheat as this darkens the color. The shell is then polished and cut. In Roman times one use for tortoiseshell was as inlay for furniture. This practice was popular in France but is now seldom used. Today plastic is usually used in place of tortoiseshell.

Tortoise is an endangered species, and it is illegal to trade tortoise products in the USA.

Shell Organics

Mohs' Hardness 2	Specific Gravity 1.08

The shell of the giant conch (*Strombus gigas*) is a layered material which is carved as cameos to show the two distinct colors of pink and white. The pink layer fades with excess strong light. Helmet shells (*Cassis madagascariensis*) are also used for cameo work. Some shells, such as the large pearl oysters (*Pinctada maxima* and *Pinctada margaritifera*) have an iridescent luster to their lining called mother-of-pearl. Shells with brightly colored blue and green shell, called paua shells and abalones, are fished for their mother-of-pearl. The larger topshells (*Trocus*) are also fished for the value of their shell.

Helmet shells are found in the warm waters of the West Indies. The *Pinctada* oysters are found off northern Australia. Abalones are found in American waters and paua shells in New Zealand.

Shells are normally carved, especially into cameos. Mother-of-pearl is used for making buttons, knife handles, inlay, and other ornaments. The thick column of topshells is sometimes turned into beads and strung as necklaces.

Ivory Organics

Mohs' Hardness 2.5	Specific Gravity 1.7–1.9

Ivory is a constituent of the teeth or tusks of all mammals. It has a rich creamy color, fine texture, and is almost perfectly elastic. The best African elephant ivory has a warm transparent mellow tint with little grain or mottling. Indian elephants have smaller tusks than African elephants, and the ivory is a denser white, more open in texture, softer to work, and yellows more easily. Both recent and fossil forms have been used. The ivory of the incisor and canine teeth of the hippopotamus is denser than elephant ivory. The exterior of walrus ivory has a much finer texture and grain than the core. The narwhal is a species of whale that lives in the Arctic; the male narwhals have an incisor tooth that may be over 6½ feet long. It looks like a spiralled, twisted tusk and has been sold as

"unicorn horn." The ivory of the boar and warthog is taken from their strong, curved teeth and is coarse with a consistency more like bone than true ivory. The cachalot whale, or sperm whale, has curved conical teeth with ivory similar to that of the boar. Most ivories fluoresce with a bluish glow under ultraviolet light. The coarser the ivory, the darker the shade of blue fluorescence.

Ordinary wood carving chisels can be used to carve ivory which, unlike bone, requires no preparation before fashioning. Carvings on mammoth ivory estimated to be about 30,000 years old have been found in caves in France. Ornamental carvings from China and Europe have been known since the thirteenth century. It was the aim

of the craftsman to keep the original shape of the ivory piece as far as possible, however odd the shape. In Japan, ivory is considered a precious material and is used for ornamental buttons (netsukes) and other decorative and functional articles. The almost-perfect elasticity of ivory makes it an ideal medium for billiard balls, fine-toothed combs, piano keys, precision scales, and rulers.

Now that there are international restrictions on the ivory trade, plastics and other materials are being introduced in its place. Ivory can be imitated by bone, deer-horn, and vegetable ivory. Vegetable ivory includes the hard seeds, or nuts of palm trees such as the ivory palm which grows in Peru and the doom palm of central Africa.

Rocks—Introduction

The movement of continental plates forces molten material from in the earth toward the surface through the rocks. This material will either cool and solidify beneath the surface or break through in a spectacular volcanic eruption before cooling and solidifying. This process constitutes the first part of the rock cycle.

When exposed at the surface of the Earth, igneous rock becomes subject to the steady attrition of wind, rain, frost, and sunshine. It is gradually worn away until it turns to rubble and, ultimately, dust. But this is not the end. The rubble and dust are carried away by the wind and by rivers, which deposit them elsewhere. Over the millennia, these deposits are compressed by the weight of new deposits on top of them. Water seeps in, causing the minerals within to crystalize and expand, or new minerals like calcite in the water to fill any gaps and crystalize into a cement that holds the compressed deposits together until

they become rock again. This is the second part of the rock cycle, which forms sedimentary rocks.

In certain circumstances, for example under conditions of extremely high pressures or temperatures, the minerals and particles in igneous and sedimentary rocks change and recrystalize into a new substance. This is the third and final part of the rock cycle which forms metamorphic rock. Metamorphic rocks can themselves change. If exposed to new pressures, the minerals within them can metamorphose into a new substance through a process called polymetamorphism. If the rocks are exposed to intense heat that causes the minerals within them to melt, the new rock will be igneous. When such rock is pushed to the Earth's surface, the process of weathering will begin, and the whole cycle will start again.

Below Metamorphic rocks, particularly regional metamorphic rocks, tend to be found in the deep interiors of mountain chains.

Plate Tectonics

The Earth is not static. The forces that shape its surface are at work all the time, slowly heaving up the mountains and then just as slowly wearing them away.

If you boil a saucepan of soup, froth and scum forms on the surface, and it moves about in lumps in response to the convection currents churning about below. This is a little like what has been going on at the surface of the Earth.

The Earth's crust is constantly being destroyed and renewed—not just the rocks of the continents, but the entire outer covering of the globe. Imagine the surface of the Earth as consisting of a number of panels, or plates, like the panels of a soccer ball. Imagine molten material welling up along one seam of a panel, and then solidifying to form the

material of the panel itself. Imagine then that the newly formed panel is constantly moving away from that seam, and is buckling down beneath the next panel and being destroyed. That is what is happening to the Earth's surface.

All this activity takes place on the floor of the oceans, and we only found out about this back in the 1960s. Throughout the oceans there is a system of ridges. These are the places where the new surface material is being created. In other areas, notably around the edges of the Pacific, there are deep troughs. These are the places where the surface material is being drawn down and destroyed. The continents are sitting embedded in these moving plates and are being shuffled around by the movement all the time.

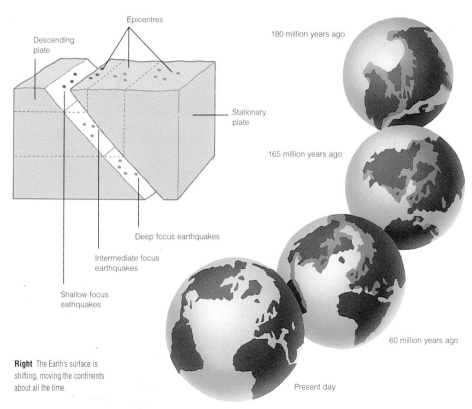

Epicentres

Descending plate

Stationary plate

Deep focus earthquakes

Intermediate focus earthquakes

Shallow focus eathquakes

180 million years ago

165 million years ago

60 million years ago

Present day

Right The Earth's surface is shifting, moving the continents about all the time.

The material of these plates consists of the crust and the topmost solid layer of the mantle which together are called the lithosphere. They move about on a spongy region of the mantle which we call the asthenosphere.

Where the material is being created, and where it is being destroyed, there is volcanic and earthquake activity. The newly formed plate material makes up the ocean floor, and so nowhere on the Earth's surface is the ocean floor more than about 200 million years old. The younger areas are found closest to the ocean ridges. Where one

ocean plate is destroyed beneath another, molten plate material rises and forms chains of volcanic islands like those that festoon the edge of the Pacific. These form in arc-shapes because of the three-dimensional geometry involved in curling the broken edge of a sphere downward.

The continental crust—the sial—is less dense than the ocean crust—the sima—and so it tends to float in it. It is too light to be drawn downward into the mantle—just as a piece of toast floating in a sink will not be drawn down the vortex of the plug hole—and so when the continent is carried to an

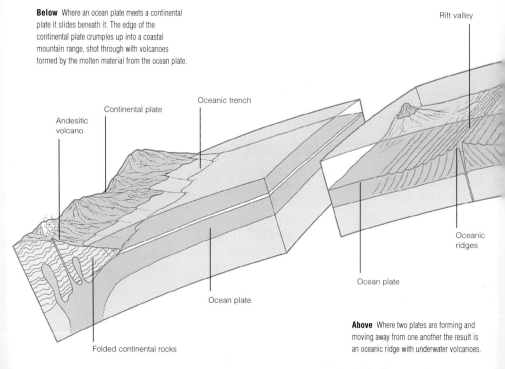

Below Where an ocean plate meets a continental plate it slides beneath it. The edge of the continental plate crumples up into a coastal mountain range, shot through with volcanoes formed by the molten material from the ocean plate.

Rift valley

Oceanic trench

Continental plate

Andesitic volcano

Oceanic ridges

Ocean plate

Ocean plate

Folded continental rocks

Above Where two plates are forming and moving away from one another the result is an oceanic ridge with underwater volcanoes.

ocean trench it stays there, crumpling up with the continuing movement. This is the reason for the active mountain chains, perforated by volcanoes, that we find at the edges of some continents. When two continents are brought together they fuse into one supercontinent, uplifting a massive mountain range along the joint. The Himalayas are an example of such a range that is now being formed. The Urals represent one that was formed 300 million years ago and is now being worn away.

The worldwide distribution of earthquake centers and of volcanic eruptions is remarkably close to the pattern of constructive and destructive plate boundaries. Such events are witnesses to the great forces that are tearing at the surface of the Earth as new material is being made and older material destroyed.

Very careful analysis can show the speed of tectonic movements. The fastest is the movement of the Australian plate, which is shifting the continent of Australia northward at a rate of 6½ inches per year. The movement of the Atlantic, at ½–1 inches a year on each side, is more typical. The Atlantic Ocean is now 32½ feet wider than it was in Columbus's time.

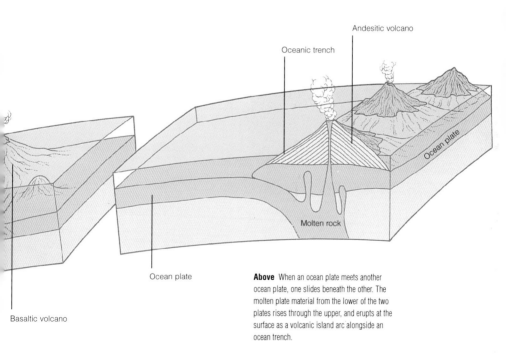

Andesitic volcano

Oceanic trench

Ocean plate

Molten rock

Ocean plate

Basaltic volcano

Above When an ocean plate meets another ocean plate, one slides beneath the other. The molten plate material from the lower of the two plates rises through the upper, and erupts at the surface as a volcanic island arc alongside an ocean trench.

Rock Deformations

The movement of the continents has left its mark on their constituent rocks. Continents that have crumpled up at the edge of a subduction zone, or have ground past one another, or have crushed up against one another to form a single landmass, contain rocks that have been affected in various ways. In the extreme form, such deformation causes metamorphism, but most often rock units are folded or simply inclined.

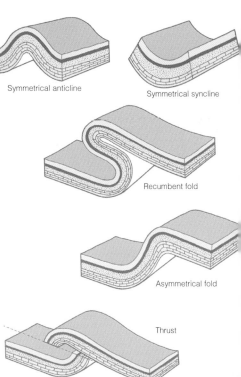

Symmetrical anticline

Symmetrical syncline

Recumbent fold

Asymmetrical fold

Thrust

Above In nature, folds are rarely simple. It is unusual to find the textbook syncline and anticline in isolation. In this example, pressure from left to right has twisted the strata into a recumbent fold at this locality in the Cape Fold Belt in South Africa.

Folded Rocks

When a layered sequence of rocks is compressed, it fractures or folds. Something as apparently solid and brittle as a bed of rock can actually fold. Push a tablecloth across the table and it will develop parallel wrinkles, at right angles to the direction of push. This is similar to what happens to the rocks of the continents. In fact, extreme forms of folds, where the different waves of rock collapse over one another as deep within the Alps' center core, are called nappes (from the French for tablecloth). When a fold sags downward it is called a syncline. When it arches upward it is called an anticline (see the diagram above).

We do not usually find an isolated syncline or anticline. More often they are found in a series, one following the other. The fold can be symmetrical, if

Above The simplest folds are symmetrical, each side being a mirror image of the other, as the anticline **top left** and syncline **top right**. Intense sideways pressure forms, in turn, asymmetric and recumbent folds, finally shearing off the limb of the fold as a thrust.

each flank dips at the same angle, asymmetrical, if one flank is steeper than the other, or recumbent, if it has turned over upon itself. Isoclinal folds are those that are so compressed that the limbs are parallel to one another.

Often the fold occurs in three dimensions, forming either a basin or a dome.

Usually we do not see a fold in its entirety in the field. We can deduce its presence by recognizing the same beds dipping in different directions not far from one another.

Things to look for in a fold

Axis The official definition of the axis is the line that moves parallel to itself to generate the fold. In more practical terms, it is the line around which the fold is bent.

Plunge If the axis is not horizontal, it makes an angle to the horizontal called the plunge.

Axial Plane this is the plane joining up the axes of the various beds in the fold. It may be vertical in a symmetrical fold, or inclined in an asymmetrical fold.

Competent beds Those that tend to hold their original shape when deformed. They tend to break rather than bend.

Incompetent beds Those that deform when they are folded.

Joints Cracks that open up because of the deformation. These can be strike joints if they are parallel to the axis, or dip joints if they are at right angles to it. Joints may form throughout the rock parallel to the axial plane. Often these tend to fan out, especially in beds of coarse sandstone.

Dip The angle at which a stratum is inclined from the horizontal.

Strike The line that a dipping bed makes with the horizontal.

Puckers or parasitic folds These form when very fine beds, such as shale, deform on a small scale as the fold forms.

The symbols are those used on conventional geological mapping.

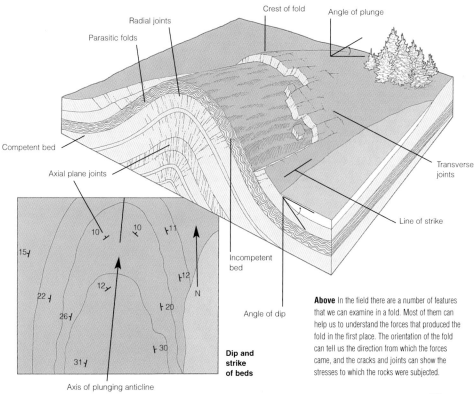

Crest of fold

Angle of plunge

Radial joints

Parasitic folds

Competent bed

Axial plane joints

Line of strike

Transverse joints

Incompetent bed

Angle of dip

N

Dip and strike of beds

Axis of plunging anticline

Above In the field there are a number of features that we can examine in a fold. Most of them can help us to understand the forces that produced the fold in the first place. The orientation of the fold can tell us the direction from which the forces came, and the cracks and joints can show the stresses to which the rocks were subjected.

Faulted Rocks

Sometimes rocks do not bend. Instead they break, and the rock masses move in relation to one another. This action is called faulting. Faults come in many different forms.

A dip-slip fault is produced when the movement is vertical, without any sideways component. The crack or the plane along which the fault moves does not itself need to be vertical, but is usually inclined. In a normal fault, one block has slipped down in relation to the other, down the inclined fault plane. This is produced by tension, as the rocks are pulled apart. A reversed fault or a thrust fault is one in which one block appears to have moved up the fault plane in relation to the other. This is caused by compression.

A strike-slip fault or lateral fault is one in which the movement is predominantly horizontal. These can be further defined by the movement that has taken place—either a left lateral fault or a right lateral fault depending on which way the opposite block appears to have moved.

More often the fault is an oblique one, in which there must have been horizontal and vertical movements.

When a block moves vertically downward between two faults, the structure is called a graben. If this forms a topographical feature on the surface it is a rift valley. If a block is left upstanding as the rock masses at each side are downfaulted, the result is a horst. A geomorphological feature so produced is called a block mountain.

Above The complex fracturing of this outcrop in Iran shows all kinds of faults, including normal faults **left**, a reversed fault **bottom center**, and a graben **top center**.

However, the faults do not always show themselves at the Earth's surface as hills, valleys, cliffs, and so on. If the faults are very old, the whole area tends to be eroded so much that no difference in the elevation between the faulted blocks can be seen. This may pose difficulties when analyzing faults, particularly in dipping strata. It may not be obvious if a particular fault is a dip-slip fault, a strike-slip fault, or an oblique-slip

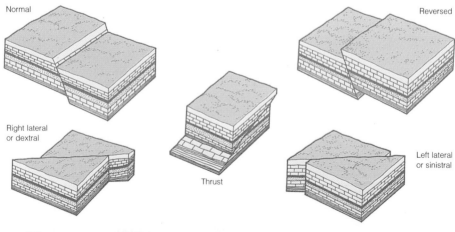

Normal

Reversed

Right lateral
or dextral

Thrust

Left lateral
or sinistral

Things to look for in a fault

The fault shown is a normal dip-slip fault.

Throw or offset The distance moved by the fault, only measurable where different beds can be matched up.

Face The surface along which the fault has moved.

Slickensides Polished scratch marks showing where one block has moved across the other.

Scarp The topographic feature produced at the surface if erosion has not worn it all flat.

Fault breccia A mass of rocky material broken and crushed by the movement of the fault. In extreme cases this may form the metamorphic rock mylonite.

Drag Often the beds at each side of the fault are distorted and folded in the direction of the fault movement. This is known as drag.

Joint A break in the rock along which there has been no relative movement is called a joint.

Left and right As in a fold, we can examine various features associated with a fault in the field, and most of these will give us some idea of the Earth forces that caused the disruption to the rocks—for example, whether the forces were tensional or compressional, and the direction in which they operated.

fault. We may have to look for other features, such as the presence of veins or intrusive igneous rocks, to estimate the displacement.

Faults can be very small, with a throw of only a few inches. However, because of the huge-scale movements of plate tectonics, some can be thousands of miles long. The San Andreas Fault of western North America runs for at least 807 miles and is caused by the relative movements of the Pacific Plate and North American Plate. It is, in reality, a swarm of right lateral faults, mostly parallel to one another. Movement along it has been in the region of 10 miles over the last two million years. It is the movement along faults such as these which causes earthquakes.

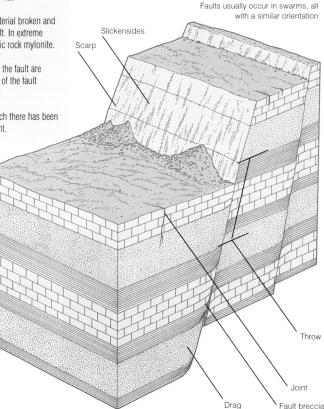

Faults usually occur in swarms, all with a similar orientation

Slickensides

Scarp

Throw

Joint

Drag

Fault breccia

Small-scale Features

Folds and faults are the most obvious features produced by the deformation of rock structures by tectonic movement. There are, however, all sorts of others.

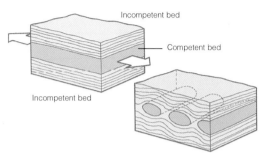

Incompetent bed

Competent bed

Incompetent bed

Boudins (above) When a competent bed surrounded by incompetent beds is subjected to a stretching strain, it may break up into sections. The incompetent material may then squeeze around it and fill in the spaces, and in cross section (**right**) the result may look like a string of sausages.

Augens (below) Similar deformations can affect the new minerals produced in metamorphic rocks. When a rock is subjected to such pressures and stresses that it metamorphoses into gneiss, new crystals, such as garnet, may form. As the rock continues to strain, the crystal may rotate and open up cracks at each side. These may fill with other minerals, such as quartz, and produce an eyelike structure called an augen.

1

Top cools quickly— jointing irregular

Main mass cools slowly— well-defined hexagonal columns

2

Cracks form across each line of tension

3

Horizontal joints split columns into blocks, with shallow depressions in top.

Columnar jointing (above 1–3) As a lava flow cools, it contracts to take up a smaller volume. The contraction takes place toward a number of random centers in the mass. These centers are evenly distributed and, as a result, the whole structure splits into a number of vertical columns. These columns tend to be hexagonal, for the same geometric reasons that honeycomb is hexagonal—it allows the largest number of units in a given space. A second type of jointing may then split each column into regular sections, so that they resemble stacks of hexagonal prisms. Many landmarks and beauty spots, such as the Giant's Causeway in Northern Ireland and Devil's Tower in Wyoming, are a result of such columnar basalts.

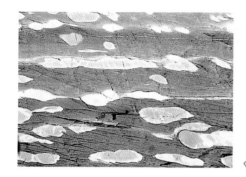

En échelon fractures (below) When two masses of rock shear past one another, the stresses set up between the two open up joints. These joints lie along the plane of the shear direction, but are at an angle to it. You can observe the same effect by spreading clay, or pastry dough, over two blocks of wood placed side by side and then moving the blocks past one another. *En échelon* joints appear in the clay or pastry.

If the stresses continue, the rock between the joints collapses and forms a fault breccia. Otherwise the angled joints fill with deposited minerals.

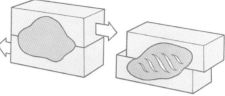

Mullions (above)
Competent beds subjected to great stress may split up into prisms oriented at right angles to the stress. The stress may then rotate them against one another, grinding off their corners and turning them into cylindrical shapes.

Dendrites (below) Often a joint is so narrow that water can only seep along it with difficulty. It does not then deposit its minerals evenly along the face, but as a kind of a gradual growth. Manganese oxides are often deposited in this way, producing a branching structure that looks like a fossil plant. This sometimes happens inside a silica mineral, producing the gemstone called moss agate.

Veins (above) Joints that are caused by tension, rather than compression, may open up. The spaces so formed tend to be filled with minerals deposited by groundwater, usually quartz but sometimes calcite. The veins so formed can be very visible when the light-colored mineral contrasts with a dark-colored rock.

These are all features that affect rocks after they have been formed. Sometimes they make such a mess of the original rock that it is very difficult to work out the history of the area. However, a useful rule is that, if structure A cuts across structure B, then structure A is younger than B. For example, if a vein cuts across a set of mullions and then is stopped suddenly by a fault, we can deduce that the mullions were formed first, then the vein injected, and then the whole system faulted.

Igneous Structures

Molten rock extruded through cracks and filling crevices solidifies into an intrusive igneous rock. The results form characteristic rock structures.

On the large scale, huge volumes of magma can rise into the continental rocks, usually melting and assimilating the continental material, and solidify in vast masses deep underground. This usually happens in the core of folded mountains, and the enormous structure so formed is called a batholith. Granite is the rock most usually found in a batholith. When the mountain chain is eroded away to its deep interior, the batholith will appear at the surface, forming broad tracts of moorland with prominent granite outcroppings. The moors of southwest England are the surface expressions of a vast batholith that lies beneath Devon and Cornwall and reaches out to the Isles of Scilly.

In general, igneous rocks are harder than the rocks into which they are injected. When the landscape is eroded away, they tend to stick out as distinct landscape features—sills as cliffs jutting out of a hillside, and dikes as wall-like structures cutting across the scenery.

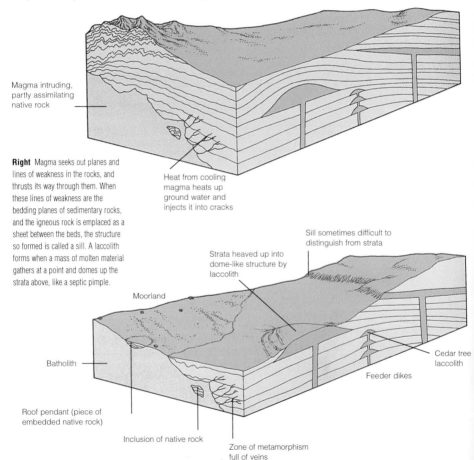

Magma intruding, partly assimilating native rock

Right Magma seeks out planes and lines of weakness in the rocks, and thrusts its way through them. When these lines of weakness are the bedding planes of sedimentary rocks, and the igneous rock is emplaced as a sheet between the beds, the structure so formed is called a sill. A laccolith forms when a mass of molten material gathers at a point and domes up the strata above, like a septic pimple.

Heat from cooling magma heats up ground water and injects it into cracks

Sill sometimes difficult to distinguish from strata

Strata heaved up into dome-like structure by laccolith

Moorland

Batholith

Cedar tree laccolith

Feeder dikes

Roof pendant (piece of embedded native rock)

Inclusion of native rock

Zone of metamorphism full of veins

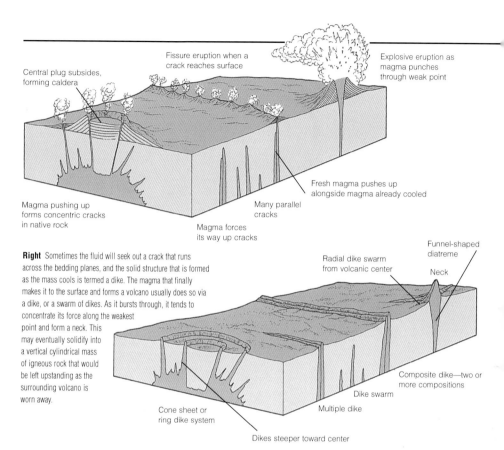

Central plug subsides, forming caldera

Fissure eruption when a crack reaches surface

Explosive eruption as magma punches through weak point

Fresh magma pushes up alongside magma already cooled

Magma pushing up forms concentric cracks in native rock

Many parallel cracks

Magma forces its way up cracks

Right Sometimes the fluid will seek out a crack that runs across the bedding planes, and the solid structure that is formed as the mass cools is termed a dike. The magma that finally makes it to the surface and forms a volcano usually does so via a dike, or a swarm of dikes. As it bursts through, it tends to concentrate its force along the weakest point and form a neck. This may eventually solidify into a vertical cylindrical mass of igneous rock that would be left upstanding as the surrounding volcano is worn away.

Radial dike swarm from volcanic center

Funnel-shaped diatreme

Neck

Composite dike—two or more compositions

Dike swarm

Multiple dike

Cone sheet or ring dike system

Dikes steeper toward center

Sill or Buried Lava Flow?

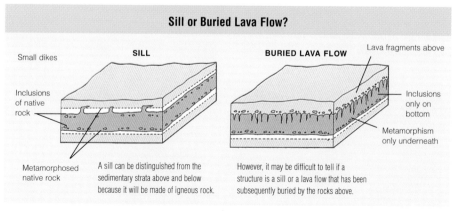

Small dikes

SILL

BURIED LAVA FLOW

Lava fragments above

Inclusions of native rock

Inclusions only on bottom

Metamorphism only underneath

Metamorphosed native rock

A sill can be distinguished from the sedimentary strata above and below because it will be made of igneous rock.

However, it may be difficult to tell if a structure is a sill or a lava flow that has been subsequently buried by the rocks above.

Sedimentary Structures

Above Ripple marks are preserved in sandstone.

An ocean bed can become a mountain, then a plain, with a succession of different plants and animals. These events can all be read in the rocks.

Sedimentary rocks are mute witnesses to their own creation. Each one could tell the story of how it formed and the conditions of the Earth's surface at the time. The nature of the rocks themselves gives us part of the story. For example, limestones form in carbonate-rich seas; rock salt forms under conditions where seawater is exposed on shallow sub-marine surfaces and evaporated; mudstones and shales form in muddy water; sandstones form in deserts or on sandy river beds.

However, it is the structures within the rocks that give us the details about the processes of their formation. Here are a few structures to look for.

Tool Marks

A sea current may carry a shell or a fragment of rock, bouncing it off the bottom and dragging it across the sea bed. The marks left can give us an indication of the direction of the current.

Usually it is not the mark itself that is preserved, but the cast made as the subsequent sediment fills the hole. When the rock is finally exposed, the fine material in which the marks were made tends to be very fragile and is eroded away quickly. The material above is coarser and sturdier—usually the bottom of a graded bed—and preserves the impression longer. This is why we more often see dinosaur footprints as three-dimensional raised surfaces on the rock outcropping than we do the original depressions made by the animal.

Ripple Marks

We have all seen wave marks left in the sand at low tide. The ripple marks, an inch or two high, that are so formed can be preserved in the bedding of the resulting sandstone.

Salt Pseudomorphs

When saltwater puddles dry out, they leave the salt as crystals. Sometimes the crystals may be fairly large, forming distinct cubes. When water returns to the area, the salt dissolves, and is washed away, but may leave behind cubic depressions which can then be filled up with later sediment. When these crystal shapes are preserved as casts in stone, they are called pseudomorphs—false shapes.

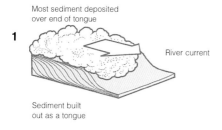

1 Most sediment deposited over end of tongue

River current

Sediment built out as a tongue

Topset beds

Foreset beds

Bottomset beds

2 Current sweeps in again

Topset beds of first deposit eroded away

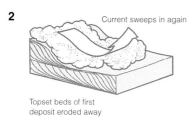

3 Final result

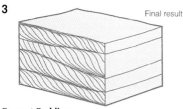

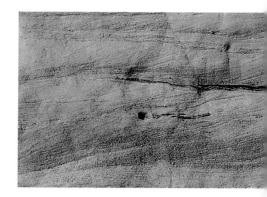

Current bedding

Dune bedding

Current Bedding

River standstones can be identified by the presence of current bedding. River sand is deposited as a tongue. Successive deposits of sand build out from the end of the tongue, in S-shaped beds—a thin layer along the top (the topset), a thick layer at an angle at the front (the foreset), and a thin layer spreading forward on top of the one before (the bottomset). Then, when the current changes, the topset and the top part of the foreset are swept off, and the tongue of sediment builds out again on top of what is left. The resulting sequence of beds shows curved structures that represent the bottom parts of the S-shapes, concave in the direction that the current is flowing.

Dune Bedding

Exactly the same thing happens when desert sands move over one another as shifting dunes. However, whereas tongues of river sediments may be a dozen or so inches thick, sand dunes can be tens of yards. The thing that distinguishes dune bedding from current bedding in a sandstone is the sheer scale of the structure.

Slump Bedding

Sometimes sandstone bedding seems to break down completely, producing a contorted mass. This is the result of sandstone beds remaining fluid, and distorting with the pressure of sand accumulating on top, or of continuing current action.

Above Flame structures

Flame Structures
When a mass of sediment is deposited suddenly on a soft layer, the mass may sink into it. The softer material may then squirt upward and be dragged away by the current. The result, in cross section, has a very sinuous, tapered appearance reminiscent of flames.

Mudcracks
Mud exposed to the sun dries out and shrinks. As it does so, it cracks into polygonal-shaped slabs. The cracks may be filled in by a subsequent deposit of sand.

Rain Pits
In dry areas the occasional raindrops may splash pits into exposed fine sediments. When turned to stone, these can be regarded as fossil weather.

Coarseness
A fast current can carry heavier fragments than a slow current. As a rule, the coarser sedimentary rocks, such as conglomerates, were deposited by faster-moving water than were the finer shales. Sometimes a current slows and stops. When this happens, the heaviest material that is carried along is deposited first, and then the lighter on top of it. The result is a bed of, say, sandstone with coarse grains on the bottom, grading to finer grains at the top.

Roundness
As rock fragments are swept along by a current, they tend to have their edges knocked off, and they become increasingly spherical.

When we see jagged fragments in a sedimentary rock we can tell that the fragments have not been transported very far. Well-rounded fragments, on the other hand, have been polished a great deal before coming to rest.

The rounded sand grains are found in desert sandstones. They have been carried out in winds, duststorms, and shifting sand dunes for millennia before finally being buried and turned to rock.

Sole Marks
When a turbidity current sweeps over an area of marine deposition, the soft fine sediment deposited at the top of the previous bed is disturbed and scoured into hollows. These hollows are reflected in the structure of the coarse bottom sediment of the subsequent bed and preserved in the final rock—on the sole of a graded bed. They may be in chains of crescent-shapes with the hollows pointing upstream, in which case they are called flute casts.

Above Flute casts

Sedimentary Sequences

Stand on the wharf of a river port and watch the river flow down to the sea. It may be that a few hundred years ago this port was on the sea itself. The sediments being washed down by the river may have been accumulating at the river mouth for hundreds of years, building up the land. If the landscape can change like that in a few centuries, imagine the changes during the vast sweep of geological time.

Such changes are recorded in the rocks. A typical rock sequence from early Carboniferous times may run, from the bottom up (it is geological convention to deal with rock strata from the bottom up, since this reflects the sequence of deposition), as follows. There may be a bed of limestone containing the fossils of marine creatures. Above this, there may be a bed of shale, still with marine fossils. Then may come a bed of sandstone—several

Left This stream bank on the Scottish-English border shows a typical early Carboniferous sedimentary sequence.

beds, in fact, that may build up into a thick sequence. This sandstone may have current bedding in it. Toward the top the sandstone may become very pale, and have fragments of carbon in it. Above this, there may be a bed of coal. Then the limestone may appear again, followed by the shale, and so on. This sequence may be repeated many times.

The fact that we described this sequence from the bottom upward reflects a fundamental law in geological study. The Law of Superposition states that in any undisturbed sequence of rocks, the oldest rocks are at the bottom.

The term "undisturbed sequence" is important here. A sequence of sedimentary rocks may be completely inverted, as in the arm of a recumbent fold. Then we have to look at the structures within the beds to see which way up it should be—graded beds grading upward, current bedding curving the right way, and so on. This is a procedure that field geologists term younging.

Another important rule is the Principle of Lateral Continuity: when we find the same rocks outcropping in different places, we can assume that they were once continuous and that they have been eroded away from the intervening region.

Analysis of a sequence will provide a history of the area reflecting, for instance, periods of inundation by sea or fresh water, times of aridity, and times of vegetable growth of varying intensity.

Left Cross-section of a typical early Carboniferous sedimentary sequence (as shown on page167). At the base (**1**), mostly beneath the rubble, is a thick bed of mudstone, deposited in muddy waters. Above this is a protruding bed of hard clay (**2**), formed from finer particles deposited in shallow cloudy water. Then comes a bed of softer clay (**3**), which formed under similar conditions but is dark with plant fragments and is less compact. This must have been formed in very shallow water for above it is a bed of coal (**4**), the outcrop of which is stained red with iron from the other rocks. The coal is overlaid by more soft clay (**5**), showing that the vegetation was flooded by shallow still water. Above this comes a sequence of thinly bedded sandstones (**6**), jutting out of the cliff face in individual beds. These were deposited in a river with a variable current. Quieter waters followed giving another bed of soft clay (**7**), and then more sand settled to produce a thick bed of massive sandstone (**8**), forming the overhang at the top of the cliff.

Unconformities

When a sequence of rocks is lifted above sea level, the wind and the rain act almost immediately to wear it down again. Erosional forces break up the exposed rocks and transport the fragments away to form new sedimentary rocks. The landscape is eventually worn flat, and the sea may cover it again.

When this happens a new sequence of sediments is built up on the eroded surface, and these eventually become sedimentary rocks. The break between these new rocks and the old rocks below is called an unconformity.

In most occurrences there is a bed of conglomerate immediately above the unconformity. This represents the remains of a shingle beach that formed on the eroded surface as the sea advanced across it. The advance of the sea is called a transgression. When the sea retreats it is called a regression. However, a regression is not easy to recognize in a rock sequence. It leaves sediments exposed to the weather, and these are then eroded, so destroying any evidence of the sea's retreat.

The presence of an unconformity is important in dating the sequence of the rocks. We have seen how we can date the geological events of an area by observing which igneous structure cuts what, and which fault breaks through what sequence. If an unconformity cuts across a dike, we can deduce that the dike was emplaced first and the rock sequence was later eroded to produce the unconformity.

The study of the sequence of rock types, and of the stories they tell, is called stratigraphy. When applying stratigraphic techniques over a large area, we can sometimes find the distribution of land and sea and the various environments at a particular period of geological time. This study is called paleogeography.

Above Angular unconformity. This is easy to identify. The beds beneath lie at angle to those on top.

Erosion and Geomorphology

The relentless movement of the Earth's surface plates causes landscapes to be uplifted and mountains to be heaved skyward; no sooner is an area of rock raised above sea level than the wind and the rain, the ice and the rivers, the sun and gravity all act to break it down once more. The shape of landscapes (geomorphology) can be seen as the temporary balance between these forces.

Visit a graveyard, preferably an old one. The recent gravestones will be fairly clean, and their inscriptions will be fresh. However, the older ones will be worn and decayed, and the oldest will be almost indecipherable. Most of the older monuments will be of the same stone—probably a local stone—and you will see how quickly that stone erodes once it is exposed by looking at the inscribed dates.

If the graveyard consists of monuments made from many different kinds of stone, you will find that some kinds weather more quickly than others. The metamorphic rock marble, for example, decays surprisingly rapidly compared to the sedimentary limestone from which it is derived.

Different climates impose different rates of weathering. Damp conditions rot material quicker than dry ones. However, under any conditions, two types of weathering can be distinguished—physical weathering and chemical weathering.

Scree slopes, such as those in the English Lake District **left**, are produced by physical weathering. Water in pores and cracks in the rock expands as it freezes, forcing the rocks apart. Biological erosion takes place as tree roots seek out joints in the rock and then split the rock as they grow, as in this Philippine example **right**. Onion-skin weathering, where a rock spalls away layer by layer, as here in Tanzania **bottom right**, is caused by both physical and chemical erosion in arid climates.

Physical Weathering

In the first of these it is the mechanical effects of wind and torrential rain, frost, and animal movements that produce the erosion.

Perhaps the most important factor in higher latitude and altitude rock erosion is frost. Rainwater seeps into pores and cracks in the rock. When this freezes to ice it expands by about nine percent of its volume, forcing open the pores and cracks. More water can then seep in and when this freezes even more force is applied. The pressure applied can be about a hundred times greater than the pressure of air in a car tire. Eventually the exposed rock disintegrates into rubble, shattered

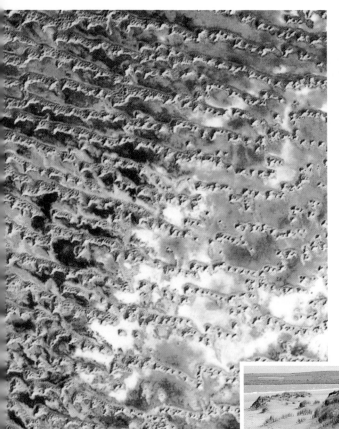

Right Limestone, consisting of the mineral calcite, is highly vulnerable to chemical weathering. The calcite dissolves in the weak acid of rainwater seeping along cracks and joints in the rock. The joints are opened up into wide gullies, called grikes, leaving rectangular blocks of rock, called clints, upstanding. This action continues underground forming caverns and potholes, where the calcite is redeposited as stalactites and stalagmites.

Left Sand dunes in the central desert of Saudi Arabia, formed by prevailing north winds. The blue is a crust of salty mud.

Inset Particles of sand, broken down and washed onto a beach by the sea, are carried along by the wind. They move slowly over the ground as small ripples and larger dunes. Eventually grasses colonize the dunes, their roots anchoring the sand in place to become a permanent landscape.

angular blocks of which lie in long slopes, termed scree, sweeping down from the jagged splintery rock faces.

In hot dry climates the difference in temperature between day and night can have a destructive effect. Rocks expand in the heat and contract in the cold. When this happens to exposed surface layers, they tend to become separated from underlying layers. This is most obvious when the rocks are distinctly bedded, with planes of weakness parallel to the surface. When it happens on massive rocks, such as granite, the result is that the rock erodes in curved slabs, a process that is given the technical term exfoliation, or the more descriptive term onion-skin weathering. This action is undoubtedly aided by what is known as pressure release, as the rocks expand after an overburden is eroded away.

The real mover in arid landscapes is the wind. The wind can pick up dry particles and hurl them along, blasting them against exposed rocks, and gradually wearing them down. Most of this action takes place close to the ground where the sand particles are being bounced along. A common result is a rock that looks like a mushroom, with a broad head and a narrow stalk that has been polished away by the sandblasting. Another result is the dreikanter, a stone that has been polished on three sides. A stone lies on the ground. Sand driven by the prevailing wind wears down one side. It becomes unbalanced and so topples over, exposing another side to be polished.

A final aspect of physical weathering is the role of living things. Trees growing in soil sink their roots into the bedrock. These roots follow cracks and expand them, splitting the rock open. Certain shellfish can even burrow into rocks, breaking them down.

Chemical Weathering

The gentle rain can often be quite harsh. It may be very acidic, either because it contains dissolved acidic industrial gases, or more probably because it has dissolved carbon dioxide from the atmosphere and formed carbonic acid.

Certain minerals are susceptible to attack by this airborne acid, notably feldspar and calcite. Granite consists mostly of quartz, feldspar, and mica. In wet climates the feldspar can react with atmospheric acid and decay into clay minerals.

This loosens the other materials in the rock and they fall out. As a result granite landscapes have china clay quarries, and white beaches of quartz and mica sand by the sea.

Limestone, which consists largely of calcite, is also eroded by acidic rain. The water seeps along joints and cracks, dissolving their sides as it goes, and these cracks are opened up into crevices called grikes, leaving the intervening rocks as upstanding blocks called clints.

Basic igneous rock, such as gabbro, is also weathered in this way. The olivine is particularly susceptible, but more to water than to the acid it contains. Water penetrates along joints and attacks all sides at once. The result is that the fresh rock is eroded away. The corners are most vulnerable and become worn off so that the mass becomes a collection of spheres—hence the name spheroidal weathering.

The Water Cycle and the Effect of Rivers

Water is in constant motion across the surface of the Earth in the surging tides, the crashing waves of the sea, and the flowing rivers. The sun evaporates water from the ocean surface and the wind transports the vapor. When conditions change, such as when the temperature drops, the vapor condenses, first to droplets that form clouds, and then to drops that form rain. When the rain falls on the land, it may sink into the soil or flow over the surface. Eventually it finds its way into streams and rivers, and flows back to the oceans. This whole sequence is called the water cycle, and it has a profound influence on the life and the landscape of the Earth.

The Ages of Rivers
Geographers and geologists acknowledge that rivers pass through three stages—youth, maturity, and old age.

Naturally, all rivers differ. Sometimes a stage is left out, with a river dropping straight out of its youthful stage in the mountains to old age on the plains. Each river varies through time also, changing its stages as mountains are worn away and plains built up.

All these stages are of interest to the geographer. However, it is the youthful stage that is most important to the practical geologist. Here the river is constantly eroding the rocks, giving good exposures and cross sections of the geology of the area. When the bedrock is worn smooth by water currents, any fossils contained often stand proud if they are made of a harder mineral. Waterfalls and rapids form over beds of harder rock, giving an instant indication of the layout of the geology.

In the mature stage the deposited debris will be more evident than the bedrock. This will be exposed on the outside of curves, where the current is fastest and eats into the bank. The bluffs of the valley may be cut down to the native rock but they are likely to be overgrown. Sometimes interesting rocks are seen embedded in the roots of dead trees washed downstream and deposited during floods. These can give an indication of what the geology is like in the mountains.

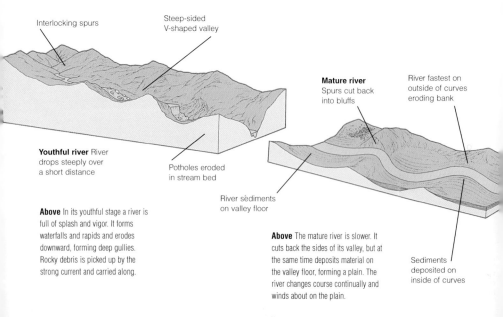

Interlocking spurs

Steep-sided
V-shaped valley

Mature river
Spurs cut back
into bluffs

River fastest on
outside of curves
eroding bank

Youthful river River drops steeply over a short distance

Potholes eroded
in stream bed

River sediments
on valley floor

Above In its youthful stage a river is full of splash and vigor. It forms waterfalls and rapids and erodes downward, forming deep gullies. Rocky debris is picked up by the strong current and carried along.

Above The mature river is slower. It cuts back the sides of its valley, but at the same time deposits material on the valley floor, forming a plain. The river changes course continually and winds about on the plain.

Sediments
deposited on
inside of curves

Trellised drainage, as in this Greenland example **right**, is the result of river capture. A river will cut back through a ridge, forming a valley that will be followed by rivers originally flowing at the other side of the ridge. A river flowing over a flat plain will naturally form loops called meanders.

River patterns

Throw water onto a rough surface. It runs off through the random hollows, skirting around the higher points, but generally flowing downhill. Rivers, in their progression from youth through

Below A river in its old age is sluggish and weak. It can no longer erode and only deposits the material washed down from the earlier stages. Meanders develop and banks, called levées, are built up at times of flood.

Old age river

River higher than floodplain

Meander

Loops as river bypasses meander

Marshes and water meadows

Crevasse splay deposited by flood

Oxbow lake formed from abandoned loop

Delta at river mouth

maturity to old age, do exactly the same, and the hollows and high points that they follow or avoid are largely due to the geology of the area. An aerial photograph of the river pattern that forms on structureless rocks, such as a vast granite batholith, shows streams and tributaries converging in a random, but even, pattern. Such a pattern is called a dendritic drainage pattern—a reference to its similarity to the branching of trees.

Dipping strata produce quite different drainage patterns. Where soft rocks alternate with hard rocks, for example shale interbedded with sandstone, the soft rocks always erode first. A river naturally tends to follow the outcrop of the softer rocks and, as a result, flows parallel to the strike. However, the higher and harder rocks will develop their own underground water levels called water tables and produce springs, and the streams from these will run down the dip of the strata to join the rivers in the soft rock valleys. This produces a rectangular river pattern with tributaries meeting main rivers at right angles—a pattern called trellised drainage pattern.

A river flowing down the dip of the strata inevitably erodes its bed. As the bed cuts deeper into the water table, the source reaches farther up into the hills. Eventually the river may cut right through the ridge of harder rock, and the river in the next valley may change its course to come

down the new gorge so formed. This is what is called river capture, and usually leaves a much reduced river trickling out of the original valley.

Any domed structure, such as the sedimentary beds heaved up over a laccolith, will produce a radial drainage pattern in which the rivers flow outward, following the dip of the strata.

An example of the radial drainage pattern is the English Lake District. The rivers flow outward from the center, but there are no dipping beds to indicate their origin. In fact, there was once a dome of younger rocks here, on which the rivers started. Eventually all the rocks that formed the dome were eroded away—not just by the rivers but by the other erosional forces too. The rivers continued along the courses that they had already established for themselves, irrespective of the new deeper geology over which they were running. This is what is known as a superimposed drainage.

In its mature stage, a river flows in a meander along its valley floor. If the whole region is uplifted, the river will begin to cut down into its

Above If a flat plain is elevated by earth movements the river may cut down into its bed, following the course of the original meander. The result is an incised meander, such as this one in Colorado.

bed. The result is a sinuous gorge following the route of the original river bed. This is called an incised meander.

Probably the most spectacular example of superimposed drainage is the Brahmaputra. Just look at it on a map: it rises in China on the north flank of the Himalayas, cuts south in a gorge through the highest mountain chain in the world to India, and reaches the Indian Ocean in Bangladesh. It was obviously there before the Himalayas existed, flowing south from the Asian continent. Then when plate tectonics brought India into collision with Asia, it began to cut down through the hills that arose, and then through the mountains that were subsequently thrust up, the rate of erosion keeping pace with the rate of uplift.

The constant shift of river patterns opens up new rock exposures for the geologist.

Underground Landscapes

The rain falling on the landscape mostly percolates into the ground. It gathers in the saturation zone, where all the pores and crevices of the rock and soil are filled with water. The top of this zone is the water table—an important concept in engineering and drilling wells. Where the water table reaches the surface, as on a slope, the water seeps out in the form of a spring.

In a limestone terrain the situation can be more complex, and more spectacular. Limestone is made of calcite which dissolves away in the carbonic acid of the rainwater. On the surface this solution takes place most quickly along the joints and fault planes, opening up crevices and separating the

Right A stream flowing onto a limestone surface may dissolve away a vertical shaft for itself, forming a sinkhole. In the underground caverns and hollows, the dissolved calcite is redeposited on the ceilings and floors in the form of stalactites and stalagmites **below**.

limestone mass into clints. This takes place underground too.

Most erosion follows the bedding planes of the limestone and the joints that tend to cut the bedding plane at right angles. It also takes place along the water table, where the surface of the water may form a stream and flow more or less horizontally. As a result a limestone terrain becomes dissolved into a series of interlocking caverns. From time to time the water table may drop. A stream in a tunnel will then erode deeply into its bed and give a tunnel that is keyhole-shaped in cross section. If the water table drops suddenly (in geological terms) the stream will begin to erode a new tunnel at the new level and leave the old one as a dry gallery. As the caverns expand, their roofs collapse, filling their floors and opening new spaces above. The collapse may cause the surface to cave in, leaving long gorges along the course of underground rivers, or broad depressions called dolines.

Vertical caves carved out by falling water are called potholes (not to be confused with the potholes that are carved out by swirling stones in a youthful river bed) or sinkholes. Surface streams flowing off an area of impermeable rock may suddenly disappear down one of these when it meets limestone.

Some calcite is washed away to sea, but much of it is redeposited in the same area. Groundwater seeping through and hanging as a drop on the cavern roof may deposit its calcite there. Not because the water evaporates away—the humidity of a typical cavern would preclude this—but because the carbon dioxide is lost from the water and it ceases to be acidic enough to hold the calcite. Accumulation of these calcite deposits builds up stalactites. When a drop hits the cave floor, the calcite is knocked out of it and an accumulation here forms a stalagmite. Different shapes of stalctite and stalagmite develop, each with a descriptive name. Water drawn along a stalgmite or a stalactite by capillary action, for example, will deposit its calcite seemingly at random and produce a twisted stalactite called a helictite.

Calcite is deposited by agitation in the underground stream as well. As an underground stream flows over an irregularity it deposits calcite, which causes a bigger irregularity, which deposits

more calcite, and so on. The result is a sequence of steps and terraces in the stream bed looking just like a hillside of terraced paddy fields—structures called gours.

When the underground stream finally reaches the surface, it may form a petrifying spring. Here the water can evaporate and deposit its calcite on anything handy. Mosses are sometimes encrusted, as are trinkets left by sightseers.

Calcite is an important mineral in cementing unconsolidated sediment to form a solid rock. A visit to a petrifying spring where the speed of calcite deposition can actually be seen is a memorable demonstration of this.

Ice

Ice can be a great rock destroyer, but it can also be a great rock mover and landscape sculptor. In tundra regions, fringing the great ice caps of the colder corners of the Earth, the permanently frozen subsoil—the permafrost—has all kinds of influences on the landscape, crazing the surface into huge polygons many yards across, or heaving up vast solid-covered, ice-filled blisters which are called pingos.

It is the work of glaciers, those rivers of ice that creep down from the snow-capped mountains, that has the greatest influence on the Earth's surface. Snow builds up in a mountain hollow, year after year. Eventually the great weight of the top layers compresses the bottom layers into ice. Under immense pressure, ice can move like putty and the whole mass creeps downhill. As it goes, its enormous weight grinds out the floor and sides of its valley, and carries the resulting debris along. Valley walls are undercut and avalanches bring more debris down onto the icy surface. A glacier is like a huge conveyor belt for rocks and stones.

This may not seem to have much relevance to the landscape of the more temperate parts of the world. However, we have just seen the back of the Great Ice Age that has affected the world for the last two million years. Much of North America, Europe, and Asia were covered in ice sheets, and the glaciers extended down from the mountain valleys in other parts of the world. Everywhere in these areas we see landforms that have been sculpted by the ice masses.

Left The great weight of a glacier grinds down the floor and sides of its valley, carrying along the debris it has torn out. **Inset** When the glacier has eventually melted, the valley will have a characteristic U-shape.

Physical Properties of Rocks

Above Igneous rocks, such as granite, are usually coarse-grained.

Field specimens of rocks are identified according to their composition, texture, and mode of origin. Each major rock type has its own range of textures.

For igneous rocks, the following descriptive terms are used:

Granular Consisting of crystal grains that are large enough to be easily seen by the naked eye, the grains varying in size from $\frac{1}{64}$ inch in andesites to over $\frac{13}{64}$ inch in granites

Aphanitic Made up of tiny crystals, which can only be identified using a microscope or powerful hand lens, they give the rock a flow texture (e.g. basalt) when they are aligned

Glassy Composed of volcanic glass; sometimes the glass may be streaky, due to aphanitic bands, and may often contain micro crystals of feldspar

Pyroclastic These are volcanic rocks in which the magma has been shattered by an explosive eruption and so may consist of tiny slivers of volcanic glass, fragments of pumice, crystals, or fractured rock; they may be unconsolidated or cemented together when fresh, and altered to clays by weathering when not (e.g. tuff, ignimbrite)

Foliated Minerals are arranged in parallel bands, sometimes contorted as a result of the way the rock flowed while it was still hot and plastic (e.g. flow-banded rhyolite)

Above Sandstone is a medium-grained sedimentary rock, with grains cemented by iron oxide.

Identification table for igneous rocks

TEXTURE	ORTHOCLASE		PLAGIOCLASE				NO FELDSPAR
	+ quartz	- quartz	+quartz	- quartz	pyroxene		+ olivine
	+ mica	+ leucite nepheline	- biotite and/or hornblende		- olivine	+ olivine	
Granular	granite	syenite	grano-diorite	diorite	gabbro	olivine gabbro	picrite peridotite
Finely granular	micro-granite	porphyry			dolerite	olivine dolerite	
Aphanitic	rhyolite	trachyte phonolite	dacite	andesite	basalt	olivine basalt	
Glassy	obsidian (massive) pumice (frothy glass) pitchstone (bitumous)			glass	tachylite (like obsidian but not translucent)		
Pyroclastic volcanic deposits	ash (unconsolidated air-falls ⅛ inch), volcanic bombs tuff (consolidated air-falls/ash flows ⅛ inch) breccia (angular rock fragments ⅛ inch)						

NOTE—gradations may occur between all types.

Sedimentary rock textures are as follows:
Clastic Consisting of broken and weathered fragments of pre-existing rocks and/or minerals and/or shell fragments, clastic rocks may have their individual components cemented together by calcite, iron oxide, etc.
Crystalline Consisting of crystals that have been precipitated from solution, which are locked together like the pieces of a three-dimensional jigsaw puzzle, thus giving the rock great strength without cementing material (e.g. limestone)
Organic Mainly composed of well-preserved organic debris, such as plants, shells, or bones (e.g. coal, shelly limestone)

The following terms are used to describe metamorphic rocks:
Slaty Finely crystalline rock in which minerals, such as mica, are aligned parallel to one another, which means that the rock splits readily along the mica cleavage planes (e.g. slate)
Schistose Minerals, such as mica, chlorite, and hornblende, are aligned in easily visible parallel bands and, because of their platy alignment, the rock splits easily (e.g. schist)
Gneissose Characterized by a coarse foliation with individual bands up to a few inches across—indeed, the foliation may wrap around larger crystals, as in Augen gneiss—and all the minerals are coarsely granular and readily identifiable (e.g. gneiss)
Granoblastic Mainly large mineral grains that have crystalized at the same time and, therefore, penetrate each other, the grains remaining large enough to be identified easily (e.g. graywacke)
Hornfels Compact, finely grained rock that shatters into sharply angular fragments (e.g. hornfels)
Banded Components occur in well-defined bands (e.g. gneiss)

Identification table for metamorphic rocks

MOSTLY FOLIATED (banded or layered structure)			
TEXTURE	NAME	COMPOSITION	DERIVED FROM
Slaty	slate	mica and quartz	shale, tuff
Schistose	chlorite schist	chlorite, plagioclase, epidote	tuff, andesite, basalt
	mica schist	musocovite, biotite, quartz	shale, tuff, rhyolate
	garnet mica schist	muscovite, biotite, quartz, and garnet	shale, tuff, rich in calcium
Gneissose	gneiss	feldspar, quartz, mica, amphibole, occasionally occurring garnet	melting of granitic or sedimentary rocks
Banded	migmatite	feldspar, quartz, biotite, and amphibole	acid and basic rocks
NON-FOLIATED (or slightly foliated)			
TEXTURE	NAME	COMPOSITION	DERIVED FROM
Hornfelsic	hornfels	dependent on the original rock	sedimentary rocks of fine grain
Granoblastic	quartzite	quartz	sandstone
	marble (R)*	calcite, calcium, and magnesium silicates	limestone or dolomite
	amphibolite	hornblende, plagioclase, quartz, garnet	basic igneous rocks

(R) - reacts with HCl

ROCKS—IDENTIFIER

Symbols

The symbols that accompany each rock in the identifier section are common symbols used to represent the rock type on a geological diagram or map.

IGNEOUS ROCKS—INTRODUCTION

Molten material welling up from within the Earth may eventually cool and solidify. The solid mass that results is called an igneous rock. There are two main types of igneous rock—intrusive and extrusive.

Intrusive igneous rocks form as the molten material pushes its way upward through the rocks, cutting across or squeezing between them, and solidifying before reaching the surface. If such rocks cool slowly, they will be coarse and have mineral crystals big enough to be seen with the naked eye. If they cool quickly, they will be fine-grained. Sometimes the molten mass begins to cool slowly, crystals of one mineral begin to form, and then the whole lot is thrust into another area where it cools quickly. This gives a porphyritic texture, with big crystals in a fine groundmass.

Extrusive rocks, on the other hand, are those that form when the liquid erupts at the surface, as from a volcano. These are always much finer than the intrusive forms. All lavas are extrusive igneous rocks.

Acidic	A rock that contains more than 66 percent silica
Intermediate	One that contains 66 to 52 percent silica
Basic	One containing 52 to 45 percent silica
Ultrabasic	A rock that contains less than 45 percent silica.

Right An extrusive igneous rock forms as molten material erupts from beneath the Earth's surface and solidifies, as here in the volcano Stromboli in the Mediterranean. **Below** an intrusive igneous rock solidifies underground, and we do not see it at the surface until the overlying rocks have been worn away. Here a mass of andesite protrudes from the surrounding softer rocks in Wyoming.

	Extrusive	Intrusive
Acidic	Rhyolite	Granite
Intermediate	Andesite	Diorite
Basic	Basalt	Gabbro
Ultrabasic		Peridotite

The terms derive from an old chemical idea that rocks are the salts of some kind of "siliceous acid"—total nonsense by modern understanding, but it does leave us with a useful and workable classification.

By applying both of the above classifications, and combining the grain of the rock with its chemical composition, we can start to define the most common types of igneous rock.

Intrusive acidic rock show large crystals, many of which are quartz. Acidic rocks tend to be lightly colored, because of the presence of quartz. Basic and ultrabasic rocks are dark. There are no ultrabasic extrusive rocks—ultrabasic rocks are rare at the Earth's surface but are thought to be the main constituent of the mantle.

As a rule, acidic and intermediate rocks form by the solidification of molten crystal material. Basic rocks are more likely to form from molten material brought up from the mantle.

This is a simplification. The true situation is much more complex. A solidifying melt goes through many stages of a process called fractionation before it becomes an igneous rock. As the mass cools the first minerals to crystalize out are usually those relatively low in silica, such as olivine, pyroxene, and amphibole. These can then sink to the bottom of the mass leaving a liquid that has become relatively rich in silica, and this may erupt toward the surface, and form acidic rocks. A liquid rising through the tubes of a volcano will find the surrounding pressure decreasing. The gassy components will fizz off, like the bubbles in champagne when the cork is popped. A volcanic eruption will be accompanied by great blasts of gas and steam, and will produce an extrusive igneous rock that has little chemical similarity to the melt that spawned it.

Another way of classifying igneous rocks is by their chemical composition. They can be rich in silica, or poor in silica. (Those that are poor in silica still have a very high proportion of silica in them, but not as high as the others.) Such a classification involves a somewhat misleading nomenclature which convention dictates that we must use.

Granite Igneous rock

Distinctive features Granular, composed of feldspars and quartz, with accessory biotite and muscovite. One feldspar may be flesh colored, while the other is white. The white feldspar may show twinning striations characteristic of plagioclase; the other feldspar is almost certainly orthoclase. The quartz appears as gray glassy grains. Biotite is black and muscovite is white or silvery, and both shine or sparkle by reflected light.

Color As above.

Texture and granularity Granular, coarse-grained, often porphyritic with feldspar crystals up to 4 inches.

Composition Orthoclase feldspar is always greater than plagioclase. If plagioclase is dominant, the rock is probably a quartz diorite. White to salmon-pink orthoclase feldspars megacrysts, set in a ground mass of glassy quartz, white-pink orthoclase, white plagioclase, black biotite, and silvery muscovite. Accessory minerals include gold-colored pyrites and silvery black magnetite.

Field associations Associated with fold mountains (e.g. Himalayas and Andes, Urals, Appalachians, and Rockies). Granites often mark position of ancient fold mountain systems.

Varieties Numerous. Immense variation in granularity and color—extremely coarse pegmatite, fine-grained microgranite, saccharoidal aplite. Orbicular has composite minerals arranged in ovoid or spherical bodies.

Uses Roadstone, building blocks, but it has poor resistance to fire as it crumbles when exposed to intense heat.

Occurrence Worldwide.

Varieties

Pegmatite

inches

Hand specimen

There is no internal structure or planes of weakness, and so it will break irregularly. The grain is usually so coarse that you can see the individual mineral crystals— the glassy quartz, the milky feldspar, and the dark but sparkling mica. The iron ore will be too small to see.

Microscopic specimen

The most obvious crystals are those of the feldspar. They will usually be twinned, each half of the twin showing a different extinction angle and fading from white to black through shades of gray. The shapeless pieces of quartz are somewhat dull and featureless. The mica will show a range of colors and will have irregular shapes. The iron ore magnetite will be present as tiny grains.

Twinned feldspar with multiple twins.

Mica with bright interference colors

Quartz

Untwinned feldspar

Left Because of the feldspar content, granites are subject to chemical weathering in moist climates. Joints are eroded and the intervening masses are left as rectangular blocks reminiscent of massive masonry. This example is at England's End.

Granodiorite Igneous rock

Distinctive features Texture, color, and the ratio of plagioclase to orthoclase, as well as the presence of quartz (polysynthetic twinning sometimes seen as fine striations on plagioclase phenocrysts). Association with granitic masses.

Color Pale to medium gray.

Texture and granularity Granular, coarse-grained, often with phenocrysts of feldspar, hornblende, or mica.

Composition More plagioclase than orthoclase, plus quartz. Minor quantities of biotite, hornblende, apatite, and sphene are also present.

Field associations Found in association with granitic batholiths. Forms large intrusive masses in the roots of mountain ranges.

Varieties Hornblende biotite granites, but these are really granodiorites.

Uses Roadstone aggregate.

Occurrence Worldwide, but particularly in Scandinavia, Brazil, Canada, USA (California has 3,500 square miles of granodiorite).

Diorite Igneous rock

Distinctive features Texture and granularity, composition, occurrence.

Color Dark gray, dark greenish-gray to black, depending on the percentage of dark minerals present.

Texture and granularity Granular, though not particularly coarse. Hornblende crystals may give it the appearance of a porphyritic texture.

Composition There is more hornblende than feldspar, and more plagioclase than orthoclase. The presence of quartz is uncommon; but, if it is present, the rock is then granodiorite (quartz diorite) rather than diorite.

Field associations Associated with both granite and gabbro intrusions, into which they may subtly merge.

Varieties Granodiorite, when minor amounts of quartz are present.

Uses Ornamental—capable of taking a high polish.

Occurrence Worldwide, but particularly in the eroded roots of fold mountains.

Gabbro Igneous rock

Distinctive features Color, granularity, predominance of pyroxene and, often, olivine. May appear to be porphyritic because of the size of the pyroxenes.

Color Dark gray, dark greenish-gray to black.

Texture and granularity Coarsely granular, but rarely porphyritic. Sometimes banded, resembling gneiss.

Composition Mainly pyroxene and plagioclase, with greater amounts of pyroxene than plagioclase or equal amounts of both. Olivine is often present, as well as grains of iron ore (magnetite and/or ilmenite) and bronze-colored biotite.

Field associations As plutons and similar large bodies, but not as large as those of granites. Also as large sheets, often containing valuable ore deposits (e.g. Lake Superior deposits).

Varieties Olivine gabbro, which is like gabbro, but also has olivine phenocrysts.

Uses Building industry, monumental since it takes a high polish, as a source of iron, nickel, and copper ores (e.g. Sudbury ores in Ontario, Canada).

Occurrence England, Scotland, Germany, Scandinavia, Canada, USA (New England, New York State, Minnesota, California, and lesser amounts in other states).

Peridotite (and other ultrabasics) Igneous rock

Distinctive features Greenish color when fresh, medium brown when weathered. Texture and composition.

Color Olive green when fresh, but weathering to dark ocher brown, due to the formation of iron oxides.

Texture and granularity Granular—saccharoidal.

Composition Made up almost entirely of small grains of olivine, or pyroxene may be present in appreciable amounts.

Field associations As small intrusions, sills, and dikes. Often brought to the surface from a great depth by volcanic activity (olivine nodules in basalt).

Varieties Dunite, which is composed of olivine only and is a pistachio green color, and picrite, which is composed of olivine plus subordinate amounts of plagioclase and is pale green. NOTE: Pyroxenite, which consists only of pyroxene, is black and has a 90-degree cleavage, and hornblendite, which consists only or hornblende, is black and has a 120-degree cleavage.

Uses As a source of valuable ores and minerals, including chromite, platinum, nickel, and precious garnet. Diamonds are obtained from mica-rich peridotite (kimberlite) in South Africa.

Occurrence Worldwide, but particularly in New Zealand, and the USA (New York State, Kentucky, Georgia, Arkansas, North Carolina, and lesser amounts in other states).

Dolerite Igneous rock

Distinctive features Color, texture. Difficult to distinguish between the hornblende and pyroxenes because of their small grain size. The plagioclase occurs as thin laths. Pyrite, bronze biotite, and iron oxide may be seen using a hand lens.
Color Medium gray to black.
Texture and granularity Granular to fine grains. Occasionally porphyritic.
Composition Pyroxene and plagioclase with larger amounts of pyroxene than plagioclase, or equal amounts of both. Olivine is also often present, as well as grains of iron ore (magnetite and/or ilmenite) and bronze-colored biotite.
Field associations As dikes and sills, often of great thickness. It may pass into gabbro at depth (dolerite is the medium-grained equivalent of gabbro).
Varieties Olivine dolerite, which is dolerite, plus olivine phenocrysts.
Uses Monumental, masonry, paving slabs, aggregate for roadstone.
Occurrence Worldwide, but particularly in the UK, Canada (Lake Superior), USA (eastern states—notably Palisades Sill—and western states as lava flows merge into basalts).

Above When dolerite occurs as a sill it is usually harder than the rocks round about. It tends to protrude from the landscape as a prominent cliff, following the grain of the land, as along the rim of this canyon in Wyoming. Columnar jointing is also visible here, produced by joints that formed at right angles to the boundary of the sill as it cooled.

Hand specimen

Because dolerate weathers so easily, it is essential to break it open to find a fresh face. It is a dark heavy rock with few light-colored minerals. Its dark color may have a greenish tinge due to the presence of serpentine produced by the breakdown of olivine. It has no internal structure and so it breaks into uneven pieces, usually with flat faces and sharp angles. Being a medium-grained rock, it will be difficult or impossible to discern the crystals with the naked eye, and a hand lens will be needed.

inches

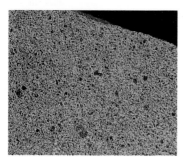

Above A fresh face of dolerite.

Microscopic specimen

Through crossed polars the magnesium-iron minerals show up in deep reds and greens. The gray feldspar crystals tend to be long and thin and embedded in pyroxene crystals, giving the so-called ophitic texture. A sample taken from the edge of the intrusion will show the more rapid cooling by the finer crystals, and may have the elongated crystals of feldspar lined up in the direction of flow.

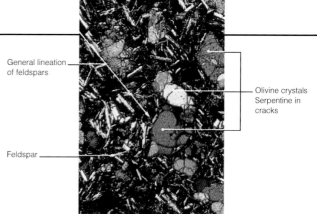

General lineation of feldspars

Olivine crystals
Serpentine in cracks

Feldspar

Rhyolite Igneous rock

Distinctive features Aphanitic, buff to grayish flow-banded rock, often containing spherulites or phenocrysts of quartz and feldspar.
Color Buff to grayish, banded.
Texture and granularity Aphanitic to very fine-grained.
Composition Same as granite, but the crystals too small to see without using a microscope.
Field associations As thick lava flows from acidic volcanoes.
Varieties Spherulitic rhyolite, which contains rounded bodies (spherules) of microcrystalline quartz and feldspar.
Uses Aggregate.
Occurrence Worldwide.

Andesite Igneous rock

Distinctive features Color and texture. Often flow-banded, and porphyritic and plagioclase phenocrysts occur as thin laths. Biotite, hornblende, and pyroxenes may be seen with the aid of a hand lens, but they can be difficult to identify because they are small.
Color White to black, but mostly gray.
Texture and granularity Aphanitic to finely granular, porphyritic, and flow-banded.
Composition Fine-grained ground mass of plagioclase, with smaller amounts of hornblende, biotite, and augite, which may occur as small phenocrysts.
Field associations Lava flows and small intrusions associated with volcanic mountain ranges.
Varieties Hornblende augite andesite, which is andesite with phenocrysts of hornblende and augite.
Uses Roadstone aggregate.
Occurrence Abundant in continental collision zones, such as the Andes, Cascades, Carpathians, Indonesia, Japan and other western Pacific volcanic islands.

Hand specimen

Rhyolites and andesites tend to be fairly light in color and light in weight due to the relative absence of magnesium-iron minerals. They can have a somewhat flinty appearance, splintering when they are struck with a hammer. Often they have a banded texture showing the very viscous nature of the liquid lava. Andesites may have a porphyritic texture, with large crystals of feldspar big enough to be seen with the naked eye.

Acidic and intermediate bombs tend not to be as streamlined as basaltic ones. As the bomb flies through the air, the surface may solidify and cool rapidly while the interior is still hot and molten. This gives rise to a breadcrust bomb which has a cracked outer layer. Hot pieces of ash may weld together as they fall, forming lumpy masses called agglomerate. When large masses of this are welded together to give a continuous rock, it is called tuff.

Rhyolite

inches

Andesite

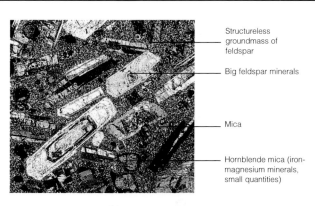

Structureless groundmass of feldspar

Big feldspar minerals

Mica

Hornblende mica (iron-magnesium minerals, small quantities)

Microscopic specimen

The microscopic view shows masses of tiny feldspar crystals. The lava cools so quickly that crystals may not have time to form, and the whole mass is an amorphous glass. Amphiboles and pyroxenes may make good crystals, having formed before the eruption.

Obsidian Igneous rock

Distinctive features Black volcanic glass, translucent on fine edges. When opaque on fine edges, the rock is tachylite (basaltic glass).
Color Black, but sometimes Indian red to brown. Has a bright, vitreous luster on smooth surfaces, and is sometimes bonded, with spherulites.
Texture and granularity Glassy. Breaks with well-defined conchoidal fracture to produce razor-sharp slivers of glass, so care is needed.
Composition Glass with the same chemical composition as granite, syenite, or granodiorite. Microscopic crystals of pyroxene may appear as whitish flecks. Microscopic iron ores oxidize to give reddish colors.

Field associations Associated with volcanic activity as rapidly chilled lava flows.
Varieties Pitchstone, which is glass with a bitumous appearance, pumice, which is highly vesiculated glass, and vitrophyre, which is glass with tiny phenocrysts.
Uses Primitive tribes use it in the making of cutting tools, arrowheads, and spearheads. Ornamental.
Occurrence Worldwide, but particularly in Scotland, the Lipari islands off the north coast of Sicily, Italy, Hungary, Russia, Iceland, Japan, New Zealand, Mexico, USA (Yellowstone Park, California, Oregon, Utah, New Mexico, Hawaii).

Microsyenite Igneous rock

Distinctive features Texture and granularity, and composition.
Color White to pinkish-gray.
Texture and granularity Granular—fine-grained to aphanitic.
Composition Orthoclase appears in greater quantities than plagioclase and there is no quartz. The small amounts of hornblende, mica, augite, and magnetite that are present can only be seen in thin sections with the aid of a microscope. Nepheline and leucite may also be present.
Field associations This is an uncommon rock, associated with syenite masses.
Varieties None.
Uses Aggregate.
Occurrence Worldwide, but particularly in the Alps, Germany, Norway, Russia, Azores, Africa, USA (New England, Arkansas, Montana, and lesser amounts in other states).

Pumice Igneous rock

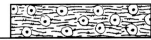

Distinctive features White or creamy white, highly vesicular rock, but weathers to a pale brown on its surface. Very low density.
Color Creamy white when fresh, but turns pale brown on surface when weathered.
Texture and granularity Vesicular.
Composition Composed principally of glass froth of granitic to granodioritic composition.
Field associations Chiefly on thyolitic to dacitic volcanoes.
Varieties None.
Uses Abrasive, cleansing powders.
Occurrence Worldwide.

Pitchstone Igneous rock

Distinctive features Black, opaque, volcanic glass that may contain irregular, whitish clusters of minerals. Resembles pitch in appearance.
Color Dull black.
Texture and granularity Glassy and breaks to produce poorly defined conchoidal fracture.
Composition Glass with the same chemical composition as granite, syenite, or granodiorite. Microscopic crystals of pyroxene may appear as whitish flecks. Microscopic iron ores oxidize, giving reddish colors.
Field associations Pitchstone originates from a rapidly chilled lava flow and is therefore always associated with volcanoes.
Varieties Obsidian, which is bright black glass with no phenocrysts, pumice, which is highly vesiculated glass, and vitrophyre, which is glass with tiny phenocrysts.
Uses Aggregate.
Occurrence Worldwide, but particularly in the Lipari islands off the north coast of Sicily, Italy, Russia, Iceland, Japan, New Zealand, Mexico, USA (Yellowstone Park, California, Oregon, Utah, New Mexico, Hawaii, and lesser amounts in other states).

Basalt Igneous rock

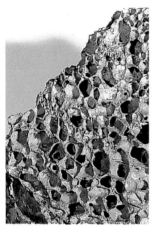

Distinctive features Texture, color, denseness, and often contorted by flow on eruption or cindery.
Color Dark greenish-gray to black.
Texture and granularity aphanitic with crystals that are too small to identify with the naked eye unless they occur as phenocrysts (e.g. augite and/or olivine). Fine-grained equivalent of gabbro.
Composition Pyroxene and plagioclase, with pyroxene appearing in greater amounts than plagioclase, or equal amounts. Olivine is also often present, as well as grains of iron ore (magnetite and/or ilmenite) and bronze-colored biotite. It

may contain olivine or pyroxene nodules brought up from depth.
Field associations As lava flows, sills, and dikes associated with volcanoes.
Varieties Olivine basalt, which is basalt plus olivine phenocrysts, and quartz basalt, which is basalt plus scarce quantities of quartz.
Uses Roadstone aggregate, source of iron ore, sapphires, and native copper.
Occurrence Worldwide, but particularly in Scotland, India (Deccan traps), Iceland, Greenland, Canada (Lake Superior has vast copper deposits), USA (Montana and western states).

Above Basaltic lava can cover large areas. When it engulfs a tree, the tree is destroyed but the lava next to the tree trunk is cooled quickly. The rest of the lava may flow or leaving a vertical tube of basalt with burned wood in the middle—a tree mold. These examples were formed as a forest was overwhelmed in Hawaii.

Hand specimen

A typical hand specimen of basalt will have a ropy texture on the outside, but will be cindery, brittle, and full of bubbles on the inside. Any hand specimen of basalt may contain bubbles, where gas was given off during eruption and the gases failed to escape before the lava solidified. In specimens of ancient basalt these bubbles may be filled with a mineral such as calcite, deposited by groundwater over millions of years.

Another good hand specimen is the volcanic bomb. This is a chunk of lava that blasted from the vent during the eruption and solidified in the air before landing.

Inches

A volcanic bomb

Eclogite Igneous rock

Distinctive features Generally coarse, green (reddish when weathered) pyroxene in which are set red garnets.
Color Pistachio green when fresh, but mottled with red when weathered.
Texture and granularity Granular —coarse- to medium-grained.
Composition Omphacite (green pyroxene), green hornblende, and pyrope-almandine garnet. Kyanite and diamond sometimes occur.
Field associations Metamorphosed gabbro, or basic magma crystalized at high pressure at great depth.
Varieties Coarse- and medium-grained varieties only.
Uses Scientific.
Occurrence As blocks in the "blue ground" that fills diamond pipes in South Africa (Kimberley), Norway, Scotland, Asia, USA.

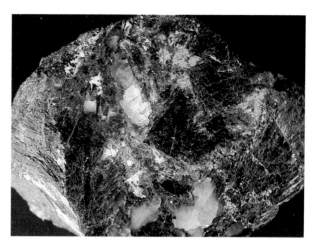

Ash (and related rocks) Igneous rock

Distinctive features
Unconsolidated, or poorly consolidated, white to black cindery ash of varying grain size.
Color Variable, ranging from pure white to black.
Texture and granularity
Pyroclastic. Unconsolidated when fresh, but consolidating to form hard volcanic tuff over geological time.
Composition Dependent on the composition of the source magma. Mostly basaltic (black) to trachytic (white).
Field associations As stratified beds of air-fall material ejected by volcanic eruptions, sometimes unstratified when formed from ash flows.
Varieties Basaltic ash, which is coarse, cindery to fine black ash, trachytic (syenitic) ash, which is coarse, cindery to fine creamy white ash, and tuff, which is dense, compact rock, varying in color from cream to yellow.
Uses Prefabricated building blocks, road surfacing, abrasives.
Occurrence Worldwide, and always associated with volcanoes.

Ignimbrite Igneous rock

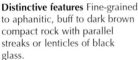

Distinctive features Fine-grained to aphanitic, buff to dark brown compact rock with parallel streaks or lenticles of black glass.
Color Pale cream to brownish to dark red-brown.
Texture and granularity Fine-grained to aphanitic, and flow foliation is often present.
Composition Usually trachytic/phonolitic to andesitic.
Field associations Exclusively produced by violently explosive volcanoes.
Varieties Sillar, which is poorly consolidated rock of same origin as ignimbrite, but in which pumice blocks have *not* collapsed to form plates of black glass and which is poorly sorted.
Uses Local building construction, aggregate.
Occurrence Worldwide— associated with andesitic to phonolitic/trachytic volcanoes.

Pyroclastics (and miscellaneous volcanic products) Igneous rock

A thick pumice deposit.

VOLCANIC BOMB Rounded or spindle-shaped rock of mainly basaltic composition ejected during eruptions.

BREADCRUST BOMB
Rounded, smooth-surfaced pumice block with cracked surface resembling cracked crust of bread, hence the name.

ACHNELITH Small, glassy volcanic bomb, sphere, dumbbell, and droplet shapes resulting from very liquid magma.

RETICULITE Lightest rock known. A basaltic pumice in which the walls of the vesicles have collapsed, leaving a network of fine, interconnecting glass threads.

PALAGONITE Submarine lava flow altered to yellowish-brown color by the formation of the gel mineral palagonite.

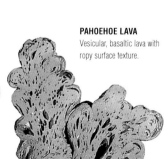

PAHOEHOE LAVA
Vesicular, basaltic lava with ropy surface texture.

SEDIMENTARY ROCKS— INTRODUCTION

As with the igneous rocks, there are various kinds of sedimentary rocks. Three main types are recognized. First there are the clastic sedimentary rocks. They are the result of some pre-existing rock's demise, and the re-cementing of its fragments to form a new rock. There are many kinds of clastic sedimentary rock, depending mostly on the size of the fragments that are cemented together.

Particle diameter

greater than 0.02 inch

These can be boulders, cobbles, or pebbles. The resulting sedimentary rock is conglomerate, if the particles are rounded, or breccia, if they are jagged and uneven.

0.00015–0.02 inch

These are the sands, and produce the sandstones of various types.

smaller than 0.00015 inch

Muds and clays come into this category, producing the clastic sedimentary rock called shale, if it is well-bedded, mudstone, if it is flaky, and clay, if it has no structure.

The second kind of sedimentary rock is biogenic sedimentary rock. Such a rock is built up of material produced by living organisms. Coal is one of the most familiar, consisting of carbon derived from masses of ancient vegetable matter. Certain limestones, when examined, are seen to consist almost entirely of fragments of fossil shells, or even of coral material cemented together as a reef.

Above Conglomerate is a coarse-grained clastic sedimentary rock, made up of rubble or gravel buried, compacted, and cemented into a whole.

Above Coal is an example of a biogenic sedimentary rock. It is made up of the accumulation of fragments of plants that were once alive.

Below Sandstone is a medium-grained clastic rock formed from sand on a beach, in a river bed, or, in this case, a desert.

Below Oolitic limestone is a chemical sedimentary rock, formed from calcite deposited on particles on an ancient seabed.

The last class is the chemical sedimentary rock. This is produced by inorganic chemical material being deposited on the floor of a sea or a lake, and building up into a solid mass. Rock salt and anhydrite occur when dissolved salts in a body of water are deposited as the water evaporates away. Certain limestones consist of calcite that is deposited in shallow water when currents bring calcite-rich waters into areas where the water chemistry is different.

It is a considerable step between a layer of rocky fragments and a sedimentary rock—between a bed of sand and a sandstone, between a heap of seashells and a shelly limestone. That step is called lithification and can be achieved by a number of processes.

In any case, sedimentary rocks are usually very recognizable in the field, because they lie in distinct layers, or beds. The analysis of the nature of the beds can tell us much about the surface of the Earth in times past.

Sandstone Sedimentary rock

Distinctive features Sand in which the grains are cemented together by secondary silica or by calcite. May be loosely cemented and soft, or well cemented and hard.
Color Buff to brownish; sometimes reddish, due to presence of iron oxides, or greenish, due to presence of glauconite.
Texture and granularity Sandy, with grains 5/64 inch and under in diameter.
Composition Sand grains (quartz), cemented by secondary silica or by calcite.
Field associations Compacted and/or cemented ancient beach, river, delta, lake, and desert deposits. Occurs as thick, stratified beds in sedimentary sequences, often showing current or dune bedding.
Varieties Quartz sandstone, which has cemented rounded or angular quartz grains, graywacke arkose, which is feldspar-rich sandstone, and calcereous sandstone, which has a high proportion of calcite, usually as cement.
Uses Construction industry.
Occurrence Worldwide.

Below Massive sandstone—consisting of thick beds with few bedding planes—will erode into sheer bluffs and towering crags, particularly when exposed to wind erosion, such as here in this dramatic example in Utah.

Above Sandstone is a porous rock and holds water very well. In well-watered regions, a sandstone landscape is able to support a prolific growth of vegetation, as illustrated by this verdant scene in France.

Graywacke Sedimentary rock

Distinctive features Poorly sorted dark gray to greenish, fine-grained sandstone.
Color Various shades of dark gray to dark greenish-gray.
Texture and granularity Granular, fine-grained.
Composition Quartz, plagioclase, and tiny rock fragments set in a matrix of microscopic quartz, feldspar, clay, and other minerals that are too small to determine without a microscope.
Field associations Formed at the bottom of ocean trenches bordering continents by avalanches of submarine sediments. Occurs in association with black shales of deep-sea origin.
Varieties Feldspathic graywacke, which is rich in feldspar, and lithic graywacke, which is rich in tiny rock fragments.
Uses None of any importance.
Occurrence Worldwide, but especially bordering ancient fold mountain ranges.

Arkose Sedimentary rock

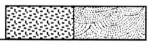

Distinctive features Sandstone-rich in feldspars. Bedding is sometimes present, but fossils are rare. It effervesces slightly in dilute hydrochloric acid, which indicates calcite cement.
Color Buff to brownish-gray or pink.

Texture and granularity Usually medium-grained but can be fine-grained. Mineral grains do not interlock.
Composition Quartz sandstone containing over a quarter feldspar with calcite or iron oxide cement. Micas may also be present.

Field associations Derived from rapid weathering, transportation, and deposition of granitic rocks.
Varieties None.
Uses Building stone, millstones for grinding corn.
Occurrence Worldwide.

Other Sandstone varieties Sedimentary rock

Grit is a coarse sandstone with very angular fragments. It was probably deposited at the mouth of a fast-flowing river.

Quartzite is a pure sandstone consisting of quartz cemented by more quartz. The term is also applied to a thermal metamorphic rock consisting of nothing but quartz.

Greensand is a coarse quartz sandstone with feldspar and mica, but containing large crystals of the green magnesium-iron mineral glauconite, formed as the sand was deposited on the bottom of the sea.

Sea earth is a very pale leached sandstone, full of root fragments. This represents an ancient sandbank on which vegetation was growing. It is usually topped by a bed of coal.

Millstone grit

Inches

Right The grains are jagged and well-sorted, which means that they were not carried far in the water that deposited them.

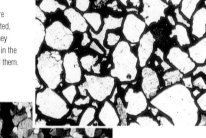

Right This sandstone is recognizable as a desert sandstone because the grains are all the same size and rounded, indicating they were blown about by the wind.

Below The mixed sizes of the grain show that this sandstone was deposited quickly.

Microscopic specimen

The analysis of sandstone through a microscope is a science in itself. According to the nature of the grains, we can tell if the sand from which the sandstone formed was derived from igneous, metamorphic, or sedimentary rocks, if the outcrops from which they were eroded were close or a long way off, and usually something about the conditions of deposition.

Iron-magnesium minerals showing that the sediment was not carried far.

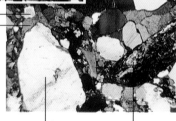

Quartz

Iron ore

Limestone Sedimentary rock

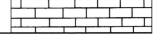

Distinctive features Whitish compact rock that effervesces in dilute hydrochloric acid. Often rich in fossils.
Color White to yellowish or gray. Black varieties are rich in hydrocarbons.
Texture and granularity Variable: compact, oolitic, crystalline, earthy-granular, pisolitic, shelly.

Composition Mostly calcium carbonate.
Field associations Deposited in ancient seas by the precipitation or by the accumulation of calcite-rich shells, etc., coral reefs, around hot springs.
Varieties Crystalline limestone, which has granoblastic calcium carbonate crystals, crinoidal

limestone, which is rich in fragments of fossil crinoids, oolitic limestone, which has tiny ooliths of calcium carbonate, pisolite, which has large (up to $\frac{5}{32}$ inch) ooliths, and reef limestone, which is rich in coral reef fossils.
Uses Cement source, building construction, blackboard chalk.
Occurrence Worldwide.

The rugged waterless nature of a limestone landscape is well known, and is due to the chemical weathering of the chief component calcite. Clints and grikes form on flat-lying limestone beds **above** forming a limestone pavement and giving a topography known as a "karst" landscape, named for the area in the former Yugoslavia. Rivers cut deep steep-sided gorges, by vertical erosion or by collapse of caverns and underground waterways. The Cévennes region of central France **right** has fine examples, such as the Gorges du Tarn and the Gorges de la Jonte.

Hand specimen

Depending on the type of limestone, the hand specimen may be a mass of fossils or it may be an even-grained, pale-colored rock.

When a biological limestone is weathered, it may show the constituent fossils in high relief. A variety of the chemical limestone called oolite consists of tiny spherical particles about 1/16 inch across, called ooliths. In a coarser variety, pisolite, the grains are pea-sized. These have formed as calcite precipitated on fragments of sand or shell, and then rolled about on the sea floor, building up like snowballs.

In the hand specimen you can distinguish between calcite and dolomite by using acid (vinegar will do). Calcite fizzes and bubbles, but dolomite does not react.

Oolitic limestone

Above Shelly limestone

Inches

Microscopic specimen

Fragments of the fossil content are usually very recognizable, with the cementing calcite visible as a regular mosaic around them. Sometimes the cementing calcite is grown from an existing calcite fragment and the shape of the original is seen as a ghost in a larger calcite crystal.

In an oolite, the concentric shapes of the individual ooliths are visible, again cemented together by a calcite mosaic.

Above Photomicrograph of a shelly limestone

Fine-grained Shales, Mudstones & Clays Sedimentary rocks

Hand specimen
Fine-grained sedimentary rocks are so soft that specimens are easily obtained.

When the rock can be split easily into thin brittle sheets, it is a shale. When it breaks into lenticular flakes, it is a mudstone. When it has little internal structure but is plastic and slippery when wet, it is a clay. If the distinction is not obvious when you hammer off a hand specimen, then apply the blade of a penknife and see how the specimen splits.

Fossils are likely to be present and these are most easily seen in shale because it splits along the bedding plane where fossils are usually aligned. Fossils of marine animals are found in deep-sea shales; freshwater shellfish and plants lie in shallow-water shales.

Very dark marine shales can be rich in carbon, showing that they were deposited in a region deficient in oxygen. Fossils in such shales may be of animals

Mudstone

that suffocated after being swept into these regions by currents. The lack of oxygen leads to the formation of iron pyrite, and this may be present as crystals or as a replacement mineral in fossils.

Clay

Varieties
Within the divisions of shale, mudstone, and clay, there are many different types. They are usually given names that are based on their economic importance.

China clay or kaolin is a white clay formed by the decomposition of the feldspars in granite.

Fuller's earth is a clay made from very fine volcanic ash, used for removing grease from wool.

Alum shale contains minerals that can be worked for alum.

Microscopic specimen
Don't bother. The constituent fragments are too fine for the technique to be of any use.

Inches

Right The fine-grained sedimentary rocks are usually very soft compared with any other rocks in the area. Where clays, mudstones, or shales are interbedded with limestone, the beds of limestone are left protruding as shelves or ridges while the intervening fine material is washed away. This gives a deceptive step-line appearance to any cliff, although its unstable nature forbids any climbing.

Shale Sedimentary rock

Distinctive features Splits easily into thin plates along well-defined planes parallel to the original stratification. Buff to gray, very fine-grained silty rock.
Color Buff to various shades of gray.
Texture and granularity Fine-grained.
Composition Complex mixture of microscopic clay minerals, plus mica and quartz.
Field associations Derived from ancient mud deposits, it occurs in most sedimentary sequences with fine sandstone and limestone.
Varieties Probably mudstone.
Uses Source of fossils.
Occurrence Worldwide.

Chalk Sedimentary rock

Distinctive features White, porous rock that effervesces in dilute hydrochloric acid. Often contains bands of flint nodules and is rich in fossils.
Color White to yellowish or gray.
Texture and granularity Fine-grained, earthy, crumbly, porous rock.
Composition Mostly calcium carbonate, with minor amounts of fine silt. Often contains flint and pyrite nodules.
Field associations Deposited in ancient seas by the accumulation of tests (tiny shells) of microscopic marine organisms.
Varieties None.
Uses As a source of cement.
Occurrence UK, France, Denmark.

Hand specimen
The rock breaks off in irregular dusty pieces because there are no internal structure or zones of weakness. Fossils are so completely encased that they cannot be removed. Any break cuts clean across the fossil. The fossils are usually formed by silica replacement, and if there are any veins present in the rock these will contain silica too. Chalk is so fine-grained that the constituent particles are impossible to see, even with a hand lens. A grayish tinge may be due to the presence of mud particles in the original sediment. A greenish tinge may be imparted by the iron silicate mineral glauconite, but only in impure chalks.

Inches

Shelly Limestone Sedimentary rock

Distinctive features Pale gray, highly fossiliferous rock. Effervesces in dilute hydrochloric acid (take care).
Color Grayish-white to buff or yellowish-gray
Texture and granularity Shelly.
Composition Mostly entire and broken fossilized shells cemented by calcium carbonate.
Field associations Represents a thick accumulation of marine shells and other calcite-rich organisms deposited in shallow water.
Varieties None.
Uses Source of fossils.
Occurrence Worldwide.

Dolomite Sedimentary rock

Distinctive features Pale-colored massive limestone that often contains small cavities. Sometimes associated with evaporite deposits of gypsum and halite.
Color Creamy white to pale brown.
Texture and granularity Coarse- to fine-grained. Often compact.
Composition Magnesium carbonate with, at times, small amounts of silica and other derived minerals.
Field associations Often interbedded with calcite-rich limestones, but may form thick massive deposits.
Varieties Sometimes known as magnesium limestone.
Uses Aggregate.
Occurrence Worldwide.

Septarian nodules Sedimentary rock

Distinctive features Ball-like structures, often enclosing shell fragment or other nuclei. Composed of sandstone or clay cemented by calcite or silica, the internal shrinkage cavities, usually filled with calcite, may be seen when the nodule is cut or broken.
Color Variable: gray to buff to dark brown with whitish-yellow calcite filling the interior, radiating cracks, and cavities.
Texture and granularity Usually fine-grained.
Composition Variable, depending on origin. Sand, silt, or clay together with calcite.
Field associations Fine-grained or clay sediments.
Varieties None.
Uses Ornamental when cut and polished.
Occurrence Worldwide.

Breccia Sedimentary rock

Distinctive features Similar to conglomerate, but rock fragments are angular and set in fine-grained matrix. Distinguished from agglomerate (its volcanic equivalent) by its sedimentary origin.
Color Variable, depending on type of rock fragments.
Texture and granularity Angular fragments of rock set in fine-grained matrix.
Composition Fragmented rocks of any kind can form breccia. The matrix is normally fine sand or silt, cemented by secondary silica or calcite.
Field associations Derived from screes and fault zones. Often found near conglomerate, arkose, and sandstone.

Varieties Named according to rock type of which it is composed.

Uses Aggregate, ornamental when highly compacted.
Occurrence Worldwide.

Coal Sedimentary rock

Distinctive features Black, dirty, hard to crumbly rock. Burns with a bright yellow flame.
Color Dull, earthy black to glistening, submetallic black.
Texture and granularity Massive, brittle.
Composition Highly compacted plant debris.
Field associations Represents remains of ancient forests that flourished, mainly on tropical deltas. Occurs mostly as thick beds in rocks of Carboniferous age, although some thin coal bands are found in rocks of other ages.
Varieties Cannel coal, which is a soft brownish-black coal, anthracite, which is brittle, black, glistening.
Uses As domestic and industrial fuel.
Occurrence UK, southern Russia, Ukraine, Africa, China, USA (Pennsylvania).

Conglomerate Sedimentary rock

Distinctive features Boulders, pebbles, or shingle, set in fine-grained matrix, sometimes resembling coarse concrete.
Color Variable, depending on the type of rock fragments.
Texture and granularity Variable.
Composition Rounded rock fragments set in a fine-grained matrix.
Field associations Derived from beach, lake, and river deposits of boulders, pebbles, and gravel. Often found near deposits of sandstone and arkose.
Varieties None.
Uses Aggregate, ornamental when highly compacted forms are cut and polished.
Occurrence Worldwide.

METAMORPHIC ROCKS— INTRODUCTION

There are two types of metamorphic rock. The first is regional metamorphic rock in which the altering force is one of pressure rather than of temperature. These are found deep within the interior of mountain chains, and are believed to constitute the lower parts of the crust. Vast tracts of the Earth's crust have been altered in this way. Different degrees of pressure produce different grades of metamorphic rock. Slight pressure—and the world "slight" is a comparative term—will produce a low-grade metamorphic rock, in which the only difference will be that the minerals will have been realigned in a different direction. Often this produces flat crystals of mica that are oriented according to the direction of the applied pressure. The result is a rock that has planes of weakness running in one direction, and that can split easily into flat slabs. Slate and phyllite are typical low-grade metamorphic rocks. At the other end of the scale, intense pressure will completely change the mineralogical makeup of the rock and produce a high-grade metamorphic rock. The chemical components may recrystalize into a totally different set of minerals from the original rock and the new minerals may form in distinct bands, often crumpled and contorted as evidence of the great pressure involved. Gneiss is the typical high-grade metamorphic rock showing distinct banding.

A typical sequence of rocks—from unconsolidated sediment, through sedimentary rock, through different grades of metamorphic rock, depending on the depth in the crust at which different conditions are found—is shown right.

The last rock in this series, hornfels, in fact belongs to the second type of metamorphic rock— the thermal metamorphic rock, sometimes called the contact metamorphic rock. Heat is the most important influence in the formation of such rocks.

Surface
Mud

3 miles deep
Shale (sedimentary)

6 miles deep
Slate (low-grade metamorphic).
Different kinds of micas develop.

9 miles deep
Schist. Garnet appears.

12 miles deep
Gneiss (high-grade metamorphic).
Staurolite forms.

15½ miles deep
Hornfels. Strange rare minerals, such as cordierite, appear.

Right Schist shows well the new minerals, such as the red staurolite and the pale blue kyanite, produced by the intense metamorphic action.

As a result, thermal metamorphic rock are less common and much more restricted in distribution than their regional counterparts. The usual place to find them is at the edge of an intrusive igneous rock, where the heat of the cooling mass has cooked the native rocks at each side. This will produce a metamorphic auriole around the igneous rock, which may only be an inch or two wide. Unlike regional metamorphic rock, thermal metamorphic rocks show no internal structure, and can often be mistaken for an igneous rock.

Different minerals crystalize at different temperatures in a metamorphic auriole, and so the mineralogy of the rock close to the intrusion will be different from that farther away. The amount of heat given off as the body cools is another important variable. The chemical constituent of the original rock determines the new minerals that are formed. In a sandstone that contains nothing but quartz fragments, the quartz recrystalizes in a more compact mosaic, forming the thermal metamorphic rock called quartzite. In a pure limestone the calcite will recrystalize to form marble. Displacement or dynamic metamorphism is local alteration caused by friction as one mass slides over another.

In all this complexity the important point to note is that metamorphism takes place in solid rock. The minerals recrystalize without passing through a molten phase. Should the minerals, at any stage of the operation, melt, then the result would not be a metamorphic rock, but an igneous one.

Slate Metamorphic rock

Distinctive features Grayish, very fine-grained, foliated rocks that split into thin sheets. Sometimes contain well-formed pyrite crystals. Found in metamorphic environments.
Color Usually shades of medium to dark gray, but sometimes a buff color.
Texture and granularity Slaty and very fine-grained.
Composition Mica, quartz, and other minerals that can be determined only by X-ray.
Field associations In areas of regionally metamorphosed shale or volcanic tuff.
Varieties None.
Uses Roofing tiles.
Occurrence Worldwide.

Inches

Hand specimen
Slate tends to be a fairly even rock, and, being fine-grained, a small sample is usually representative of the whole emplacement. Its color is usually a dark gray but, according to the precise mineral content, it can be green, blue, or reddish-brown. A hand lens may reveal the mica flakes that give the rock its cleavage, but often they are too small.

Welsh slate

Schist Metamorphic rock

Distinctive features Schistose and mostly composed of biotite, muscovite, and quartz. Sometimes contains green chlorite, or garnets, or staurolite and kyanite.
Color Variable: streaky, silvery, black, white, or green.
Texture and granularity Schistose with mineral grains that are platy or aligned.
Composition Mostly muscovite, biotite, and quartz but sometimes some green chlorite is present. May also contain large, well-formed crystals of garnet.
Field associations Zones of contact or regional metamorphism.

Varieties Greenschist, which is soft schist rich in green chlorite; mica schist, which is rich in micas; garnet mica schist, which is mica schist rich in garnets; staurolite-kyanite schist, which is mica schist, rich in these minerals; and amphibolite schist, which is mostly amphibole and plagioclase.
Uses Source of minerals for collectors.
Occurrence Worldwide, adjacent to large, igneous intrusions or in eroded roots of fold mountain systems.

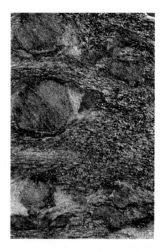

Inches

Hand specimen
The broken face of a hand specimen of schist will sparkle in the sun because of the mica crystals. The crystals may be big enough to be seen with the naked eye, but if not you will definitely see them with a hand lens. The other minerals, particularly the index minerals that show the grade of metamorphism, should be looked for too. Garnets will be readily recognizable by their deep red color and their other properties, and kyanite should be obvious by its light blue color. The other index minerals may be difficult to detect without trained help.

Gneiss Metamorphic rock

Distinctive features Coarse-grained, pale-colored gneissose rock, containing abundant feldspar.
Color Whitish to dark gray—with the darker varieties containing more biotite.

Texture and granularity Gneissose, coarse-grained.
Composition Mostly feldspar, with quartz, mica, hornblende, and garnet.
Field associations In roots of eroded fold mountain systems.

Varieties Depends on the source rock. Granitic is the most common, but basic varieties also occur.
Uses Construction, ornamental, aggregate.
Occurrence Worldwide, but always in roots of fold mountain systems.

Above We see gneiss in places where ancient mountain ranges have been worn down to their bases. A landscape of gneiss, such as here in the Scottish isles, tends to be rounded and smooth. This is not just because erosion has been acting on it for so long, but also because the rock tends to be of a fairly even hardness with few of the cleavage planes we associate with other forms of regional metamorphic rock.

Hand specimen

When you hammer off a specimen, it will not usually split along the foliation plane, such as schist does. The resulting specimen will be irregular and cut across the different bands.

The minerals in gneiss form crystals that are big enough to be seen with the naked eye. Light-colored layers of quartz and feldspar alternate with darker mica-rich, amphibole-rich, and pyroxene-rich layers. The crystals can be so big that you can identify them from their physical properties. Sometimes the mineral bands and structures are so big that it is easier to study them in outcrop than in hand specimens.

Inches

Microscopic specimen

A big crystal found in gneiss will show evidence of having been stressed—indicated either by an internal structure that appears to have been pulled and twisted about, or by such optical properties as the exinction angle differing across its area. Large crystals of feldspar may also have broken up into a mosaic of finer grains.

Band of finer crystals— contrast with quartz produces banding in rock

Interlocking grains of quartz

Quartzite Metamorphic rock

Distinctive features Compact, hard, very fine-grained rock, which breaks into sharp angular fragments. Quartzite is always associated with other metamorphic rocks, while cemented sandstone is always associated with other sedimentary rocks.
Color White to creamy white.
Texture and granularity Granoblastic and very fine-grained.
Composition Interlocking sand (quartz) grains, often with silica cement.
Field associations In zones of regionally metamorphosed sandstones.
Varieties Local varieties based on color.
Uses Aggregate, monumental.
Occurrence Worldwide.

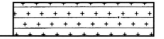

Marble Metamorphic rock

Distinctive features Fine- to coarse-grained granoblastic that effervesces in dilute hydrochloric acid. Often banded with various colors and sometimes veined.
Color Variable: white, cream, gray, red, green, and often streaky with light and dark patches.
Texture and granularity Fine- to coarse-grained, granoblastic.
Composition Calcium carbonate.
Field associations In zones of regionally metamorphosed limestone.
Varieties Many, depending on the color and banding, e.g. Connemara marble, which is pale green.
Uses Building and ornamental
Occurrence Worldwide.

GLOSSARY

Acicular Needle-shaped mineral form, often radiating from a base.

Adamantine Bright mineral luster, like that of a diamond.

Amorphous Without shape, not crystalline because there is no regular internal structure.

Aqua regis Mixture of one part of hydrochloric acid to one part of nitric acid. Capable of dissolving gold.

Asterism Star effect seen in a gemstone cut and polished *en cabochon*.

Basal cleavage Cleavage parallel to a mineral's basal plane.

Batholith Mass of igneous rock formed irregularly from an intrusion of magma deep in Earth's crust.

Bedding The layers in which sedimentary rocks are deposited.

Bedding planes The dividing lines between bedding strata.

Birefrigence The difference between the maximum and minimum refractive indices of a doubly refractive stone.

Botryoidal Resembling a cluster of grapes.

Carat Abbreviated to ct. The internationally recognized unit of weight used in gemmology equivalent to 0.2 grams, divided into 100 "points."

Chatoyancy Iridescent luster visible in thin bright lines due to the presence of inclusions.

Chelsea Color Filter Device used to aid identification of gemstones. When a stone is viewed through it, all the spectrum colors except red and green are cut out, revealing underlying colors visible to the naked eye.

Cleavage The plane along which a crystal will naturally break due to a weakness within the atomic structure.

Conchoidal Describes a crystal that breaks with concentric cavities.

Crystal A form bounded by flat faces.

Crystal system The six main groups into which crystals are classified according to their shape.

Deposit Where one or more minerals have formed in sufficient quantity to make extraction viable.

Dichroism see *Pleochroism*.

Diffraction The splitting of white light into the colors of the spectrum as light passes through narrow slits, for example in a spectroscope.

Dike Igneous intrusion of great length but limited thickness which often fills a vein or fracture plane.

Double refraction When crystals split rays of light by different amounts to give a range of refractive indices.

Drusy cavity A hollow space within a rock that is filled with a collection of secondary materials.

Dull Luster with little reflection.

Earthy Luster with no reflection

En cabochon Convex cut used for opaque gemstones or to show asterism or chatoyancy.

Evaporite A mineral formed when aqueous solutions evaporate.

Extrusive When molten rocks or lava flow out of the Earth's surface.

Faces The flat external faces of a crystal.

Feldspar The most common mineral group. Feldspars make up about 60 percent of the Earth's crust.

Feldspathoid A mineral similar in structure and chemistry to feldspar, but with less silica.

Fire Properly called dispersion, the splitting of white light into spectral colors when it passes through a gemstone.

Fluorescence Temporary emissions of light waves to give colors not normally seen.

Form Describes a number of identical flat faces that make up a crystal. More than one form may be needed to describe a crystal.

Fossil Any trace left by organic life in rock.

Fracture The uneven breaking of a stone, the direction of which is not related to the atomic structure of the crystal.

Granular Appearing grainy or in grains.

Habit The characteristic form of a crystal.

Hackly Fracture with a rough surface.

Hardness The resistance of a substance to scratching, abrasion, and penetration.

Hemimorphic A crystal which develops differently at the ends of each axis.

Inclusion Cavities, fragments of crystal, or other substances found within the crystalline structure of a gemstone.

Intrusion Igneous rock that, as magma has been forced into older rock.

Iridescence Interference of light in the internal structure of a stone, causing white light to split into the spectral colors.

Luster How a mineral shines, due to the light it reflects.

Magma Molten rock in the Earth's mantle.

Massive A sedimentary rock that shows no bedding.

Mineral A naturally occurring inorganic substance with a constant chemical composition and internal atomic structure.

Metallic Luster like metal.

Metamorphism Rock transformation from one state to another; caused by heat and pressure.

Mohs' hardness scale Empirical scale for measuring hardness.

Pegmatite Dikes of igneous rock, caused by the cooling of residual liquids from magma, which give an ideal growing region for crystals.

Placer deposit Minerals deposited, probably in alluvial conditions or on a beach, because of their high specific gravity or resistance to weathering.

Platy Of a mineral with broad flat crystals.

Pleochroism Occurs when a stone appears to be two (dichroic) or three (trichroic) colors or shades of body color when viewed from different angles.

Point One hundredth of a carat.

Pseudomorph Crystal with the apparent form of another.

Refractive Index Abbreviated to RI. A constant relationship between the angle at which light enters a crystal and the angle of refraction.

Reniform Kidney-like shape of some minerals.

Scree Slope of broken rocks that have been weathered off an exposed outcrop.

Specific gravity The weight of an object compared to the weight of an equal volume of water.

Streak The color of the powder of a mineral.

Trichroism See *Pleochroism*.

Twinning Growth of a crystal in two different directions from one face.

Vein Thin band of mineral, usually in rock.

Vitreous Luster like glass.

Volcanic pipe Lava vent.

Weathering The breakdown of rocks by climatic forces.

FURTHER READING

Liddicoat, R., *Handbook of Gemstone Identification*, Gemmological Institute of America, 1977

Mercer, Ian, *Crystals*, British Museum (Natural History)/Harvard University Press, 1990

Pallant, Chris, *Rocks and Minerals*, Dorling Kindersley, 1992

Schumann, Walter, *Gemstones of the World*, NAG Press, 1997

Symes, Robert F., *Rock and Mineral*, Dorling Kindersley/British Museum (Natural History), 1988

Webster, Robert and Jobbins, E. A., *Gemmologists Compendium*, NAG Press, 1986

INDEX